The Kettle

2010

The Melting Pot Genealogical Society was organized in September 1976 as the result of a course in the study of genealogy which was offered at Garland County Community College (now National Park Community College). Inez Cline, then Garland County Historian, was the instructor for the nine week course. At the end of the course, the students were interested in forming a genealogical society for Hot Springs and Garland County. Ms. Cline agreed to work with them. She suggested that they call the group "The Melting Pot." The first meeting was held on September 9, 1976, at St. Gabriel School. The MPGS Library has been located in several places in the past, and it is now locateda6 649-B Ouachita Avenue.

The Melting Pot Genealogical Society is a 501-C-3 non profit organization devoted to the research and preservation of historical and genealogical data and other information. All contributions are tax deductible.

In Appreciation

The beautiful cover for this year's publication of *The Kettle* in 2010 was painted for The Melting Pot Genealogical Society by Hot Springs' native and watercolorist, Richard Stephens.

Richard's work has been in major watercolor exhibits from coast to coast, he received the best of show award in the 2006 and 2009 Annual Mid-Southern Watercolorist Exhibitions, he was selected among the "Top Ten Emerging Watercolorists in the Americas" featured in the magazine "Watercolor Magic", he was selected for inclusion in "Splash 10", the semi-annual publication of the top collection of watercolor paintings in the United States, published by North Light Books, he was the recipient of the Hanor-Westfall Memorial Fund for Artists art purchase award for display in the administration building of the Arkansas School for Mathematics, Sciences and the Arts, he has consistently participated in the monthly Hot Springs' Gallery Walk, he held a three month joint exhibit with Gary Simmons at the Hot Springs Convention Center, and he has a painting on display at Hot Springs' Museum of Contemporary Art in the Ozark Bath House. And, following in the footsteps of his schoolteacher parents, Richard conducts watercolor workshops around the country.

Thank you, Richard; we are honored to have your work represent us on the cover of *The Kettle*.

To view more of Richard's work, visit his website at www.raswatercolors.com

CONTENTS 2010

This has been an extraordinary year for me, as editor of *The Kettle*. In beginning to make contacts concerning possible stories for this year's publication, I have crossed the country with e-mails looking for people, information, locations, etc. My wanderings on the "net" have taken me to Singapore, Florida, California, New Mexico, New York, Illinois, Missouri, Iowa, and of course, all over Arkansas. I have truly discovered the meaning of the phrase "*it's a small world*," and to give you an idea of how that goes ...

Linda Miller, our past president, received an e-mail through the "Random Acts of Genealogy Kindness" website from Pamela Tremé in Land O' Lakes, Florida. Pamela was working on her family history and needed an old obituary. She contacted Linda, and Linda helped her and suggested she might want to consider having her story included in *The Kettle, 2010.* As a result, Pamela sent a copy of her story - and thus a long, interesting tale began. We realized very soon that her story was intertwined with people we all knew, or knew of, in Hot Springs, and we found that our current president, Margie Hill, had grandchildren that were members of Pamela's family.
- Pamela's story is: <u>Discovering Maxine</u> (see pages 63 - 69)

Not only have we gotten Pamela's story for *The Kettle*, but we have "the other side" of the family here in Hot Springs. Maxine's daughter, Evelyn Owen, married Burton Sargo, and their daughter, Jan Sargo Thomason, a member of The Melting Pot and Maxine's granddaughter, has written the Sargo's story.
- Jan's story is: <u>The Sargos of Garland County</u> (see pages 77 - 90)

Finally, with a cemetery transcription that has been updated for 2010, Patti Vance Hays and Charleen Cook Nobles added the burial place for many of the people in the above two family stories.
- <u>Rockdale Cemetery</u> (see pages 70 - 76)

- The <u>Harley Edward Greene</u> story (see pages 29 – 48) was another story that caught my interest, but since we had the "Bump Family Story" in *The Kettle 2009*, it seemed appropriate to wait for 2010. These stories are similar: in location (Bear City or Bear, AR); in proximity of the families who lived within a very short distance of each other on Brady Mountain Road; and in the profession of the family head (cabinet and furniture makers); so I asked Jan and Andrew Myers, a great grandson of Harley Greene, to wait for 2010. They very graciously agreed, and we have corresponded from Arkansas to New York for most of a year. I made a trip to see the home that Harley built by hand, and the present owners, stepson of one of Harley's grandsons living in Arkansas, allowed me to visit inside and take many pictures. I am grateful to him for this addition to the Harley Edward Greene Story.

Then...Richard Stephens agreed to design and paint the watercolor for our cover! What a delight for all of us...

And finally, a very special thanks to Esther Todd McCallum at Seiz Signs for all of her computer know-how. I could not have done it without her help almost daily.

Caroline Seiz Campbell, editor

The Melting Pot Genealogical Society's
Officers and Board Members

The officers and board members of The Melting Pot Genealogical Society for 2010 are (seated left to right) Margie Weatherford Hill, President; Charleen Cook Nobles, Vice President;
(standing) Mary Powell Booles, Librarian; Debra Slater Garner, Corresponding Secretary and Researcher; Caroline Seiz Campbell, editor of *The Kettle*; Twila Ackley Brown, Recording Secretary; and Nell Soward Brown, Treasurer.

Not shown are: Pat Soward Brown, Registrar; Marguerite Holzer Robbins, Assistant Corresponding Secretary; and Barbara Golden Erdmann, Assistant Librarian.

The Melting Pot Genealogical Society is alive and well, and the year 2010 has been an eventful year. We began the New Year with a novice president, and not quite a full slate of officers for a short time. It was very evident we were going to miss having Linda Miller, our past president, at the helm. However, she was always available for help and advice, and she guided me through the first few weeks. Thanks to her, I soon settled into the job at hand.

Barbara Thexton became second in command as our Vice President, but soon had to leave for family health reasons. Charleen Nobles stepped in, and filled that position very capably. I continued to act as Recording Secretary, as well as President, until Twila Brown saw our need and volunteered to take that position. Even though we had been conducting business, having all positions filled sure made the work easier. Every Board Member does an excellent job in the position she fills, and it has been a pleasure to work with this group of ladies.

Our meetings each month have been entertaining, educational, and related to the research, compiling, and preservation of family and community histories. Our programs and speakers are chosen specifically to further our desire to help others record their own life stories.

Late in 2009, we saw the results of many weeks, months, and even years of work on the big Garland County book. The finished product is a great book! The Melting Pot Genealogical Society members and the Garland County Historical Society members who spent so much of their time collecting information, proofreading, editing, and finally seeing the work done can surely be proud of their work. The book has almost been sold out and more have been ordered. Good job!

I would like to acknowledge and say a big, big thank you to our two Corporate Members, Simmons First 2008, and Seiz Sign Company 2009, as well as our 2010 Benefactors, Hot Springs Community Foundation (ARCF) and the Hot Springs High School Class of 1949. We appreciate the ongoing support of the community in our efforts to preserve the past and assist in genealogical research.

The MPGS Library is open to the public on Monday and Friday from 10:00 AM to 2:00 PM. If we had more volunteer librarians, we could offer more hours for the use of our books and resources. Your Librarian, Mary Booles, is continually working to update and improve the library. If you would like to be involved, please drop by the library and let Mary know.

During this year we have seen some of our members, or their family members, pass away. Some of us have endured health problems and dealt with that. Such is life, and those things, along with happy events, such as marriages, new babies, educational accomplishments, career successes, military service, and many other factors make a persons life story unique. Not even your siblings have the same stories to tell. Please consider writing your personal story. It will someday be very important to your descendants.

I thank you for a very interesting and rewarding year. I have met new people and become better acquainted with the ones I already knew. Thanks to each officer for making my job more pleasant and much easier.

Sincerely,

Margie Hill

DEDICATION

Garland County Veteran's Memorial

This 2010 publication of *The Kettle* is dedicated to the men and women of our armed services, both past and present. We honor their dedication to the United States of America and to maintaining our freedoms.

The Veterans' Memorial project began after the 2000 Veterans' Day Parade. Each year a critique is held following the Parade, and as the meeting was breaking up, MSGT Bill Sexton said that he had been to his home state recently and that his County had erected a Veterans' Memorial. He asked, "Why don't we have one of these?" The room was silent until John Barron stated, "Let's meet and talk this over." A meeting was held at the Red Cross Building in January 2001.

Approximately twenty people attended the meeting and the possibility of creating a fitting Memorial for our many Veterans was born. Officers for this long term commitment were: Morris Cash, Chairman; Bill Sexton, Vice Chairman; Ken Johnson, Secretary; and Richard Ennis, Treasurer. It took eighteen months to become a 501 c (3) Corporation, and then the fundraising began.

Ten members contributed $100 each as the first Donors, and this money was used to purchase five hundred Lapel Pins to be sold for $5.00 each as the first fundraiser. The catalyst for the project was the action of State Senator Terry Smith, who secured a $110,710.00 Grant from the State of Arkansas for the Memorial.

DEDICATION

After this, contributions were slow coming in, and it was at this time that Tom Wilkins and Dick Antoine volunteered to be Fund Raising Co-Chairmen. Their "It Just Makes Cents" campaign brought in close to ten million pennies, and then we knew we would have a Memorial!

Once there was a sufficient amount of funds, drawings and specifications were put out for construction bids. Dick Holden, Hot Springs Monument Company, and Butch Martin, Marco Construction Company, were the successful bidders, with construction beginning in late 2009 at 118 Orange Street.

The committee of 15 dedicated members is proud of what they have accomplished in building this Monument with the help of citizens of Garland County. The ten years of hard work by the group have made it possible to give proper recognition to our real heroes. One thousand one hundred fifty six (1,156) Commemorative Bricks have been placed. New bricks will continue to be added each year.

The Garland County Memorial Site is for all Veterans, from all branches of military service, and from all wars. It is not just for Garland County Veterans.

(Note: Graphic design work to remove building from background of Veteran's Memorial was done by Douglas Eddie Rice, Royal, Arkansas)

BENEFACTORS

Hot Springs Community Foundation

The Melting Pot Genealogical Society applied for a grant through the Hot Springs Community Foundation.   The Foundation generously awarded a grant of $500.00 to MPGS to be used to help offset the cost of publication of this edition of *The Kettle*.

Hot Springs High School Class of 1949

The Hot Springs High School Class of 1949 met in Hot Springs in October 2009 for its 60th year Reunion. There were 181 students in the graduating class.

Following the Reunion, the planning committee members met and decided to give checks for $750 each to: The Melting Pot Genealogical Society, The Caring Place, Jackson House, Charitable Christian Medical Clinic, and $830 to Garvan Woodland Gardens which hosted two of the class activities over the weekend.

Representing the Class of 1949 at this presentation was Alma Nell Soward Brown (middle) presenting check to Margie Hill, 2010 MPGS president (on left) and Linda Miller, 2009 MPGS president (on right).

THE MELTING POT GENEALOGICAL SOCIETY WELCOMES 2009 CORPORATE MEMBER

In early November 2009, the first copy of the The Melting Pot Genealogical Society's annual publication, *The Kettle*, was presented to David Hamilton, President of Seiz Sign Company at 1231 Central Avenue, by Caroline Campbell, Editor of *The Kettle*.

Hamilton said "As one of Hot Springs' oldest businesses, Seiz Sign Company is pleased to become the 2009 Corporate Member of The Melting Pot Genealogical Society. This year's publication of *The Kettle* continues the Melting Pot's hard work in documenting historical and genealogical information in and for Garland County."

Our 1925 Dodge Brothers Touring Car
By Foster Manning

We bought this car from a long-time friend of ours (he selected the colors) in 1990. It was fairly complete but lacked floor boards and the interior including seat frames or the top. It also did not have headlights, a steering wheel, wood top bows, running boards, clutch, front fender support spacer, rear spare tire bracket and frame, or wheel caps. However, it did have all the bright work redone in original nickel plate.

The greatest problem was finding someone that could do the interior duplicating the original style and color and not require sending the car so far away that it would be difficult to check on regularly. During this time the car was stored in Wenatchee, Washington and later moved to Coeur d'Alene, Idaho where we had built a log family retreat.

As luck would have it and with the help of new friends, we finally located a lady about 30 miles south of our place in Idaho that was willing to take on the job. We had photos we had taken in New Zealand of similar completed cars and an original owner's manual that had photos of the car and accessories when new. Work started in September of 2006 and completed (except for final mechanicals) in April 2007. We had it on the road testing in May and drove it in the first parade on May 15th. A friend and I painted a new trailer to match the Dodge.

Locating original missing parts was a real challenge of perseverance and we still lack a few minor items that most people would not notice. The car is a joy to go for rides in and we receive smiles and waves wherever we take it. We drive it each year in the annual parade "Lost in the 50's" at Sandpoint and the "Car d'Lane" in Coeur d'Alene.

Patricia was busy locating appropriate period costumes for us and another couple to enhance our lovely 1925 Dodge. Meet us in Idaho and we'll give you a ride.

Foster and Patricia Manning
(Note: Foster Manning is a member of the Hot Springs High School Class of 1949, one of our Benefactors 2010)

ANCESTORS
OF
HARRIET SUSAN "SUE" NOONER

NOONER, Harriet Susan "Sue"
b. 05 September 1932
Benton, Saline County, AR

NOONER, Elihue Columbus
"E.C."
b. 08 Mar. 1906
Mt. Tabor, Garland Co., AR
d. 09 July, 1961, Hot Springs,
Garland Co., AR

NOONER, Dennis Decatur
b. 15 Nov. 1868   Ava
McCool Twp., Perry Co.,AR
d. 12 November 1914
Mt. Tabor, Garland Co.,AR

NOONER, Elihue Washington
b. 20 August 1823
Chickasaw Co, MS
d. 12 August 1905
Ava, Perry Co, AR

TURNER, Barbara Clarinda
b. 07 February 1842
Tuscaloosa, AL
d. 10 January 1916
Ava, Perry Co, AR

TEDDER, Harriet Mariah
"Hattie"
b. 28 November 1873
Dardanelle, Yell Co, AR
d. 05 July 1966
Hot Springs, Garland Co,
AR

TEDDER, David Putman
b. 08 April 1845
Cherokee Co, GA
d. 10 September 1918
Tulsa, Osage Co, OK

PULLEN, Mary Jane
b. 13 May 1843
GA
d. 11 January 1905
Garland Co, AR

MEREDITH, Ruby Rebecca
b. 05 November 1907
Stillwater, Yell County, AR
d. 28 March 2001
Hot Springs, Garland Co., AR

MEREDITH, Franklin (NMN)
b. 01 April 1880
Baxter Twp, Garland Co, Al
d. 22 July 1945
Hot Springs, Garland Co, Al

MEREDITH, David Henry
b. 01 January 1848, AL
d. 12 May 1921
Garland County, AR

GAMBLE, Rebecca Ann "Becky"
b. 14 February 1846
Crows Creek, Jackson Co.AL
d. 06 December 1903
Garland Co, AR

MELTON, Susan Alice
b. 07 January 1882
Gladstone, Garland Co, AR
d. 22 Mar 1975
Hot Springs, Garland Co, Al

MELTON, Marion Columbus
"Lum"
b. 16 June 1848 DeKalb, GA
d. 14 April 1930
Garland Co, AR

NOLES, Cynthia Virginia
b. 25 September 1859
Guntersville, Marshall Co, AL
d. 28 December 1943
Hot Springs, Garland Co, AR

Note: (NMN) is used where there is no middle name

Garland County Marriages - "G"

Compiled by Patti Vance Hays

Picture taken from the Internet
(Couple unknown)

These records are from the second master index (Books 39-70)
and not from actual records (listing is continued from prior editions)

Garland County Marriages - "G"

Groom	Age	Bride	Age		Date	Book
Gabbert, Joseph McKinney	58	Benninger, Mrs Florence	41		04/19/1948	58-298
Gabler, Arthur L	51	Taylor, Ina	38		07/14/1945	53-130
Gade, William	69	Bolinger, Zada E	68		10/12/1959	69-93
Gaimari, Mario C	26	Shinsky, Betty Lou	23		06/06/1950	61-12
Gaither, Alfred William	31	Anderson, Freda Mae	20		03/11/1944	50-534
Gaither, Calvin L	23	Huddleston, Thelma Lee	19		05/05/1949	59-488
Galante, Dan	52	Schendel, Verna	32		01/17/1951	61-457
Gallagher, Richard W	21	Raineri, Ann	18		06/08/1947	57-111
Gallaher, Carl B	26	Gallaher, Ogden	17		07/10/1948	58-516
Gallaher, Carl B	24	Ogden, Opal Irene	16		02/22/1947	56-387
Gallaher, Willis E	26	Mashburn, Iva Lena	26		05/11/1952	63-64
Gallo, Benjamin J	25	Scollo, Antoinette	22		05/29/1952	63-102
Gallogly, Charlie L	72	Frencis, Lulla B	63		05/31/1947	57-91
Galloway, C A	47	Anderson, Pearl Carraia	53	Col		63-541
Galloway, Johnny	37	Cope, Mary Ellen	25		05/16/1960	69-321
Gamble, C F	58	Nevius, Mrs Ann	54			57-501
Gambrell, Bradley McCoy	21	Moore, Lois Evelyn	19		09/29/1961	70-393
Gamer, Elmer M	43	Greenlee, Kathryn	27		06/01/1946	55-95
Gammeter, Gordon Crawford	22	Dold, Ollie Linda	18		07/05/1958	68-26
Gammill, Alva W	56	York, Hazel	39		12/10/1949	60-270
Gandy, W D	51	Tarver, Mildred	34		11/08/1948	59-126
Gann, Boyd Jr	26	Dixon, Virginia Ruth	19		04/30/1945	52-530
Gannon, Herbert R	30	McNeff, Alice L	20			60-381
Ganson, Woodrow W	26	Hignight, Dorothy N	20		01/19/1944	50-392
Gant, Albert Emanion	19	Scott, Mildred	17		11/17/1947	57-541
Gant, Alex	27	Walkins, Hattie	30	Col	06/28/1943	49-487
Gant, Cecil Charles	22	Jackson, Loyce	19	Col	03/11/1945	52-352
Gant, H L	24	Moore, Disseree	16		03/22/1947	56-520
Gant, Hal Jesse	26	Hawkins, Esther Marie	18	Col		51-495
Gant, Zollie	22	White, Almeta	17			56-568
Gante, Alex	32	Grant, Hazel	24	Col	10/03/1946	55-541
Gantt, Allen	34	Burton, Virgie Mae	18	Col	05/17/1944	51-89
Gantt, Hershell	23	Amos, Pearline	21	Col	12/16/1943	50-326
Gantt, Hollie Lee	21	Taylor, Ruthie Mae	18	Col	01/04/1947	56-249
Garatt, John W	22	McHughes, Sarah L	16		03/24/1947	56-505
Garber, Alvin S	22	Jett, Barbara	17		02/09/1952	62-558
Garcia, Edmond	24	Chopin, Ruby	23		01/02/1959	68-279
Gardner, A J	64	House, Mrs Mary J	62	Col	12/25/1951	62-493
Gardner, Billy John	26	Lipsmeyer, Patricia	20		03/01/1957	67-67
Gardner, Calvin D	23	Perlmann, Ruth B	23		03/23/1946	54-359
Gardner, Clifford	22	Luker, Jacqueline	19		05/03/1947	56-640
Gardner, Elza T	21	Jones, Margaret	19		09/24/1949	60-148
Gardner, Frank M	45	McCullah, Kate Irene	30		08/07/1948	58-589
Gardner, James Allen	37	Chandler, Mildred Geraldine	22		02/17/1945	52-270
Gardner, Joe W	56	Singleton, Etta Lee E	36		04/20/1945	52-496
Gardner, Kenneth	18	Turner, Floy Dean	18		04/11/1953	63-589
Gardner, Lester	43	Borman, Nellie	37		07/06/1952	63-165
Gardner, Mose M	23	Hamilton, Ruthie Mae	22		03/04/1950	60-434
Gardner, Ren Winard	23	Hignight, Venetta	20		01/13/1943	49-90
Gardner, Robbie Joe	19	Reed, Betty	18		02/07/1953	63-492
Gardner, William	33	James, Mary Ella	27	Col	05/23/1959	68-417
Gardner, William F Jr	28	McMullen, Charlotte	26		09/19/1953	64-159

Garland County Marriages - "G"

Groom	Age	Bride	Age	Col	Date	Book-Page
Garfield, Harry A	36	York, Violet	45		10/02/1954	65-97
Garfunkel, Walter	52	Cooper, Pearl Wheatley	41		09/17/1958	68-138
Garibay, Antonio M	19	Lynn, Lorene	20		05/03/1948	58-335
Garibay, Jack Seaton	20	Gray, Patricia Ann	19		04/14/1961	70-113
Garibay, James L	20	Newcomb, Nell	18		05/02/1957	67-129
Garland, Kenneth M	20	Lindsey, Lucille	22		10/03/1946	55-532
Garland, Wallace	26	Holliman, Vira Mae	19	Col	07/21/1951	62-217
Garner, Billy B	26	Rigsby, Mary Lee	25		06/21/1946	55-195
Garner, Bobby Dwayne	20	Cogburn, Katherine	19		12/18/1961	70-493
Garner, Carl Otis	32	Austin, Mary Marie	25		10/25/1943	50-217
Garner, Charles Edward	19	Terry, Pauline	18		08/30/1950	61-192
Garner, Doyle	20	Jester, Mary Jo	18		07/02/1959	68-490
Garner, Eldon J	24	Randall, Pauline Eleanor	20		10/20/1945	53-442
Garner, Etril	21	Bates, Ruth	18		01/14/1944	50-384
Garner, Ezra B	48	Hutchinson, Lena	42		08/31/1957	67-251
Garner, Garald	31	Jones, Christine	25		05/31/1957	67-163
Garner, Harle Davis	20	Tackett, Bonnie Yvonne	22		04/16/1960	69-293
Garner, Harvey	41	Day, Paula R	43		05/11/1946	55-9
Garner, Herbert Ronald	19	Bonds, Nell Jean	19		09/05/1958	68-126
Garner, Howard Ray	21	Calloway, Mary Edna	18		06/04/1949	59-559
Garner, Jody	19	Williams, Johnnie Marie	17		08/10/1958	68-73
Garner, Joe Bob	19	Phillips, Nancy	17		03/17/1955	65-314
Garner, John F	21	Black, Jeanette	19		02/09/1946	54-230
Garner, L D	53	Hefley, Winnie Jane	37		04/16/1945	52-481
Garner, Leland D	18	Palmer, Clara	18		12/22/1945	54-26
Garner, Leonard Bill	24	English, Mildred Vernon	18		08/25/1945	53-260
Garner, Newton E	23	Moore, Mrs Aline T	26		04/04/1944	50-598
Garner, Ralph L	33	Davis, Doris Gwendolyn	18		02/03/1961	70-21
Garner, Raymond E	25	Rhine, Virginia Claudine	24		07/22/1949	59-565
Garner, Robert J	22	Loy, Myrna	19		03/31/1956	66-293
Garner, Rube Silas	21	Morehead, Wanda Willidene	19		03/07/1947	56-453
Garner, Sidney P	25	Wilson, Anna Bell	34		12/23/1943	50-343
Garner, Toy E	50	Moncus, Bertha	39		04/01/1943	50-581
Garner, Utril	24	Hawkins, Hester Ellen	16		09/23/1948	59-50
Garner, Utril	21	Tisdale, Pauline	18		02/04/1943	49-151
Garner, Utril	24	Scott, Kathline	18			58-487
Garner, Walton	22	Matthews, Laverne	18		02/24/1945	52-304
Garner, William	23	Bates, Ruth	20		09/13/1947	57-336
Garner, William E	27	Mickens, Evelyn	19		10/11/1951	62-371
Garner, Willie J	22	Crane, Patricia	18		06/19/1959	68-464
Garner, Wilmer	21	Cummings, Gloria	18		08/12/1946	55-358
Garner, Wilmer	21	Loyd, Anna Mae	19			57-258
Garner, Wilmer	21	Otwell, Doralina	20		04/24/1948	58-307
Garner, Wilmer	23	Smith, Hilder May	17		06/19/1951	62-149
Garner, Wilmer E	23	Johnson, Lillian E	19		02/16/1950	60-401
Garrard, O L	33	Buckles, Beuhlah Bell	23		10/15/1949	60-168
Garratt, Doyle	23	Sutton, Dorothy Louise	19		11/23/1949	60-234
Garratt, Thomas O	18	Steelman, Ruth	19		09/09/1961	70-364
Garrett, Bailey	66	Jones, Mrs Mattie R Velia	65		01/26/1952	62-539
Garrett, Chester W	27	Hopson, Clariette	18			50-47
Garrett, Clifton E	30	Gentle, Thelma	26		08/29/1958	68-99
Garrett, Curtis	23	Washington, Dorothy	22	Col	10/11/1957	67-321
Garrett, D H	23	Williams, Gloria Dell	19		04/26/1956	66-333

Garland County Marriages - "G"

Garrett, David Bailey	65	Smith, Essie M	60		08/09/1950	61-149
Garrett, Delbert H	22	Waites, Bettye Jane	19		05/23/1952	63-92
Garrett, G R	23	Morris, Maxine	19		06/14/1947	57-129
Garrett, Garland Weldon	37	Mathews, Ethel Elaine	28			62-216
Garrett, Irvin J	32	Walters, Mary Edna	26			63-127
Garrett, Lawrence A	27	Hutchinson, Jean M	33		11/21/1947	57-553
Garrett, Louis Gipson	23	Wheatley, Carolyn	20		10/26/1946	56-49
Garrett, Melvin	39	Garrett, Vernell	28		08/25/1958	68-111
Garrett, O W	50	Arnold, Marie	34		07/30/1944	51-289
Garrett, Rellis	21	Hanlon, Violet	18		04/17/1943	49-322
Garrett, Rogie	18	Taylor, Patsy	16		10/12/1953	64-190
Garrett, Sidney M	23	Funk, Julia Ophelia	20		07/04/1951	62-172
Garrett, Vander	44	Linville, Louella	24		12/07/1944	51-632
Garrett, Wayne	27	Berry, Irene W	28		08/04/1945	53-177
Garrett, William LaEarl	34	Brown, Margarett	27		08/29/1949	60-86
Garrish, Frank B	58	Raver, Wreatha	43		07/05/1947	57-195
Garrison, John Edward	22	Green, Billie Helen	21		08/10/1952	63-205
Garrison, John N	56	Shaw, Bessie Bernice	24		04/13/1953	63-592
Garrison, Kenneth E	19	Page, Bettye Jane	19		09/11/1945	53-300
Garrison, Ralph	63	Klauch, Gertrude Viola	56		09/25/1950	61-248
Garvan, Francis P Jr	47	Alexander, Verna Cook	50		06/29/1960	69-384
Gary, Joseph	56	Schumacher, Edith	50		02/14/1953	63-497
Gasaway, Jerry Wayne	18	Skates, Reba Charlan	19		02/18/1961	70-37
Gasnell, Alvin	28	Storey, Viva Eileen	23		06/05/1946	55-105
Gaston, Herbert Lee Jr	23	McKinley, Sarah Elizabeth	22		10/28/1960	69-521
Gaston, Leroy B	28	Sill, Mina R	20			59-545
Gateley, Ralph M	22	Nichols, Marjorie	20		10/31/1953	64-217
Gates, Anthony Allyn	21	Moore, Dorothy Lee	19		03/03/1959	68-336
Gates, James A	21	Waldrop, Carolyn Sue	16		05/29/1958	67-554
Gates, Leonard	22	McCarthy, Violet	21		01/16/1943	49-102
Gates, Owen	21	Taylor, Woodie Vie	19		08/20/1946	55-381
Gates, W F	50	Gates, Mary E	40		03/19/1955	65-316
Gatewood, Charles	38	Stringer, Lanelle	26		08/12/1943	50-35
Gathings, Robert O	29	Ferguson, Nedra O	22	Col	06/03/1956	66-393
Gatlin, William	34	Neal, Zoie	27			56-587
Gatson, Calvin	20	Ficks, Nettie	21	Col	09/14/1947	57-373
Gaudard, R	51	McGuire, Etta Bell	26		12/21/1945	54-30
Gault, Johnnie	46	Hayes, Marie	43		01/13/1945	52-114
Gaunt, N David	32	Heard, Kathryn Jeanette	21		11/10/1948	59-133
Gauthier, Paul K	41	Williams, Jerry Lynn	27		06/11/1961	70-217
Gavilsky, William	32	Helmak, Ann M	32		05/18/1946	55-35
Gay, Glen Harold	21	Priddy, Jane Evelyn	19		11/03/1950	61-246
Gay, McConico B	21	Huggins, Gwenn	18		02/16/1947	56-409
Gay, Ronald Dean	20	Maddox, Almeda Ann	20		01/25/1957	67-25
Gee, Donald	23	Gee, Mary	19		02/24/1951	61-526
Gee, Howard	21	Bennett, Wanda Lee	18		08/22/1945	53-178
Geiske, Paul J	65	Cooper, Gracella Beatrice	51		07/01/1961	70-251
Geltz, Earl T	54	Heckert, Elva	54		05/08/1947	56-612
Gensler, Ray Arden	37	Stanfield, Virginia #	31			60-209
Gentile, Leonard	46	Montgomery, Cleo	29		05/09/1946	55-3
Gentry, Edward	22	Nobles, Pansy	19		02/23/1943	49-196
Gentry, Howard	21	Carter, Marguerite	19		11/18/1944	51-572
Gentry, James	21	Cockrell, Betty Alice	16		05/10/1948	58-354
Gentry, Joseph B	21	Bailey, Gladys	18		03/21/1946	54-404

Garland County Marriages - "G"

Verna Cook Alexander

And

Francis P. Garvan, Jr.

June 29, 1960

Verna Cook Garvan is the Benefactress of Garvan Woodland Gardens

This picture of Verna Garvan was furnished by GWG, Hot Springs, AR

Garland County Marriages - "G"

Groom	Age	Bride	Age		Date	Book-Page
Gentry, R L	22	Sholes, Mary	20	Col	12/09/1946	56-184
Gentry, Walter (Jewell)	21	Henderson, Muriel Agnes	18		12/04/1948	59-172
Gentry, Willie	36	McCroy, Lucile	37		12/16/1949	60-276
Gentry, Willie	36	McRoyce, Lucille	35		07/21/1949	60-27
Gentry, Wilton Martindale	27	Parham, Pauline	21		07/18/1946	55-287
George, Alvie E	21	Dawson, Bessie Sue	17		11/09/1943	50-254
George, Archie Merritt	48	Sims, Purity Modean	27		08/12/1960	69-433
George, Arthur L	26	Hays, Ruby Dell	24		10/18/1947	57-478
George, Barton R	31	George, Helen Mae	23		03/30/1949	59-420
George, Billy Alphonso	18	Jackson, Helen	19	Col	09/08/1953	64-140
George, Billy Gene	23	Sanders, Yvonne	18		06/28/1957	67-199
George, Clarence A	38	Howell, Leathie Parker	34		02/24/1944	50-481
George, Edward	35	Carter, Adell	29		02/10/1949	59-314
George, Edward	35	Holt, Roger Lee	29		01/06/1947	56-281
George, Edward	49	Harper, Nona Mae	40	Col	02/21/1957	67-59
George, Edward F	28	Kemp, Patsy F	19		03/01/1957	67-441
George, Elmer	21	Timbs, Viola	19		11/14/1950	61-330
George, Fred	40	Goldstein, Helen M	30			65-472
George, Glen	18	Black, Evelyn	16		11/13/1953	64-227
George, J T	61	Vandeveer, Margaret R	39		01/30/1954	64-351
George, Lawrence A	55	Dornauf, Margaret	50		05/07/1952	63-63
George, Louis	18	Stanley, Dinna	19			59-265
George, Orie	38	Steward, Irene	40		07/13/1946	55-272
George, Ralph David	21	Storey, Ellene	21			52-528
George, Ralph David	21	Moore, June Elizabeth	18		07/10/1945	53-120
George, Tommie E	44	Eckard, Erlene E	42		01/05/1949	59-256
George, Vernon	21	Ware, Ruth	18		12/26/1946	56-241
Geraths, Henry A	37	Hicks, Frances Margaret Houser	32		09/17/1946	55-483
Gerber, Louis	68	Berman, Sadie	65		03/03/1961	70-59
Gerber, Sidney M	21	LeBow, Lillian	24		12/07/1946	56-182
Gerhardt, Wayne G	52	Cox, Edith June	34		01/09/1945	52-98
Gerhart, Charles W	31	Simpson, Sibley Bernice	19		05/17/1945	52-600
German, Roscoe H	26	Akins, Estie Irene	21		08/11/1945	53-220
Germany, J B	55	Germany, Marie	52		12/01/1960	69-557
Gervais, Fred J	51	Morris, Marie H	52		05/21/1951	62-90
Geurin, C D	23	Haynes, Faye Erlene	18		05/15/1948	58-373
Geurin, Carlus A	24	Callahan, Eva Mae	18		12/24/1946	56-223
Geurin, Charles	20	Blakley, Mary Sue	16		11/20/1959	69-133
Geurin, Edward	22	Hefley, Jo Ann	18		02/11/1961	70-30
Geurin, G M Sr	51	Morrison, Edith	53		03/22/1952	62-601
Geurin, James M	20	Sherrill, Gwen C	17		06/07/1952	63-121
Geurin, James P	21	Sparks, Marilynn	20		06/19/1955	65-460
Geurin, Samuel M	70	Fisher, Mary Julia	64		03/24/1946	54-412
Geyer, R P	73	Spencer, Nellie	47		07/11/1960	69-401
Giampietro, Leonardo	50	Toccia, Vittorina	42		03/16/1951	61-549
Gianakopoulas, James George	31	Pappas, Anna Jean	22		11/27/1955	66-158
Gianelloni, Damien Edward	58	Hall, Lulu Vera	56		08/08/1959	69-3
Gibb, Edward W	62	Wassell, Ruth May	56		01/04/1956	66-208
Gibbon, Joseph P	49	Owens, Elaine	38		05/03/1948	58-331
Gibbs, James F	27	Fason, Ima Jean	22		11/14/1946	56-96
Gibbs, Maurice M	44	McDaniel, Lorene	31		02/14/1943	49-173
Gibbs, William D	23	Grantham, Mary Ann	22		01/15/1953	63-457

Garland County Marriages - "G"

Gibson, Alvin Thomas	21	Myers, Juanita W	18		05/23/1943	49-399
Gibson, Berry	49	Graves, Elsie	30		07/21/1943	49-539
Gibson, Claude	35	Shipp, Clover Blevins	37		12/21/1948	59-210
Gibson, Harry B	28	Anderson, Betty	21	Col	04/02/1954	64-448
Gibson, Hubert L	37	Roberts, Maureen	22		12/23/1946	56-232
Gibson, Jack D	26	Sheppard, Leona Pearl	23		06/12/1948	58-432
Gibson, James	24	Walker, Mazola	24		10/22/1944	51-490
Gibson, John Cannon	21	Jensen, Shirley Ann	26		11/04/1961	70-445
Gibson, Nathaniel W	27	Bland, Mary Frances	21	Col	10/18/1946	56-25
Gibson, Oren	19	Emory, Mildred Inez	18		12/02/1944	51-605
Gibson, Robert Louis	21	Springs, Georgia Mae	18		08/30/1945	53-271
Gibson, Samuel	32	Hamilton, Faye	27		07/12/1945	53-119
Gibson, Vernon	21	Hutzel, Elizabeth J	17		06/17/1949	59-592
Gibson, Vernon	32	Collins, Effie Elaine	35		10/12/1960	69-509
Gideon, Alvin Luther	22	Nichols, Marjorie	19		07/30/1948	58-557
Gideon, Doris	20	Tillery, Wilma Jean	17		01/16/1954	64-333
Gideon, Thomas Lester	21	Harris, Mabel Lucille	18		03/06/1943	49-227
Gideon, Thomas R	58	Wusson, Virginia	39		09/07/1959	69-40
Gigerich, Walter C	46	Kettelkamp, Virginia	33		09/26/1943	59-132
Gilbert, Howard J	24	Lewis, Francis Almeda	27	Col	09/04/1953	64-145
Gilbert, John L	25	Garrett, Freda	18		06/27/1958	68-19
Gilbert, Mack	21	Young, Nina Jean	22		09/17/1949	60-142
Giles, Alvis	27	Bailey, Frances Kathleen	22		11/18/1943	50-275
Giles, Augusta	21	Livingston, Jessie Mae	20	Col	03/28/1943	49-274
Giles, Herbert	57	Blakely, Dorothy	39		03/26/1946	54-420
Giles, John Thomas	38	Green, Margaree	18	Col	08/05/1945	53-182
Giles, Samuel	21	Cheaster, Elosie	18			51-136
Gilk, Bud	23	Mort, Rose	20		12/02/1945	53-578
Gilkey, Eugene W	31	Graham, L Lenera	24		01/11/1945	52-103
Gilkey, Opal	25	Peters, Josephine	20	Col	02/25/1946	54-311
Gilkey, Opal	38	Durfield, Cecil	39	Col	05/06/1958	67-525
Gilkey, Wilbert	24	Garner, Doenis	21	Col	11/04/1947	57-509
Gilkey, Wilbert	31	Perkins, Willye Ruth	21	Col	05/22/1955	65-398
Gill, Australia	24	Skinner, Coralee	23		11/18/1949	60-226
Gill, Australia	25	Frazier, Emma Lee	19	Col	01/07/1952	62-527
Gill, E L	57	Johnson, Flora	48		09/16/1944	51-405
Gill, Henry P	48	Schalestock, Mary	43		03/07/1954	64-409
Gill, J L	36	Gill, Emma	36		02/28/1945	52-314
Gill, John H	43	Dancer, Lessie	34		06/04/1947	57-103
Gillan, Richard P	20	Selph, Peggy	20		09/29/1946	55-517
Gillemand, Leslie Charles	19	Rachilla, Shirley Allene	18		09/12/1958	68-135
Gillen, Henry N	54	Forde, Bennie Jean	55		04/29/1944	51-48
Gillespie, Arthur	25	Gant, Evelyn	18	Col	03/09/1954	64-413
Gillespie, Grant C	20	Calhoun, Mozelle	18		02/04/1960	60-380
Gillespie, O C	18	Thomas, Linda	18		03/24/1961	70-84
Gillespie, William R	50	Palmer, Iona Faye	41		10/18/1944	51-480
Gilley, Joseph W	29	Conner, Cletice I	25		08/04/1952	53-200
Gillham, C W	20	Burrough, Carolyn	22		01/02/1959	68-282
Gillham, Charles	19	Terry, Mildred	18		05/25/1945	52-626
Gillham, Charles Douglas	19	Vawter, Bonnie Sue	18		04/19/1950	60-522
Gillham, Enoch N	39	Roach, Mary M	32		10/23/1943	50-214
Gillham, James Lowell	26	Savage, Lydia Jane	19		03/30/1946	54-433
Gillham, Thomas L	24	Cox, Bonnie L	16		11/26/1953	64-246
Gillham, Virgil	28	Deaton, Numida Marie	28			59-589

Garland County Marriages - "G"

Al Ginsburg, Lois Thornton, Bob Thornton, Hannah Thornton, Frank Thornton

Alfred Ginsburg

and

Lois Thornton

January 29, 1948

Garland County Marriages - "G"

Groom	Age	Bride	Age	Race	Date	Book-Page
Gillham, W R	31	Roach, Geneva	20		06/05/1959	68-437
Gilliam, Claud H	23	Biggerstaff, Lillian Jean	18		11/27/1946	56-149
Gilliam, Cleve H	68	Harlin, Ethel	52		08/03/1958	68-66
Gilliam, Cleve H	69	Calaway, Mittie E	61		02/12/1958	67-431
Gilliam, Richard Lynch	23	Holder, Ann Denham	17		11/18/1953	64-221
Gilliam, Robert Newell	24	Moss, Marie Neal	22		06/20/1946	55-187
Gilliard, Thomas	25	Johnson, Austerine	27	Col	08/09/1945	53-205
Gillis, Henry B	30	Pasley, Lois Lorene	22		03/18/1944	50-546
Gillman, Leo J Jr	26	Eldridge, Doris E	28		01/01/1953	63-439
Gilman, Walter A	33	Davis, Mary Lou	20		06/20/1948	58-449
Gilmore, Frank	60	Baggett, Clessie	54		06/04/1946	55-114
Gilmore, Monroe	22	Cockrill, Dorothy	23		12/02/1961	70-473
Gilmore, Shirrell Jr	31	Allen, Connie Lorene	26		05/17/1952	63-84
Gimbel, Daniel J	25	Poe, Barbara	19		10/26/1957	67-332
Ginsburg, Alfred	23	Thornton, Lois	23		01/29/1948	58-100
Gioia, Archie L	36	Roach, Ida M	37			52-548
Gipson, Albert	40	Cunningham, Susie	50		02/20/1949	59-335
Givens, Paul Edward	23	Piper, Ann Elizabeth	21		10/26/1957	67-333
Gladden, Albert Austin	67	Rowton, Goldie	62		12/03/1957	67-357
Gladden, James F	22	Cortez, Mary D	20		10/26/1961	70-430
Glanton, Luther T Jr	37	Stevenson, Willie I	29	Col	06/26/1951	62-137
Glasgow, Thomas Edison	21	Gibson, Mary Lousie	18		06/11/1946	55-132
Glass, E A	46	Harper, Euniceteen	34		06/26/1948	58-466
Glass, Hyman S	48	Schweitzer, Ann R	35		10/30/1946	56-60
Glasscock, William Alonzo	27	McGillvray, Betty Rose	28		08/11/1954	65-22
Glasshofer, Sheldon	21	Goldstein, Bonita	18		05/18/1952	63-76
Glaves, Alexander E	26	Biedron, Mary Josephine	30		01/27/1945	52-145
Glaze, B F	74	Glaze, Vivian Thomas	37		11/05/1951	62-408
Glaze, Harold J	22	Harris, Mildred Pauline	18		06/15/1948	58-418
Glenn, Elmer L	49	Bruce, Ethel F	37		01/30/1943	49-122
Glenn, Elmo C	69	Denning, Leila	63		03/20/1959	68-352
Glenn, William	49	Cummings, Faye	55		08/01/1959	68-533
Glickman, Sam M	51	Dougher, Marguerite	50		11/22/1945	53-543
Glidewell, Billy F	23	Burrough, Martha Ann	17		04/25/1952	63-44
Glidewell, Charles G	21	Grandstaff, Jewel Dean	19		08/01/1946	55-319
Glidewell, Clarence H	33	McGee, Alexandria Christine	18		02/20/1948	58-139
Glidewell, Edwin Freeman	28	Myers, Emma Jean Elizabeth	27		09/03/1949	60-105
Glidewell, Fred Jr	20	Perry, Buna Harriett	19		02/04/1943	49-145
Gloor, Oscar Jr	22	Kimbrell, Patty Carey	21		12/26/1952	63-419
Glosky, Francis John	33	Witherspoon, R Minnie	34		06/21/1948	58-456
Glosser, Benjamin	39	Halcyk, Olga	24		02/19/1953	63-507
Glover, Billie J	21	Wagner, Mamie Marie	19		03/27/1954	64-429
Glover, Charles Edward	25	Lashley, Loretta Mae	23		10/09/1956	66-544
Glover, Eugene	21	Ticer, Maxine	19		04/17/1953	63-597
Glover, Grant	43	Bates, Julia M	23	Col	12/18/1953	64-275
Glover, James D	21	Swan, Alberta	18		06/11/1948	58-386
Glover, John	55	Watkins, Heddy	35		03/24/1947	56-530
Glover, William A	40	Wacaster, Rosalie	34		05/11/1953	63-622
Glyn, James E	38	Nickles, Marelee	28	Col	06/07/1948	58-420
Goble, Edward Alden	39	Scott, Mary Jane	27		10/16/1954	65-113
Goddard, Charles Vance	48	Towell, Kanta Lee	43		01/17/1947	56-318

Garland County Marriages – "G"

1952

Oscar Gloor, Jr.

and

Patty Carey Kimbrell

December 26, 1952

1965

**Oscar Gloor, Jr., Patty Kimbrell Gloor, Oscar Gloor IV
Heather Anne, Storm Robert, and Theresa Regina**

Garland County Marriages - "G"

Godfrey, Charles Wesley	22	Thornton, Barbara Lee	18		10/19/1953	64-204
Godwin, Carroll Dean	19	Turbyfill, Ethylene Ann	18		11/25/1948	59-164
Godwin, Dannie L	18	Culps, Thelma J	20		01/09/1955	65-228
Godwin, G T	80	Clay, Mintia	65		07/25/1945	53-156
Godwin, J C	50	Crawford, Memphia Killian	39		02/04/1957	67-39
Godwin, J V	21	Donohue, Jean	22		07/22/1957	67-228
Godwin, Jesse	57	Scott, Thelma	45		08/06/1960	69-430
Godwin, Jewel Gilbert	37	Underwood, Mary Estell	38		05/14/1945	52-579
Godwin, Lester	23	Qualls, Janett	18		12/31/1959	69-184
Godwin, Morlton	20	White, Leona	16		07/17/1957	67-224
Godwin, Raymond E	20	Gleason, Dorothy B	18		10/04/1951	62-359
Godwin, Silas Leo	19	Powell, Hazel	17		08/11/1955	66-23
Godwin, T E	35	Boone, Versie Mae	29		08/06/1943	50-6
Godwin, Wilford R	18	Veazly, Irene	17		07/10/1950	61-89
Goedecke, Jim Harry	22	Chancellor, Methel Wilma	18		12/18/1950	61-397
Goessman, Herbert	20	Wynn, Dolorase	17		06/12/1955	65-441
Goff, Ray	21	Hill, Lois	18		08/01/1943	49-495
Goglin, Richard J	28	Aarvold, Jean M	25		01/27/1945	52-172
Goines, Tommy	18	Ragsdale, Peggy	17		08/07/1961	70-305
Goines, Troy	41	Jackson, Lois Virginia	33		10/13/1961	70-383
Goins, Harold C Jr	20	Howell, Johnnie B	17		10/29/1958	68-187
Goins, Jewel W	21	Baker, Bertha	18		02/03/1945	52-190
Goldberg, Max	50	Krasner, Jeanette	40		03/09/1947	56-457
Golden, Baushausen	70	Merriott, Louisa	58		01/18/1947	56-327
Golden, Billy Charles	19	Whisenhunt, Jackie Patricia	16		04/16/1955	65-354
Golden, Bobby	22	Qualls, Joyce	16		03/15/1957	67-82
Golden, Bobby E	24	Lacy, Sharon Joyce	19		10/11/1959	69-87
Golden, Granville	68	Westfall, Helen	55		12/12/1955	66-172
Golden, Henry	70	Horton, Era	60		10/08/1959	69-83
Golden, Hiram C	25	Kitchen, Natalie	17		02/06/1958	67-422
Golden, James Oliver	24	Skates, Essie Murlene	26		02/23/1961	70-46
Golden, Jimmy L	19	Mitchell, Retha Mae	18		04/04/1952	63-11
Golden, Kenneth R	29	Golden, Dortha Jean	27		05/27/1955	65-411
Golden, Marion Blaine	22	Johnson, Wanda Aletta	20		10/06/1956	66-542
Golden, Marshall	18	Ray, Dena	16		05/17/1957	67-146
Golden, Morlton	26	Rowland, Joyce	18		04/20/1948	57-401
Golden, Morris	62	Morell, Mrs Eva	58		03/21/1947	56-514
Golden, Raymond	19	Tate, Lola	16		05/03/1947	57-5
Golden, William Roy	21	Harbin, Mary Ann	18		09/02/1950	61-203
Golden, Winfred	21	Martin, Emogene	18		01/09/1947	56-293
Goldstein, Barney	32	Kline, Ellen	25		04/06/1945	52-433
Goldstein, Frank	36	Shapiro, Doris	23		06/26/1946	55-205
Goldstin, Rev J W	73	Ponder, Evelene	32			57-238
Goldston, James W	80	Harris, Sarah	61	Col	05/15/1954	64-499
Goldston, Rev J W	71	Raymond, Lucille	66	Col	03/26/1945	52-406
Goldston, Rev J W	73	Raymond, Lucille	68	Col	08/19/1947	57-306
Gomance, Dale	25	Parker, Wanda Mae	20		05/21/1955	65-404
Gomez, Jose Santos	22	Saraliva, Alejandra	21			66-631
Gomoll, Franklin D	18	Graves, Sue	16		07/02/1953	64-68
Gonzales, N J	30	Brown, Virgie	30		11/02/1945	53-484
Goodale, Thomas Franklin	19	Terry, Susie Marie	23		11/22/1961	70-457
Goodman, Homer C	21	Newton, Maxine	18		08/07/1943	50-9
Goodman, John H Jr	19	Slaight, Mary Frances	18		12/27/1961	70-514

Garland County Marriages - "G"

Goodman, Selmar A	31	Perkins, Lola Bell	23		03/27/1945	52-413
Goodner, Stephen Lester	19	Henry, Ione Alice	18		02/26/1960	69-233
Goodrich, Ray E	24	Henry, Helen	16		07/06/1945	53-109
Goodson, Robert	24	Hopson, Nellie	18		05/17/1957	67-148
Goodwin, Arthur P	30	Dalton, Jean	24		12/25/1949	60-282
Goodwin, Charles R	56	Bumpus, Maude	58		06/08/1947	57-113
Goodwin, Charles Ray	44	Lindsey, Lucille	20		02/19/1944	50-471
Goodwin, Ernest Howard Jr	23	Yenawine, Maxine	20		02/05/1950	60-367
Goodwin, Herbert	46	Evans, Elvessa	36	Col	03/30/1954	64-443
Goodwin, Hosea	55	Porter, Dymple	55	Col	12/15/1953	64-271
Goodwin, Hosea	50	King, Janie	33		11/24/1948	59-163
Gookin, Jerry H	24	Sims, Betty Lou	19		12/08/1961	70-484
Goolsby, Ovie	31	Henson, Lessie Florene	23		02/09/1946	54-116
Goosh, William	22	Toliver, Verna	28		05/10/1948	58-358
Gordon, Charles W	44	Spahn, Margie Whittlesey	40		01/31/1947	56-365
Gordon, Clayton E	21	Whitley, Dorothy Raye	19		09/11/1948	59-19
Gordon, Fletcher Ross	20	Jester, Helen Ruth	20		09/29/1951	62-348
Gordon, Fred Raymond	62	Deschene, Esther Marie	41		12/26/1950	61-406
Gordon, Isaac Jr	21	Brown, Maybell	18	Col	08/23/1945	53-253
Gordon, Joseph Douglas	19	Thornton, Billye Joe	18	Col	04/01/1946	54-451
Gordon, Joseph M	24	Harvey, Thelma	26		11/02/1959	69-109
Gordon, William E	37	Ried, Sallie	23			60-54
Gordy, Jack	61	Kregor, Pearl	48		06/25/1951	62-161
Gore, Louis John	66	McCoun, Mattie Lee	55		04/08/1959	68-371
Gorman, Michael J	67	Edwards, Mattie	55		03/01/1946	54-330
Gortney, Charles L	31	Petty, Betty Jo	19		08/08/1959	69-2
Gose, Samuel Thomas	24	Hahn, Eva	26		11/23/1946	56-134
Goslee, Charles Robert	19	Crum, Peggy Lou	19		11/20/1945	53-544
Goslee, John H	48	Brown, Etta	40		10/25/1958	68-179
Goslee, Thomas M	27	Watson, Helen	27		01/06/1950	60-319
Goss, Ernest	34	LaFont, Mayme	33		02/07/1946	54-220
Gossage, Billy Wayne	21	Cash, Gay	20		09/12/1955	66-78
Gossage, James W	21	Blocker, Dolores	20		04/19/1954	64-469
Gossage, Robert Lee	20	Hendrix, Shirley	17		02/04/1961	70-20
Gossett, Moses M	24	Gordon, May	24		06/11/1948	58-430
Gossett, Otto Charles	22	O'Neal, Naoma M	18		12/17/1942	49-25
Gossett, R L	24	Frances, Hazel Elaine	18		11/01/1944	51-520
Gostee, James E	21	Lewis, Alice Jean	17		03/31/1961	70-93
Gott, Otis Ray	65	Zeamer, Corrine E	55		03/03/1956	66-267
Gottfried, Joseph	41	Russell, Juanita	35			62-423
Gottlieb, Burton Miller	24	Dose, Mildred Bertha	23		12/17/1953	64-274
Goucher, Ronald	21	Childers, Celeste	20		02/09/1961	70-28
Gough, Cecil Leo	30	Bright, Marjorie M	25		02/16/1951	61-511
Gould, Henry	26	Cunningham, Nell R	20		01/17/1947	56-302
Gouy, Floyd L	18	Henry, Virginia	18		08/10/1948	58-591
Goza, Hurn	35	Sleeper, Alice	23		02/10/1945	52-238
Grable, Billy G	18	Neal, Eva Juanita	18		12/14/1946	56-196
Gradomski, Stanley	54	Hamenko, Helen	47		01/30/1947	56-357
Grady, Albert C	26	Harris, Lucille	34		07/02/1952	63-163
Grady, John E	34	Hahne, Dolores A	19		03/04/1952	62-581
Graff, Emmitt R	35	Woody, Lillian	25		03/26/1948	58-235
Graff, W G	38	Graff, Mildred O	36		05/05/1951	62-59
Graham, Clarence Edward	41	Womack, Ouida Ann	33		01/31/1953	63-487
Graham, Ellis B	55	Ham, Addie	59		06/01/1948	58-407

Garland County Marriages - "G"

Graham, Ernest E	44	Wise, Rena	44		02/21/1945	52-287
Graham, H A	36	Brewer, Sue Woods	35		12/06/1945	53-556
Graham, James W	23	Carpenter, Louise	21		12/01/1944	51-607
Graham, John Robert	54	Austin, May J	57		10/28/1944	51-511
Graham, Joseph	28	Johnston, Opal	34		06/29/1961	70-246
Graham, Kenneth D	21	Ginger, Juanita Lillian	18		01/20/1943	49-109
Graham, Virgil Lee	57	Glover, Mattie L	40	Col	06/22/1944	51-178
Graham, Willie	40	Smith, Aline	22		07/13/1946	55-268
Grammas, Mark	45	Beckwith, Ethelyn	29		11/22/1943	50-283
Grammer, Gordon	31	Garrett, Mary	20		05/11/1947	57-21
Grant, Arlie Richard	20	Roberts, Daisy Verna	18		10/30/1943	50-229
Grant, Carroll	19	Keltner, Linda Delores	20		01/04/1960	69-188
Grant, Coy	25	Chancellor, Ida	25		05/02/1945	52-535
Grant, Grover L	27	Howard, Baxter L	29		10/17/1944	51-477
Grant, Hamilton Jr	18	Beverly, Ann	19	Col	02/19/1954	64-383
Grant, Harry D	57	Green, Ruth Mae	42		04/30/1949	59-483
Grant, Harry K	24	Warford, Edith K	21		04/17/1943	49-323
Grant, Herbert M	27	Diedrich, Elna	21		09/01/1945	53-278
Grant, Huey P	19	Powell, Fern	21		04/23/1954	64-470
Grant, Hugh	25	Cathey, LaNelle	22		12/30/1944	52-68
Grant, Lamar	22	Jameson, Emma Jean A	20		05/01/1945	52-519
Grant, O B	63	Stone, Tommie	51		11/07/1957	67-340
Grant, Virgil S	32	Chupp, Pauline	31		10/09/1945	53-408
Grant, W C	45	Hilton, Polly E	44		11/06/1955	66-142
Grant, Walter Jr	21	Logan, Rachel	18		08/30/1956	66-508
Grant, Willie Lee	19	Pleasants, Imogene	16	Col	01/02/1951	61-437
Grant,, Joseph Tolbert	19	Frazier, Georgia Etta	19		09/22/1950	61-242
Granthum, Albert	29	Nations, Marie	23			49-479
Granthum, Henry	55	Caldwell, Hattie	55		04/09/1946	54-481
Gravel, Orville	36	Butts, Dorothy Merolane	34		04/08/1944	50-613
Graves, Beverly Ira Jr	22	Ramseur, Mary Bland	19		07/12/1944	51-247
Graves, Billy Ray	19	Oates, Carolyn LaVerne	18		08/04/1961	70-301
Graves, Bruce	23	Lowder, Joyce	21		09/09/1961	69-468
Graves, Charlie R	37	Maddon, Virginia	20		12/31/1959	69-181
Graves, Debert Jr	22	Wright, Carilyn	20		06/10/1960	69-332
Graves, Denver	31	Pittman, Hilda	31		03/19/1956	66-281
Graves, Elmer	18	Crain, Elwanda	18		10/09/1949	60-157
Graves, Frank	65	Broughton, Mary L Graves	64		02/15/1962	70-560
Graves, George O	18	Breshears, Vera J	16		01/24/1953	63-477
Graves, Herman R	19	Hefley, May Lee	17		09/07/1946	55-451
Graves, Howard E	24	Corsette, Virginia Lee	20		08/01/1953	64-109
Graves, James	50	Gray, Dorothy	42		09/29/1947	57-419
Graves, James	23	Walton, Lula Pearl	18		12/23/1944	52-19
Graves, James C	54	Sullivan, Dora	53		07/25/1951	62-230
Graves, James C	47	Robertson, Katherine	33		04/20/1944	51-23
Graves, James L	22	Marshall, Murlene	21		08/19/1955	66-38
Graves, Leo Aaron	22	Valantine, Katie Jewell	19		10/31/1960	69-524
Graves, Mack E	26	Knight, Freda Mae	27		06/17/1944	51-109
Graves, Odis O	40	Hobgood, Alice Ruth	44		02/04/1962	70-547
Graves, Oliver	21	Noles, Electa	21		02/25/1957	67-61
Graves, Othel	32	Wike, Ila Mae	28		04/20/1946	54-519
Graves, Preston A	21	Sharp, Arceal	16		06/03/1946	55-102
Graves, Rual	24	Wilson, Norma Jean	18			56-576

Garland County Marriages - "G"

Sherman and Gertrude (Terry) Graves
with their first two of twelve children, <u>Carolyn</u> Linda and <u>Richard</u> Sherman

Sherman Graves

and

Gertrude Terry

April 20, 1943

Garland County Marriages - "G"

Graves, Rual L	21	Blessman, Blossom	21		09/17/1943	50-121
Graves, Rual L	25	Wilson, Norma J	18		12/16/1947	57-611
Graves, Russell	21	Skates, Eva Jo	18		02/03/1947	56-366
Graves, Sherman	19	Terry, Gertrude	18		04/20/1943	49-330
Graves, Stanley R	20	Davis, Patsy Fern	18		07/16/1949	60-22
Graves, Vestel I	33	Muldoon, Margarete R	32		06/17/1950	61-36
Graves, W Vestal	51	Bagley, Margaret L	47		07/31/1943	49-564
Graves, Wallace M	47	Graves, Blanche Kathy Clement	35		03/30/1955	65-337
Graves, Woodrow	18	Lockwood, Helen Lorraine	18		07/21/1961	70-284
Gray, A W	45	Ward, Eugenia	41		03/24/1953	63-553
Gray, Gilbert	59	Sweeney, Parthenia	43		03/26/1943	49-263
Gray, Harry	68	Fox, Emma	70		06/02/1946	55-84
Gray, Jerry C	32	McBride, Eunice	28		04/10/1956	66-310
Gray, Jimmy Luther	25	Lawrence, Frances A	22		05/09/1957	67-137
Gray, Joe Bob	24	Dawson, Laura May	23		07/31/1949	60-47
Gray, John	21	Toatley, Mattie Lee	18	Col	04/01/1946	54-448
Gray, John George	42	Meeks, Margaret Elizabeth	38		10/14/1954	65-109
Gray, Leo	46	Arnold, Effie May	40	Col	08/02/1943	49-572
Gray, Lyman F	28	Warwick, Ollie Mae	23		01/27/1945	52-179
Gray, Merwin Leon	18	Cox, Thelma Mae	17		02/01/1953	63-483
Gray, Myron M	20	Sorrell, Rachel Louise	18		04/28/1949	59-478
Gray, Patrick	49	Heckman, Ruth	31		08/20/1959	69-15
Gray, Roy Gene	25	Hill, Connie Sue	21		07/24/1955	66-3
Greeley, Martin	66	Paddock, Minnie	57		06/01/1956	66-385
Green, Albert Lee Roy	22	Waldron, Patricia	17		11/02/1948	59-105
Green, Albert Leroy	35	Klech, Eula Lee	34		03/24/1961	70-80
Green, Albert W	34	Coleman, Mildred	27		04/27/1947	56-619
Green, Carroll Bernard	37	Ritter, Anna Marie	35		06/04/1955	65-433
Green, Cecil B	29	DuVall, Juanita	23		12/23/1944	52-42
Green, Charles E	21	Otwell, Myrtle	19		04/29/1951	62-44
Green, Delbert R	21	Morgan, Willie	18		08/21/1943	50-50
Green, Donald Louis	18	Johnson, Maxcine	17	Col	11/10/1958	68-202
Green, Donald Louis	21	Mack, Valeria	21	Col	08/29/1961	70-347
Green, Earl G	41	Smith, Gladys	30			53-445
Green, Earl George	45	Green, Mrs Mabel	48		07/13/1959	68-506
Green, Fred R	56	Parker, Annette Pauline	33		03/12/1949	59-381
Green, Harold L	32	Garner, Betty	24		06/13/1953	63-630
Green, Howard	22	Burr, Juanita	21		05/20/1946	55-42
Green, Ira M	41	Croft, Pearl Elizabeth	32		07/14/1946	55-270
Green, J D	22	Kight, Clarice	18		04/22/1944	51-32
Green, James	54	Furlow, Florence	46	Col	03/28/1946	54-423
Green, James O	36	Smith, Uva Kinsey	21		08/09/1944	51-300
Green, John F	71	Starkes, Pleggy	57		07/10/1943	49-510
Green, Junius	29	Ferguson, Anna Bell	28	Col	03/13/1947	56-472
Green, Lee W	34	Baldwin, Olivia	21		09/16/1944	51-401
Green, Leroy C	26	Frohling, Edna V	26		10/08/1945	53-397
Green, Leslie F Jr	29	Hooper, Elva Jean	24		03/25/1960	69-256
Green, M M	63	Hooper, Bertha Adeline	54		07/07/1947	57-198
Green, Matthew	50	Johnson, Gertrude	43		06/30/1944	51-212
Green, Onis C	51	Smith, Martha	38		07/30/1959	68-482
Green, Prince Lee	43	Newborn, Doris	35	Col	08/17/1960	69-446
Green, Ray E	29	Blackmon, Doris	18		10/07/1946	56-5
Green, Roosevelt	30	Lee, Jewel	27		06/14/1943	49-454

Garland County Marriages - "G"

Green, Spencer L	39	Rivers, Ruby	23		10/17/1953	64-200
Green, Victor J	47	Porter, Mary L	27		02/24/1943	49-205
Green, Wilbur Edmond	33	Young, Leona	25		11/08/1944	51-381
Green, William	46	Taylor, Posey	38		03/06/1949	59-328
Green, William	46	Taylor, Posey	38			59-209
Green, William B	23	Pounds, Janiece	21		07/22/1956	66-466
Green, William Elbert	24	Johnson, Emma Sue	21		04/01/1960	69-266
Green, William J	26	Hickerson, Josie Geraldine	19		04/04/1944	50-589
Green, William Johnny	19	Love, Mary Ella	16	Col	12/22/1951	62-484
Greenan, James O'Brien	22	Cooper, Iris Nadine	18		08/09/1944	51-311
Greene, Allen	34	Larrieu, Dorothy	38		03/02/1951	61-534
Greene, Donald Owens	28	Adams, Ella May	21		05/07/1954	64-484
Greene, George W	39	Grisam, Lucy Anne	39		09/13/1945	53-272
Greene, Harold H	23	Tedford, Wilta	22		10/08/1951	62-360
Greene, Hollis E	23	Barnes, Bonnie L	27		07/01/1946	55-220
Greene, Hollis E	32	Rhine, Virginia C	26		01/28/1956	66-235
Greene, James E	28	Reed, Helen Y	26	Col	10/14/1956	66-551
Greene, James M	33	Greene, Gladys M	33		11/18/1949	60-227
Greene, John H	21	Muldrow, Jessie	21	Col	04/05/1946	54-463
Greene, John R	45	Underwood, Bertha Maye	29		11/26/1945	53-562
Greene, Samuel	60	Pryor, Viola	39		12/22/1948	59-220
Greenfield, Charles R	61	Whitaker, Charlotte E	29		07/02/1959	68-486
Greenlaw, Willie L	20	Sanders, Lydia Marie	19		03/08/1946	54-357
Greenlee, Elmer H	38	Bailey, Betty Joan	38		10/09/1958	68-168
Greenroyd, Loy	44	Wilson, Mary	38		06/14/1957	67-185
Greenwald, Henry Lewis	37	Padgett, Verna Dee	31		02/05/1960	69-218
Greenwood, Charles	24	Chambers, Thelma	29		02/17/1943	49-186
Greenwood, Earnest Rufus	19	Morris, Mabel Lean	18	Col	12/24/1957	67-385
Greer, Sidney	21	Hardwick, Dorothy	21		05/08/1952	63-65
Greeson, Elmer M	31	Byram, Verona	28		09/29/1945	53-372
Greeson, Raymond E	24	Pippin, Gwendolyn	27		10/11/1945	53-409
Greeson, Ronald Eugene	18	McCullough, Patricia Ann	16		02/28/1957	67-442
Gregg, Lloyd G	33	Gregg, Ruby J	26		06/24/1951	62-157
Gregg, Thomas Kelly	27	Williams, Melba Ruth	22		04/04/1955	65-344
Gregory, John	53	Gore, Mrs Lola	51		01/17/1949	59-280
Gregory, Ralph H	21	Phillips, Daisy	19		12/09/1943	50-315
Gregory, Richard	41	Williams, Dorothy	37		05/06/1961	70-138
Greguras, John E	34	Singletary, Hilda	27		03/15/1958	67-462
Greis, James Joseph	23	Wright, Vonda Coralea	21		03/24/1946	54-406
Greis, Ralph T	24	Crittenden, Marie	31		03/19/1945	52-370
Grevas, James	22	Lambros, Kathryn	20		03/01/1947	56-449
Grevious, William Jr	33	Hopson, Opal Lee	28	Col	06/01/1957	67-164
Grice, D L	37	Owens, Mary Lillian	33		05/26/1961	70-173
Grider, J D	33	Chambers, Willie Lee	20		12/27/1953	64-291
Griffie, W H	69	Searcy, Laura	79		01/09/1959	68-286
Griffin, Douglas E	38	Hale, Dolly V	30	Col	02/22/1946	54-299
Griffin, Jesse C	18	Smith, Mary Lee	18		10/07/1944	51-446
Griffin, Leo D	27	Williams, Janet	22		09/23/1955	66-86
Griffin, Leonard	29	Miller, Jodie Marie	27			53-404
Griffin, Mack S	62	Dicks, Marie	45		06/29/1956	66-443
Griffin, Maurry D	41	Pilkerton, Errine	34		08/12/1943	50-31
Griffin, Richard R	23	Mosley, Rebecca Louise	18		06/04/1945	53-18
Griffin, Ruby J	67	Golightly, Elizabeth	68		07/13/1959	68-504
Griffith, A C	25	Rogers, Martha Ann	16		06/01/1943	49-419

Garland County Marriages - "G"

Griffith, A C	31	Griffith, Irma	23		10/29/1949	60-188
Griffith, Bobby	18	Smith, Norma	17		08/22/1958	68-105
Griffith, Clyde B	26	Cook, Mary Lucille	28		10/31/1945	53-460
Griffith, Glenn J	41	Stanfiell, Dorothy Louise	27		08/03/1944	51-298
Griffith, Hugh Jr	22	McClain, Geneva	19		08/17/1946	55-383
Griffith, James M	36	Wood, Ida	31		05/07/1948	58-344
Griffith, Randolph	19	Cook, Imogene	18		01/08/1945	52-92
Griffith, Samuel Edward	18	Willis, Thelma Dean	16		12/17/1951	62-478
Griffith, Samuel Edward	22	Griffith, Thelma D	21		03/17/1956	66-280
Griggs, Fred E	21	Montgomery, Christine Louise	19		06/23/1951	62-156
Grigsby, Ben	43	Armstrong, Lois	30	Col	08/26/1945	53-158
Grigsby, Harold Johnson	22	Malone, Dorothy Mae	22		07/15/1944	51-251
Grigsby, William	48	Ritchie, Dora	42			56-448
Grillette, Ira Lee	48	Berry, Nancy M	56			63-460
Grim, H G	20	Kerr, Betty June	19		04/20/1945	52-491
Grimes, George Paul	22	Cox, Phoebe Ann	21		02/27/1960	69-235
Grimes, Starlin D	22	Stanley, Ida Jean	19		02/09/1946	54-241
Grimes, Troy	39	Hall, Ella V	23			58-11
Grimes, Troy	42	Hall, Elve	24		06/06/1949	59-564
Grimes, W F	30	Fisher, Elizabeth	30		06/21/1949	59-602
Grinnis, Walter S	33	Grisham, Lila Lucille	26		07/01/1946	55-224
Grinnis, Walter S	31	Duren, Evelyn L	22			51-573
Grisham, Chester	22	Breshears, Mamie Pauline	18		08/27/1943	50-70
Grisham, G W	18	Lawler, Lillian	26		10/06/1945	53-398
Grisham, G W	25	Grisham, Lillian	30		09/14/1952	63-260
Grisham, Gene	24	Marrs, Violet	21		05/27/1955	65-406
Grisham, Harold	20	Johnson, Duan	18		12/15/1960	69-576
Grisham, Howard D	18	Richardson, Tressie P	19		02/17/1961	70-36
Grisham, Ira	20	Hardin, Eloise	18		04/15/1949	59-442
Grisham, Irven	40	Chambers, Ruby Lee	28		09/04/1943	50-92
Grisham, J D	19	Harris, Lucille	17		03/04/1944	50-509
Grisham, Ronald Lee	18	Graves, Alice Joan	16		02/11/1961	70-32
Grisham, Roscoe E	20	Cotnam, Margaret Marie	18		12/04/1944	51-616
Grisham, Roscoe E	22	Rhodes, Agnes	26		12/23/1946	56-230
Grisham, Vernon	24	Wilburn, Geraldine	20		04/04/1948	58-249
Grizzard, Render	18	Hendricks, Judy	17		03/01/1962	70-576
Groslin, William Edne	59	Matthews, Hattie	57		06/03/1950	60-604
Gross, Clarence	37	Chamber, Atrice	27		04/13/1948	58-282
Gross, David	31	Weiss, Betty	22		05/30/1945	52-638
Gross, Eldon	25	Isebrand, Doloris	22			59-477
Gross, Herman Ray	22	Whisenhunt, Evelyn	22		12/25/1943	50-351
Gross, Jack	38	Spindler, Lily	32		08/13/1947	57-288
Gross, Jerry Dale	18	Benson, Martha Ann	18		06/05/1955	65-434
Gross, L E	30	Walters, Velma Smith	26		05/15/1944	51-85
Gross, Maurice W	54	Cohen, Leah	42		12/26/1950	61-417
Grous, Anthony Charles	36	Grous, Mrs Kathleen	25		07/22/1946	55-295
Grove, Hugh	53	Windom, Agnes	42		01/29/1949	59-297
Grubb, Lloyd L	54	Fisher, Clara D	52		11/28/1959	69-141
Grubb, Maurice T	48	Connell, Judy M Haycock	46		06/29/1949	59-620
Grumbach, Norman	38	Risner, Charline Bridges	21		11/07/1944	51-543
Grunewald, Gordon H	26	Jacobs, Florence C	27			51-534
Grunt, Arthur H	24	Hesselbein, Nadine C	22		02/01/1944	50-419
Guellich, Walter A	25	Thomas, Katherine Berneice	24		04/01/1945	52-401

Garland County Marriages - "G"

Groom	Age	Bride	Age		Date	Book-Page
Guerin, Dorce	26	Burton, LaVerne	21		02/10/1961	70-26
Guest, Cecil E	28	Ristvedt, Berenice V	37		04/09/1949	59-433
Guidry, Monte Vaughn	30	Bassham, Carollyn Ruth	20		11/17/1956	66-580
Guillioli, Guillermo	34	Mitchell, Jerelene L	24		12/19/1948	59-204
Guillory, Joseph H	25	Wetzler, Mary M	25		12/09/1943	50-313
Guinee, Walter S	27	Penn, Jacqueline	22		01/02/1956	66-206
Guinn, Clyde	19	Blake, Gracie	18		11/15/1948	59-142
Guinn, Ervin	21	Ray, Evelyn	33	Col	02/14/1957	67-51
Guinn, Fred	27	Belle, Virginia	19	Col	01/09/1953	63-449
Guinn, Fred	22	Bell, Virginia	18		10/18/1949	60-167
Guinn, Fred	22	Brooks, Maxine	22		04/04/1947	56-559
Guinn, J C	33	Roach, Ruby	27		08/24/1959	69-22
Guinn, James Willie	23	Moore, Lois Marie	21	Col	02/05/1945	52-220
Guinn, Jesse Jr	24	Johnson, Annie Louise	19	Col	02/05/1958	67-418
Guinn, Joseph Felix	50	Banks, Ernestine	50		06/24/1961	70-232
Guinn, Melvin D	21	Standefer, Majory L	18		05/27/1950	60-603
Gullatt, Ulysses	25	Haskin, Joe Hazle	20	Col	01/14/1953	63-453
Gullatt, Ulysses S Jr	26	Gullatt, Jo Hazle Haskin	21	Col	11/09/1953	64-224
Gullett, Thomas T	29	Griffin, Barbara K	22		10/08/1953	64-183
Gullett, Thomas T	31	Massey, Ruth	22		07/27/1956	66-471
Gulley, J D	22	Butler, Louise	21	Col	12/17/1958	68-249
Gullion, H C	46	Lester, Jewel	26		01/14/1946	54-124
Gunsalus, Clifford W	23	Snarr, Gwendolyn	22		06/29/1946	55-215
Gunter, George Walter	45	Baker, Alice Lucile	42		09/18/1947	57-385
Guoynes, Lee M	33	Harlan, Nadyne C	29		04/18/1951	62-28
Gurdin, Harry	36	Robinson, Lillian	25		10/19/1946	56-38
Gurley, James H	32	Briggs, Francis E	26		11/22/1947	57-552
Gussi, Robert	23	DeCocco, Geneva	24		10/16/1961	70-416
Gutherie, Bill	20	Tillery, Wanette	18		12/14/1959	69-153
Guthrie, James D	33	Burchell, Carolyn	21		04/29/1960	69-306
Gutierrez, Robert White	40	Hammons, Virginia	28		11/20/1946	56-116
Guy, Elton E	45	Bloxsom, Odelle K	43		04/25/1944	51-37
Guy, Vernon B	24	Armitage, Mureta	21		09/09/1945	53-296
Guye, Herman	27	Brown, Evelyn	18	Col	06/28/1945	53-89
Guye, Robert L	32	Wingfield, Clopatria	24	Col	01/28/1946	54-185
Guye, Theodore	18	Nelson, Minnie	19	Col	04/19/1958	67-507
Guyton, Jessie	49	Langston, Alice	48	Col	05/05/1951	62-57
Gwin, William James	21	Norman, Barbara Lou	21		12/24/1954	65-212

GARLAND COUNTY, ARKANSAS:
OUR HISTORY AND HERITAGE

The Garland County Historical Society and The Melting Pot Genealogical Society held a wine and cheese party in December 2009 at the Hot Springs Convention Center to introduce the newly published *Garland County, Arkansas: Our History and Heritage*. The book is a compilation of places, events, businesses, industry, and family histories from our area. The book represents several years of research by the two organizations.

The book may be purchased at The Melting Pot Genealogical Society Library, 649-B Ouachita Avenue or at The Garland County Historical Society, 328 Quapaw Avenue. To order by mail, contact: mpgs@att.net or gchsweb@gmail.com. The price of the book is $50.00, if picked up and $60.00, if mailed.

Other books offered at this event included *The Record* by the GCHS, *The Kettle* by the MPGS, and several books about Hot Springs' past by Orval Allbritton. These books are available at the GCHS and the MPGS Library.

GARLAND COUNTY, ARKANSAS:
OUR HISTORY AND HERITAGE

Representing The Melting Pot Genealogical Society at the event was:
Caroline Seiz Campbell, editor of *The Kettle,* Mary Powell Booles, Librarian, and (not shown) Linda Miller, President, Marguerite Robbins, co-editor of the Heritage Section.

In publishing *Garland County, Arkansas: Our History and Heritage*, several names were lost in the process of merging the two indexes of this 700 page book. The list of names from the genealogical heritage section which were omitted is given below.

Aaron, Issac, 443
Aaron, Susan, 443
Abbington, John, 544
Abbott, Alfred Bemont, 390
Abbott, Greeley Thomas, 518
Abbott, Hat, 390
Abbott, Imogene, 390
Abbott, Samuel Bemont, 390
Abbott, Shirley Jeanne, 390
Abell, Martha, 482
Abernathy, Billy, 391, 495, 592
Abernathy, Esther, 608
Abernathy, Jennifer Lynn, 391
Abernathy, M. F. "Bill", 391
Abernathy, Mamie, 596
Abernathy, Mamie Ruth, 391, 593, 625
Abernathy, Mamie Ruth Stranburg, 390, 391, 406, 495, 503, 528, 587, 593, 594, 596, 617

Abernathy, Scott William, 391
Abernathy, Stacy, 417
Abernathy, William Howard "Billy", 391
Ackrenden, Margaret, 401
Adams, Ara Tracey, 621
Adams, Earl, 621
Adams, Elizabeth Jane, 574
Adams, Ernest Clyde, 456
Adams, Frances Ella, 400
Adams, Frances Marvin "Frank", 391
Adams, Ida Francis, 533
Adams, James, 600
Adams, John "Jon", 391
Adams, Lockie Lee, 578
Adams, Mae, 487
Adams, Margaret Helen, 485

Errata for the publication may be found at: www.garlandcountyhistoricalsociety.com/hherrata.html

Harley Edward Greene

Harley Edward Greene

Paternal Ancestral Lineage

By Andrew Myers (great-great grandson)
(New York)

5. Harley Edward Greene, son of George Washington Maxington Greene and Persis Viola Hazard, was born 9 SEP 1861[1] in Spafford, Onondaga, New York.[2][3] On 14 OCT 1889 he married Frances Ellen Parks in Montgomery County, Arkansas.[4] He died 18 DEC 1931 in Bear, Montgomery, Arkansas. **Frances "Fannie" Ellen Parks,** daughter of Abraham "Lum" Columbus Parks and Tabitha Hodges.[5] She was born 1 SEP 1862 near Marshall, Searcy, Arkansas and died 1 FEB 1926 in Mill, Garland, Arkansas.[6] Both are buried at Greenwood Cemetery in Hot Springs, Garland, Arkansas. [7]

Photo of Harley Greene; received from Herbie Meeks, Arkansas.

Harley Greene was born in the very small rural community of Spafford, just thirty miles southwest of Syracuse, New York and just off the east bank of Skaneateles Lake. The town was formed April 8, 1811 from the military townships of Sempronius, Marcellus and Tully and received its name from Horatio Gates Spafford, LL. D., author of the <u>Gazetteer of New York</u>.[8] Spafford is nestled in a thick lush forest amongst the rolling hills of upstate New York. One can only imagine the work that was involved by the early pioneers in clearing the land for their crops, with primitive tools and draft animals. Passing through town, all around are the vacant farm fields surrounded with rock walls that were built over 150 years ago, where vast green fields meet forests of old growth hardwoods. Residents are scattered with an occasional clustering of neighbors. Many residents of the area, like Harleys' great grandfather John, fought in the War of 1812.

Most of the fighting took place on the Great Lakes and around New York City, leaving Central New York largely untouched. My wife wrote this of our visit to Spafford, "walking through the fields and the forests that border Spafford and Borodino, I imagined myself transported in time to that era. The scent of the air, fresh as spring although it was autumn, the gorgeous reds and yellows of the leaves rustling in the wind, and the calls of wildlife alerting all to my unwelcome presence, could not be that different today than when the area was settled. What was Harley's childhood like here in this beautiful peaceful place? I imagined Onondagan Indians scouting through the woods to spy on me and the faint sound in the distance of the steam mill. There is an eerie feel to the place, almost hostile, as if the spirits that rest here are being disturbed. I came to a ridge that overlooks the valley, a place

Photo of Harley Greene (left) & James Columbus Parks (right)

Harley Edward Greene

indescribable in its majesty. I sat in awe, drinking in the scenery."

Around 1880, George moved his family to Windsor, New York,[9] probably so his wife Persis could care for her father, E.A. Hazard. According to one family story, at about the age of sixteen, Harley married, although the brides name is unknown. Disapproving of the marriage, Persis had the marriage annulled. She then sent him to Oxford, England to receive an education. He received his training in fine woodworking and later returned to the states. Upon his arrival in the US, he boarded a train headed to Arkansas, never to return home.[10] [11] Harley settled in Royal, Arkansas where he met his new bride, Fannie, and they were married on the 14th day of October 1889.

Tin type photo of Persis V. Hazard as a child; received from Herbie Meeks.

Harley was rather tall and of somewhat muscular build, but was very kind and loving, adored by all who knew him-- especially his grandchildren. He was very devoted and protective of his family. Every evening around 4 o'clock he would go around locking everything up. "I was so young at the time, it scared me," claimed Viola Austin, "I think he did it because he was protecting his family. Grandma was Indian and it was supposed to be kept secret."[10] He had only one eye, losing the other in a hunting accident. He was an avid reader, very intelligent and very talented. He was Justice of the Peace for years, but his main profession was carpentry, masonry and woodworking. He built furniture: rocking chairs, grandfather clocks and footstools among other things, shipping it nationwide. He also made watches and other jewelry as well. He would ship truck loads of rocking chairs to Missouri and California. His craftsmanship and talent is

(Left to right) Addie & Mabel Greene in the chair made by Harley.

best seen in his hand carved furnishings. He made three hand carved grandfather clocks to be wedding gifts for his daughters. His eldest daughter, Mable received hers (pictured to the right), but Harley ran into financial difficulty and sold the other two, their whereabouts now unknown. He also made "savings boxes" as they were called by his grand daughter Imogene. He gave one to each of his daughters and their husbands, which have been handed down in each family.[10] [12]

Now in possession of Viola Austin. Photo received by Herbie Meeks.

Harley Edward Greene

He began building his home on Brady Mountain Road around 1890 and completed in 1901. Referred to by family as "The Heritage Home," it is a Queen Anne Victorian, 2-story home. It was among the most elaborate and fanciest of homes in Bear City at the time. Of all the Victorian Houses, the Queen Ann often called the most romantic and feminine; receiving its name from Ann, Queen of England, from a time when Art and Science flourished during her reign in the 1700s. American Queen Ann style homes became a fashion statement in the

All Photos of Harley Greene's Home;
taken by Caroline Campbell, Editor of The Kettle.

1800s, during the American industrial revolution, and were lavishly decorated. Harley's home was no exception—decorated with spindle work along the porch roof, delicate turned bracketed posts and fish-scale walls beneath a decorative gable, his house definitely gave the townsfolk something to admire. At the entry the visitor is greeted by vibrant stained glass windows and a

hand carved decorative door. Harley's fine architectural skills are put to work on the inside as well, including all of the hand made furnishings and décor. Harley's home has been described as *"absolutely breathtaking"* by those

Harley Edward Greene

who remember it in its original condition. There was a small library inside full of all sorts of books which, according to his granddaughter, Viola, was her favorite place to spend time, disappearing for hours to read there. "Oh how I loved getting into all those books," said Aunt Vi.[10]

Dallas Bump said the home has a reputation for being haunted.[13]   Our family does have its ghost stories. In one, Harley's mother, Persis, had gone to Arkansas for a visit and to meet Harley's family. As the story was told to me by my grandmother

Helen, long after Persis had passed, Harley and some friends were playing cards, smoking cigars and drinking when all of a sudden they all swore they saw Persis coming down the stairs shaking her finger at them in disapproval of their actions. Other family members we have interviewed say that sounds like something she would do. For many of the Christians in our family who do

not believe in ghosts, including myself, researching this family has been a test of my beliefs. I have yet to have an encounter with any of my ancestors' ghosts. My wife, on the other hand, could tell you stories from dreams and research of this family that make the hair stand up on my neck.

After nearly 100 years and many different owners, The Heritage Home was purchased by family in 1990. In 2005 restoration began and a stunning job they have done. Today, Harley's home is on the National Register of Historic Places and if you can catch the owners at home, they'd be happy to give you a tour.

In early spring of 1931, Ralph and Gladys Kresge were headed to Texas from Binghamton, New York for Ralph's job transfer. They stopped to visit Harley in Arkansas while traveling. As a wedding gift Harley gave Gladys a footstool that he had made (pictured to the right).

Stool made by Harley; Photo taken by author Nov 2009.

Harley Edward Greene

Harley and his son-in-law Edward Wehunt, built the Palestine Baptist Church in Bear, Arkansas, a beautiful example of fine stone masonry.

Photo of the Palestine Baptist church; taken by Dale Myers in the 1970s.

The Great Depression tested many families and the Greenes' were no exception. Harley, with his wife, three daughters and their families, worked in staves mills. "Grandpa would buy tracts of lumber and sell the lumber to beer companies to be used to make beer barrels, wooden kegs for beer. When the timber was gone we would move somewhere else and start over. We travelled around together like a band of gypsies; this is how we grew up. We were a close family," said Jean Meekins.

Fannie Ellen Parks, loving wife, devoted companion and best friend of Harley. She bore Harley six children, three sons and three daughters. Only the daughters survived, the boys all dying in their first year of life and ending the Greene name on this line.

Fannie was of Indian blood from the Choctaw tribe. Family stories told by Fannie claimed her mother walked the Trail of Tears or in the Cherokee language *Nunna daul Tsuny* which means "The Trail Where They Cried".[14]   A senseless act in American History; The Trail of Tears was first implemented by Andrew Jackson with the passage of the Indian Removal Act of 1830.

Photo of Fannie Ellen Parks, age 18.

Photo of Fannie & Cossie (Beauchamp) Parks

This was the relocation and movement of Native Americans from their homelands to Oklahoma and beyond. The Choctaw were the first to be removed and became the model for the remaining removals. The Cherokee were the last to be removed in 1838. As many as 46,000 Native Americans were removed opening up 11 million acres to be

Harley Edward Greene

settled by the white man. They were marched more than 1,000 miles, a harsh and tragic journey. Many Native Americans died while traveling and many others suffered disease and starvation.

A Tintype photo written on the back "wife of Lum Parks" Received from Herbie Meeks.

Tabitha Hodges was the wife of Abraham "Lum" Parks and referred to by him as Ok Lo Hah.[15] A family story from the Hodges family claims that three siblings, Jesse M, Emaline, and LaFayette were orphaned in the Butler Creek area near Iron City, Tennessee while walking on the "Trail of Tears". The three orphans were then brought to Searcy County, Arkansas to "be with relatives." [16] Could there have been four orphans and our Tabitha one of them? Truly, an interesting family story, the details yet to be fully discovered.

Harley Edward Greene and Fannie Ellen Parks had the following children:

i. Infant Son born 15 May 1890 [17] probably near Hot Springs, Arkansas and possibly died in the same place shortly after his birth. He is buried at Greenwood Cemetery in Hot Springs, Arkansas.

ii. George A Greene born 15 Apr 1891 probably near Hot Springs, Arkansas and possibly died in the same place on 19 Jul 1892.[18] He is buried at Greenwood Cemetery in Hot Springs, Arkansas.

iii. Willie T Greene born 20 Aug 1892 [19] probably near Hot Springs, Arkansas and possibly died in the same place on 3 Sep 1892. He is buried at Greenwood Cemetery in Hot Springs, Arkansas.

iv. Mable Viola Greene born 6 Oct 1894 [20] in Roswell, Chaves, New Mexico. In 1916 she married Mack Jesse Standridge. They settled for a short time in Arkansas and Missouri, later moving to California during World War II and raised a family. She died 26 Jul 1982 in Sunnyvale, Santa Clara, California and is buried alongside her husband at Mission City Memorial Park Cemetery in Santa Clara, Santa Clara, California.

v. Addie Persis Greene born 20 Aug 1898 in Arkansas.[21][22] The majority of her early life was spent in/around Bear and Hot Springs Arkansas.[23][24][25][26] At the age of 21, she married Edward Gayle Wehunt,[27] the son of Edward Austin and Lilly Cordelia (Beck) Wehunt,[28] on 21 Sep 1919 by P. P. Gilham, JP in Royal, Garland, Arkansas. About 1956, they moved to the Anderson, California area and raised a family of five children. She died on 17 Jan 1968 at Memorial Hospital in Redding, Shasta, California of bronchopneumonia and is buried alongside her husband in Anderson District Cemetery in Anderson, Shasta, California. [29] Edward Gayle Wehunt was born 18 DEC 1899 in Mena, Polk, Arkansas. He was a skilled carpenter and mason, having assisted Harley in building the Palestine Baptist Church in Bear, Arkansas. [30] Edward died 29 JUN 1977 at Mercy Medical Center in Redding, California of acute circulatory failure.

vi. Fannie Ellen Greene was born 8 APR 1901 probably in Bear, Arkansas and died 24 APR 1988 in Norman, Montgomery, Arkansas. She married Lee Monroe Meeks who was born 15 NOV 1896 in Silver, Montgomery,

Harley Edward Greene

Arkansas.[31] He died 16 DEC 1974 in Santa Clara County, California.[32] Both are buried at Mt. Hope Cemetery in Morgan Hill, Santa Clara, California.[33] [34]

6. George Washington Maxington Greene, son of Henry M. Greene and Ann Mariah Coon, was born 17 APR 1835 in Spafford, Onondaga, New York.[35] On 31 MAR 1861 he married Persis Viola Hazard in Great Bend, Susquehanna, Pennsylvania.[36] He died 31 AUG 1898 in Homer, Cortland, New York of tuberculosis. **Persis Viola Hazard,** the daughter of Edward Allen Hazard and Elizabeth Ann Rowley. She was born 28 FEB 1843 in Windsor, Broome, New York and died 25 DEC 1933 in Liberty, Susquehanna, Pennsylvania.[37] George is buried in the family plot with his parents at Spafford Cemetery in Spafford, New York. [38] Persis is buried alongside her son, Arthur, at Rose Hill Cemetery in Hallstead, Pennsylvania.[39] [40]

Photo of George W.M. Greene

George was born and raised in rural Spafford, New York. His grandfather, John, a pensioner of the war of independence, settled with his family in Spafford shortly after the turn of the nineteenth century.

He was a mason by trade and a follower of Christ. He met his wife, Persis, on a religious retreat in Great Bend, Pennsylvania; both their parents were ministers of the Baptist Church in their communities. He is described as being quiet and very stern, yet humble.[41] Persis applied for a Widow's Civil War Pension, however, it was indicated that his regiment was not mustered into service.

Photo of George & Persis' home on Dubois St., Hallstead, Pennsylvania. Left to right; Libbie, Persis, Arthur. Scanned by author Jul 2008.

Harley Edward Greene

The original photo of the home is of the old fashion postcard type. If you look closely, you can see Persis standing there in the front, her daughter Libbie on the left and son Arthur holding his mules on the right. Arthur was very proud of those mules and often told stories of them.

Prior to 1880 he moved his family to Windsor, New York, most likely so Persis could care for her father, Edward Allen Hazard, as they are found living with him on the federal census for that year, he died on May 29, 1882.[42] [43] After the death of Persis' father, George bought a 2-story brick home in Great Bend (now Hallstead), Pennsylvania on Dubois St in 1883 from Lydia Law Brooks. The original parcel, before partitioning in later years, belonged to the Dubois family. [44]

Photo of George & Persis' home on Dubois St.; taken Jul 2008 by Andrew Myers.

I found George's home still standing and occupied. I was very saddened to see that the original brick was covered with vinyl. The current owner purchased the home from her father. It is the home that she and her siblings grew up in. She was very polite and gave us a tour and permission to take as many photos as we wanted. I showed her the original photo and she stated that is exactly what the home looked like when her parents purchased it. There was a vault upstairs which they removed. Apparently the home had been converted first to a library and then to a bank. The chimney had to be rebuilt and her father reframed and covered up many

Harley Edward Greene

of the windows because they made the home too difficult to heat. She and her husband have considered restoring it back to the original condition and a copy of the original photo was left with them as she requested, in case they choose to follow that path. When her parents first decided to sell the home, her older sister declined the offer, because she was convinced the home was haunted. As a teenager she would often see a tall thin man with a mustache standing at the top of the stairs. So, the younger sister and her husband purchased it. She said growing up she had always heard someone walking around the home at night and even now occasionally hears the footsteps and the creaking of the floor boards. Of course, out of curiosity, we had to leave her with the photo of George and our contact information. A couple of weeks later she called to say her sister had confirmed that our George was the apparition her sister had seen so frequently.

When you walk out of the house in Hallstead, a lush thick forest on the edge of a creek greets you. The old ruins appear to be that of an old grist mill. The poison ivy was so thick beyond the wall we dared not to venture out even if we had gotten permission to do so. But looking through you could see that the remains of this old building go as far back to the water's edge.

Arthur and his wife, Cora, made their home up the road from Persis. His home was an old wooden shack with dirt floors for many years. Long gone after all these years and no trace of its existence was to be found during our travels.

Persis Viola Hazard was a very stern and loving follower of the Lord. She was raised in the Baptist faith, her father being a former Baptist Minister, and in later years is found in newspaper articles attending the Friends Society Church and a huge supporter of their functions along with her daughter Libbie. She was your typical pioneer wife, having worked hard on the homestead. Every night

Photo of Persis Greene
Volume XXXIII

Harley Edward Greene

before bed Persis would put hot (cayenne) pepper in hot water to drink. She claimed it helped to keep her warm at night. She was
quite the seamstress as well; she made all of her and her children's clothes as well as for her grandchildren.   She made both the communion dresses for Gladys Mason and Max Greene.

Persis' sewing table, the "Pitcher" Lamp was Persis' wash set. The bowl broke many years ago, so Gladys had the pitcher turned into a lamp. Photo taken by Andrew Myers July 2008.

Her father, Edward, made her a sewing table as a gift, which Persis cherished and passed on to her daughter Libbie.

According to the family stories of her son, Arthur and daughter, Libbie; Arthur had married Nettie Terboss at the age of 16. They had one child, Max Arthur Greene who was born 25 Aug 1894. Persis did not approve of this marriage because Arthur was too young and on the

1900 Federal census Arthur is recorded as divorced. She also did not approve of Libbie's marriage to

Merton Mason because he was agnostic and was abusive to Libbie and the children.[41] [45]

Above: Gladys Mason in communion dress; Scanned by Jan Myers Nov. 2009.

Below: Max Arthur Greene in communion dress; provided by Herbie Meeks.

George Washington Maxington Greene and Persis Viola Hazard had the following children:

    a. Harley Edward Greene born 9 Sep 1861 in Spafford, Onondaga, New York and died in Bear, Garland, Arkansas. He is buried at Greenwood Cemetery in Hot Springs, Arkansas. [Subject of this Article]

    b. Elizabeth "Libbie" Viola Greene born 26 Aug 1870 in Spafford, Onondaga, New York.   On 26 Jun 1895 to Merton Marvin Mason, son of Marvin Mason and Cemira Lovena Gilmore, in Hallstead, Susquehanna, Pennsylvania. They resided in Binghamton, Broome, New York their entire married lives. Merton was an upholster having a large shop in the rear of his home on 6 ½ Morgan St. and very well known in the community. Libbie was a teacher early in life and later became a homemaker after the children were born. She was a member of the Friends Society Church and a frequent hostess for many of their functions. She lost her sight to diabetes in old age and died 14 Nov 1931 in Binghamton, NY. She is buried at Chenango Valley Cemetery in Binghamton, NY. [46] [47] [48] [49]

    c. Arthur Fred Greene born 17 Dec 1872 in Spafford, New York. He was first married in approx. 1888 to Nettie Terboss. They had one child Max Arthur Greene, born 25 Aug 1894 probably in Hallstead or Great Bend, Pennsylvania. Max was

Photo of Libbie (Greene) Mason

Harley Edward Greene

Photo of Arthur
Fred Greene

a Sergeant in the Army during WW1 and died November 10, 1918, the day before Armistice Day. His Unit (79th) Division had been cited for bravery) and he is buried at Meuse-Argonne American Cemetery in Romagne, France. On the Montfaucon Monument the words of General Pershing are memorialized: "The Meuse-Argonne offensive (in which over 1,000,000 American soldiers fought) was suddenly conceived, hurried in plan and preparation, complicated by close association with a preceding major operation, yet brilliantly executed and prosecuted with an unselfish and heroic spirit of courage and fortitude that demanded eventual victory. It stands out as one of the very great achievements in the history of American arms." Arthur married second Cora B Benedict sometime after 1900 and raised a family of 4 children. Arthur was an Ironworker by trade working for the Hallstead Railroad, a line that ran to Spafford, NY. He had fallen off a handcar and suffered a compound fracture to his left leg, which had to be amputated. He struggled the remaining years of his life to provide for his family. Arthur died 20 Feb 1945 in Scranton, Lackawanna, Pennsylvania from Erysipelas, a serious bacterial infection in the skin. He is buried at Rose Hill Cemetery alongside his wife, mother and son in Hallstead, Pennsylvania. [50 51 52 53]

Unidentified Photo believed to be Henry M. Greene; Received from Herbie Meeks.

7. Henry M. Greene, son of John Greene and Mary Hill, was born 16 Apr 1796 in Hoosick, Rensselaer, New York. On 07 Apr 1831 he married Ann Mariah Coon in Marcellus, Onondaga, New York. He died 06 Apr 1879 in Spafford, Onondaga, New York. **Ann Mariah Coon,** was born 10 Oct 1813 in Marcellus, Onondaga, New York and died 09 Nov 1874 in Spafford, Onondaga, New York. Both are buried at Spafford Cemetery in Spafford, New York. Henry does not have a headstone to date. [54]

Although Henry was 16 at the onset of the War of 1812 it appears that he did not serve in that conflict, though his father, John, served his country as a Lieutenant in that war. He was, however, a second corporal in the 62nd NY rifle Co., which served much the same role as the National Guard of today. Though he served in peacetime, we have no doubt that he would have proved his mettle in battle as his family has, both before and since.

The image, on the next page, is of Henry Greene's promotion paper, the original document is in possession of Harley's great grandson, Richard Macchi of Texas. The document reads:

Harley Edward Greene

"By Barber Kenyon Captain of the Rifle Company of the 62nd Regiment of infantry in the State of New York to Henry Greene Greeting. You being appointed Second corporal in my company by virtue of authority in me vested, Repaying special trust_ in your patriotism courage and and (sic) good conduct I do authorize and empower you the said Henry Green to act as Second corporal in my Company. You are therefore carefully and dilligently (sic) to do the duty of a Second

Corporal in my Company according to the Rules and directive of the Malitia (sic) of this State and you are hereby required to pay due obedience to your superior officers and all officers and soldiers under you are hereby Required and directed to obey you as Second corporal for all of which this shall be your sufficient warrant. Given under my hand and seal this 22nd day of May 1821."
~ Signed ~ Barber Kenyon Capt

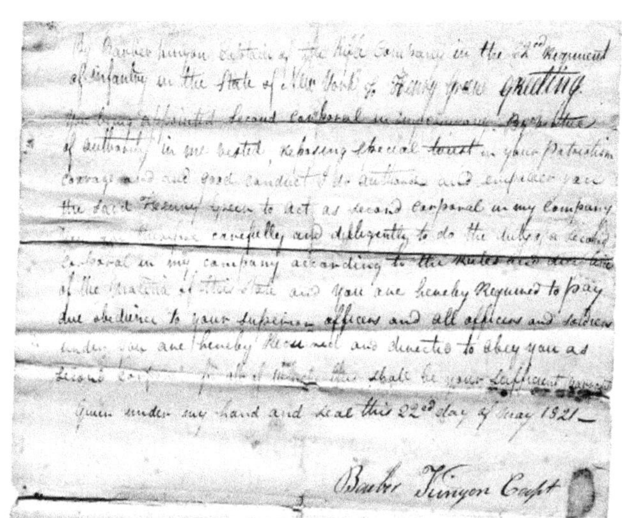

Henry M. Greene and Ann Mariah Coon had the following children:

a. Albert G. Greene born 11 Aug 1832 in Spafford, Onondaga, New York and died 28 Mar 1878 in Skaneateles, Onondaga, New York.. married 3 Dec 1852 in Scott, Cortland, New York, Melissa Wheeler. He is buried at Spafford Cemetery in Spafford, New York.

b. Alexander Greene born 15 Dec 1833 in Spafford, Onondaga, New York. He married in Scott, Cortland, New York, Matilda Rounds, daughter of Russell and Lydia (Harrington) Rounds. He was a blacksmith by trade and resided Spafford.

+

c. George Washington Maxington Greene born 17 Apr 1835 in Spafford, Onondaga, New York and died in Homer, Cortland, New York. He married 31 Mar 1861 Persis Viola Hazard in Great Bend, Broome, New York. He is buried at Spafford Cemetery in Spafford, New York. Persis is buried at Rose Hill Cemetery in Hallstead, Susquehanna, Pennsylvania

d. Mary A. Greene was born 12 Jun 1836 in Spafford, Onondaga, New York. She married Nov 1855 Erastus Griffin in Auburn, Cayuga, New York. She died 20 Jan 1861 in Otisco, Onondaga, New York.

e. Henry "Harry" M. Greene was born 6 Jul 1839 in Spafford, Onondaga, New York. On 2 Jun 1864 he married in Preble, Cortland, New York, Phidelia Riggals who was born 13 Jun 1849 in England and died 19 Sep 1919 probably in Preble, New York. Henry died in 1918 in Preble, New York.

f. Lucy Maria Greene was born 7 Sep 1840 in Spafford, Onondaga, New York. She first married 24 May 1864 in Auburn, Cayuga, New York George L. Hinds who was born in 1843 and died 18 Dec 1878. She married second Charles H. Sweet and resided in Carthage, Missouri.

g. Martha L. Greene was born 3 Apr 1842.

Harley Edward Greene

h. Rhoda A. Greene was born 30 Nov 1844 in Spafford, Onondaga, New York. She lived for a time in Brooklyn, New York. She died 22 Mar 1905 unmarried in Tully, Onondaga, New York. Her obituary reads: "Preble, Feb 20--Miss Rhoda Green, sister of Harry Green, died suddenly of heart failure of Friday evening at Hotel Tracy at Tully. Her remains were brought to Preble. The body was placed in the vault, from which place it will be taken to Spafford for burial in the spring. She was 60 years of age." [55]

i. Benjamin S. Greene was born 5 Mar 1846 in Spafford, Onondaga, New York and died 22 Mar 1847 probably in Spafford, New York.

j. Caroline Greene was born 18 Apr 1847 in Spafford, Onondaga, New York. She married 20 Oct 1869 in Syracuse, Onondaga, New York, Devillo Norton the son of Seymour and Sally (Lyman) Norton.

k. Frances Greene was born 12 Jan 1849 in Spafford, Onondaga, New York and Married in George Springer. They resided in Brooklyn, New York.

l. Orlando M. Greene was born 18 Jan 1851 in Spafford, Onondaga, New York. He died unmarried 16 May 1874 in Spafford, New York. He is buried at Spafford Cemetery; [photo of headstone taken] his headstone inscription reads: "Around my bed stood those that wept, and sighed to part with one so dear, But he in Jesus gently sleeps, Without a groan, without a fear."

m. Helen Greene was born 18 Jun 1853 in Spafford, Onondaga, New York. She married William Dennis. They resided in Auburn, Cayuga, New York.

8. John Greene, son of Christopher Greene of "Revolutionary memory,"[56] [57] was born 6 May 1761 in Preston, New London, Connecticut.[58] Before 1793 he married Mary Hill possibly in Hopkinton, Washington, Rhode Island. He died 25 Jul 1850 in Spafford, Onondaga, New York[59] and is buried in Stanton Yard Cemetery (no stone), Spafford, Onondaga, New York.[60] **Mary Hill,** was born between 1764-1768 probably in Rhode Island or Connecticut.

John served as a private in the Revolutionary War and was a Lieutenant in Thaddeus M. Wood's Regiment during the War of 1812. Often referred to as the "Second American Revolution" by historians, the War of 1812 was a war fought between the United States and Great Britain and lasted till 1815. There were many causes of the war, one cause was Britain had restricted trade, impeding on America's trade with France. The Native Americans, united by Tecumseh to oppose white man's westward expansion in the early 1800s and they joined forces with the British side during the war. The battles in New York State, occurred primarily in the Niagara frontier, a focus for both the British and American armies to control the Great Lakes and St. Lawrence River Corridor; one might recall the efforts of the famous Lake Erie hero, Oliver Hazard Perry (A distant cousin to Harley Greene). A large portion of the residents of Spafford participated in the war. Some smaller battles occurred in Rensselaer, Oswego and Queenstown; all are in the proximity of Spafford.

It's likely that he was a Seventh Day Baptist and lived fairly close to the church in Scott. His son, the Rev. Joel Greene was a reverend at this church and records indicate he was ordained by two church Elders one of whom was named John Greene. His son Henry is also believed to have been a Baptist Minister according to family stories, although no documentation has been found

Harley Edward Greene

to prove Henry or John were preachers. John was on the subscription list in 1843 for the Black River Journal, a religious newspaper owned by his son Joel until 1846, when he sold it.

It is probable that he travelled and settled in Onondaga County with some of his brothers. According to his Revolutionary War Pension, he claimed he was living in Plainfield, Connecticut before he enlisted into service at the beginning of the war and after peace. He then moved to Maple Town, Rensselaer, New York and on to Hoosick, Rensselaer, New York. His first four children are recorded as being born in Hoosick between 1793 - 1799. He then removed to Petersburg, Rensselaer, New York around 1800, then he removed to Nelson, Madison, New York, residing there for six years and then moving on to Otisco, Onondaga, New York for another six years. Based on these calculations and census records it would appear that John settled in Spafford about 1816.

There is a Mariam Greene buried in Spafford Cemetery in a row behind where Henry Greene is buried. Mariam Greene is the wife of Jeremiah Greene and two recorded daughters of Mariam are Loraine Greene who married Thurston Carr and Maria Greene who married Hiram Mason. Though it remains to find supporting evidence, a biography of Reverend Joel Green, published in 1880, has stated that his grandfather was the "Colonel Christopher Greene, of revolutionary memory." Although an earlier newspaper article from 1843 did not use a military title, stating only that his name was "Christopher Green, of revolutionary memory." After searching for soldiers of the Revolutionary War, the only Christopher Greene found was a Revolutionary War Hero who was brutally murdered at Red Bank by a band of Tory rebels, in retaliation for leading the first regiment of black soldiers against the crown. He has a monument in New Jersey and Congress awarded a sword to him for his heroic defense of Ft. Mercer against unreasonable odds, an event lauded by his cousin the General Nathaniel Greene and General George Washington.   Col. Christopher Greene's children are fairly well documented, as would be expected of a war hero and cousin of Nathanael Greene: there is no John among them. Unless dates and birthplaces of the Colonel's other children are wrong, a highly unlikely scenario for such an historical figure, there is no logical way for our John to fit. However, there is a Christopher Greene born in 1735, son of John and grandson of William Green, all who were from Preston, Connecticut, who fit the time frame for our John Green. John says in his Pension application that he was born in Preston, Connecticut. This must all be thoroughly researched out, as it would upset the best conjectures of the last hundred years. This Christopher does not fit the description of Joel's biography, but it wouldn't be the first time a family tradition proved false.
                    The Saga Continues….

John Greene and Mary Hill had the following children:
      i. Mary   b. 1 Jun 1793 d. 6 Oct 1852 m. Seneca Stevens
      ii. Christopher b. 16 Apr 1794 d. 6 Apr 1867 m. Elizabeth Newman
      iii. Henry M., Sr. b. 16 Apr 1796 d. 6 Apr 1879 m. Anna Mariah Coon
      iv. Rev. Joel   b. 4 Aug 1799 d. 27 Apr 1883 m. Nancy Frink
      v. Esther Hill   b. 23 Mar 1801 d. 4 Feb 1888 m. Samuel W. B. Sanford
      vi. Amon L. b. 15 Jul 1803 d. 1868 m. Eunice Belknap
      vii. Electa b. 11 Jul 1810 d. 1871 m1. Horton Applebee m2. unk. Ray
      viii. John, Jr. b. abt 1800 m. Lucy Stoddard
      ix. 2 unknown sons & 2 unknown daughters

Harley Edward Greene

The Ancestral Lineage of the author
back to Harley Edward Greene
Andrew Roland Myers

1.   **Andrew Roland Myers,** son of Dale Lawrence Myers and Mary Ellen Spotts. He married Janet "Jan" Laura (Collar) Miller. **Janet Laura (Collar) Miller,** daughter of William Peter Collar and Gloria Bishop. Issue: Acacia Myquala Paris Myers & Andrew William Lawrence Myers.

2.   **Mary Ellen Spotts**, daughter of Roland Edward Spotts and Helen Addie Wehunt. She married Dale Lawrence Myers. **Dale Lawrence Myers,** son of Andrew Jackson Hicks and Edith White; adopted by Arthur Otho Myers and Bessie Elvira Hicks. Issue: Andrew Roland Myers & Mary Melissa (Myers) Smith.[61] [62] [63] [64]

3.   **Helen Addie Wehunt,** daughter of Edward Gayle Wehunt and Addie Persis Greene, was born 26 May 1921 in Hot Springs, Garland, Arkansas. She married 19 Apr 1940 in Los Angeles, Los Angeles, California Roland Edward Spotts. She died 29 Jun 2005 in Gresham, Multnomah, Oregon. **Roland Edward Spotts,** son of Edward Abraham Spotts and Ruth O. Cubbage, was born 3 Mar 1917 in Battle Creek, Ida, Iowa. He died 12 Apr 1980 in Portland, Multnomah, Oregon. Both are buried at Mount View Memorial Garden in Forest Grove, Washington, Oregon. Issue: Shirley Ann, Kenneth Edward, Mary Ellen, Penelope Sue (died in infancy), Ruth Helen, Deborah Jean, Stephen Roland.[65] [66] [67]

4.   **Addie Persis Greene,** daughter of *Harley Edward Greene* and Fannie Ellen Parks, was born 20 Aug 1898 in Hot Springs, Garland, Arkansas. On 21 Sep 1919 in Royal, Garland, Arkansas she married Edward Gayle Wehunt. She died 17 Jan 1968 in Redding, Shasta, California. **Edward Gayle Wehunt,** son of Edward Austin Wehunt, was born 18 Dec 1899 in Mena, Polk, Arkansas and died 29 Jun 1977 in Anderson, Shasta, California. Both are buried at buried at Anderson Cemetery, Anderson, Shasta, California. Issue: Helen Addie, Paul Harlie, Imogene "Jean", Joseph Doyle, Grace Juanita Louise.

5. *Harley Edward Greene*

Harley Edward Greene

About the Author

I hope you have enjoyed reading about my family as much as my wife and I have enjoyed researching them. Although it has been an emotional roller coaster for us during this journey thus far and continues to be, it is more than worth it.

My name is Andrew Roland Myers. I have always had an interest in my roots, fostered by my parents, grandparents and especially my uncle, Raleigh D. Carothers. However, it was not until the early 1990's that I began to research my family history in earnest. When I married my wife, Jan, I found that her passion and research abilities complemented my own. Together, with our children, we enjoy traveling to our ancestors stomping grounds, learning their stories and following in their footsteps. Transcribing cemeteries and creating memorials on Findagrave.com has become an offshoot of this, as a service for those researching from afar, to preserve the information found on headstones that are often deteriorated and will soon be illegible.

I was born and raised primarily in Oregon with the exception of our traveling during my father's missionary work: we made two trips around the States and spent 2 years in the Philippines. My parents still reside in Oregon, my wife and I moved to upstate New York in early 2005. We live a rural life here in Upstate with our animals and dream of the day we will be truly self-sufficient. In my spare time I enjoy restoring abandoned heirlooms and building our house.

While my family's history is rich, my wife and I are working hard to preserve our own memories and those of our parents while we can. I am selfish and like to speak for myself…I want to tell my own stories! It is our wish that someday we will have preserved enough of our stories that our great grandchildren won't be left guessing to fill in the blanks of our lives.

Works Cited
For The Ancestral Lineage of
Harley Edward Greene

[1] Death Certificate, Harley E. Greene, file date "nd", file no. 604, Bear, Garland County; Arkansas Department of Health, 4815 West Markham Slot 44, Little Rock, AR 72205;. Copy in possession of author.

[2] *1870*; Census Federal Census [online ancestry.com] *Spafford, Onondaga, New York*; Roll *M593_1061*; Page: *718A*; Image: *688*; Family History Library Film: *552560*.

[3] Edward Allen Hazard, Letter to Daughter, 12 Jan 1873. [The original handwritten letter is in the possession of Chris Hazard. Letter used with permission. One of Edward's daughters was visiting her sister Persis, in Spafford to help Persis after the birth of her son Arthur. Arthur was 2 weeks old at the time the letter was written and his death certificate states he was born in Stafford, NY[sic] should be Spafford, NY.] Copy in possession of author.

[4] Marriage Certificate, Harley E Greene to Fannie E. Parks, 14 OCT 1889, Montgomery County, Arkansas, County Clerks's Office, 105 Hwy 270 E#10, Mount Ida, Arkansas, 71957, bk B, pg 405. Copy in possession of author.

Harley Edward Greene

---

[5] *1870 Federal* Census [online ancestry.com], *Sulphur Springs, Searcy, Arkansas*; Roll *M593_64*; Page: *51B*; Image: *102*; Family History Library Film: *545563*.

[6] Death Certificate, Fannie E. Greene, filed 2 FEB 1926, #565, Mill, Garland County; Arkansas Department of Health, 4815 West Markham Slot 44, Little Rock, AR 72205;. [Only surnames given for parents] Copy in possession of author.

[7] Greenwood Cemetery Transcription, online <http://www.rootsweb.ancestry.com/~armpgs/greenwood_cemetery.htm> Patti Vance Hays, compiler [pvhwdh@cablelynx.com], updated 10 MAR 2010; print out dated 12 MAR 2010.

[8] History of Spafford, NY [online http://history.rays-place.com/ny/onon-spafford.htm] [History of Onondaga County, New York with Illistrations and Biographical Sketches by Professor W. W. Clayton, pub. by D. Mason & Co., Syracuse, NY 1878].

[9] *1880 Federal* Census [online ancestry.com], Windsor, Broome, New York, Roll *T9_811*; Family History Film: *1254811*; Page: *533.2000*; Enumeration District: *62*; Image: *0446*..

[10] Viola "Aunt Vi" (Standridge) Austin, grand-daughter of Harley & Fannie Greene, Oral Interview, 13 Mar 2010 by author via phone [notes taken].

[11] Herbie Meeks, [herb1926meeks@alltel.net] Message to Andrew Myers, 2 Mar 2008 [This message gives a brief overview of various family members from his recollection.] Copy printed and in possession of author.

[12] Imogene "Jean" (Wehunt) Meekins, grand-daughter of Harley & Fannie Greene, Oral Interview, 1 APR 2009 by Jan Myers via phone [notes taken].

[13] Donald Harington, *Let Us Build Us A City: Eleven lost towns*, (Harcourt Brace & Company, Orlando, Florida, 1986) p.385, 411, 420

[14] "The Trail of Tears" online <http://ngeorgia.com/history/nghisttt.html> Golden Ink Internet Solutions, copyright 1996/1997, print out dated 14 April 2010.

[15] Land Patent from Abraham Parks to Ok Lo Hah, filed 1 Apr 1857 (Choctaw Scrip 80 acres), Batesville, Arkansas, Document No. 601C, Bureau of Land Management, 7450 Boston Blvd, Springfield, VA 22153. [Act/Treaty of Dancing Rabbit Creek, August 23, 1842] Copy in possession of author.

[16] Joyce (Moore) Hodges [<jehodges@moose-mail.com> or 17952 168th St. South, Bonner Springs, KS 66012]. "Hodges." < http://jehodges.tripod.com/Hodges.html> date unknown. [This webpage gives her Hodges Family history, unsourced.] Printout dated 14 April 2010.

[17] Photograph of Infant Son headstone, Greenwood Cemetery, Hot Springs Arkansas. Taken by Patti Hays [pvhwdh@cablelynx.com], APR 2009. Copy in possession of author.

[18] Photograph of George A Greene headstone, Greenwood Cemetery, Hot Springs Arkansas. Taken by Patti Hays [pvhwdh@cablelynx.com], APR 2009. Copy in possession of author.

[19] Photograph of Willie T Greene headstone, Greenwood Cemetery, Hot Springs Arkansas. Taken by Patti Hays [pvhwdh@cablelynx.com], APR 2009. Copy in possession of Drew & Jan Myers, Norwich, New York.

[20] Mabel Viola (Greene) Standridge, Online Memorial, <online http://www.findagrave.com/cgi-bin/fg.cgi?page=gr&GRid=22054139>, by Charles Austin [aka CLA], 9 OCT 2007, [memorial #22054139], printout dated 12 Mar 2010.

[21] Death Certificate, Addie Percy Wehunt, filed 19 JAN 1968, Local registration no. 4500, file number 37 page 320; Registrar of Vital Statistics, Assessor-Recorder Office, Shasta County, California. Copy in possession of author.

[22] Memorial [Funeral] Obituary for Addie P. Wehunt, pub. by The Record-Searchlight, Redding, California; 18 JAN 1968.Addie P. Wehunt, Obituary. [Memorial Obituary distributed to family at the time of the funeral giving a brief overview of her life and surviving family members.] Copy in possession of author.

[23] *1900 Federal* Census [online ancestry.com], *Bear, Montgomery, Arkansas*; Roll *T623_69*; Page: *4A*; Enumeration District: *127*.

[24] *1910Federal* Census [online ancestry.com], *Bear, Montgomery, Arkansas*; Roll *T624_59*; Page: *2B*; Enumeration District: *76*; Image: *309*.

[25] *1920 Federal* Census [online ancestry.com], *Hot Springs Ward 6, Garland, Arkansas*; Roll *T625_63*; Page: *2A*; Enumeration District: *84*; Image: *951*.

[26] *1930Federal* Census [online ancestry.com], *Bear, Garland, Arkansas*; Roll *75*; Page: *1A*; Enumeration District: *4*; Image: *579.0*.

[27] Marriage Certificate, E. G. Wehunt to Addie Green, 21 SEP 1919, Garland County, Arkansas, County Clerks's Office, 501 Ouachita Ave Rm 103, Hot Springs, Arkansas, 71901, bk marriages, pg 573. Copy in possession of author.

---

[28] Death Certificate, Edward Gayle. Wehunt, filed 5 JUL 1977, Local registration no. 4500, file number 451 page 165; Registrar of Vital Statistics, Assessor-Recorder Office, Shasta County, California. Copy in possession of author.

[29] Photograph of Edward & Addie Wehunt headstone, Anderson District Cemetery, Anderson, California. Taken by Kathy O'Brien [obrien.kathy@att.net], MAR 2009. Copy in possession of author.

[30] Photograph of Palestine Church, Bear, Garland, Arkansas. Taken by Dale Lawrence Myers [421 Second St, Fossil, Oregon 97830], JUN 1970. [Church built bet. 1920-1930; confirmed by Jean Meekins & Viola Standridge] Copy in possession of author.

[31] Lee Meeks, *World War I Draft Registration Cards, 1917-1918* [online ancestry.com] *Montgomery County, Arkansas*; Roll *1530564*; Draft Board: *0*. [Original data: United States, Selective Service System. *World War I Selective Service System Draft Registration Cards, 1917-1918*. Washington, D.C.: National Archives and Records Administration. M1509, 4,582 rolls. Imaged from Family History Library microfilm.]

[32] Lee Meeks, *California Death Index, 1940-1997* [database on-line]. Provo, UT, USA: Ancestry.com Operations Inc, 2000. Original data: State of California. *California Death Index, 1940-1997*. Sacramento, CA, USA: State of California Department of Health Services, Center for Health Statistics.

[33] Lee Monroe Meeks, Online Memorial, <http://www.findagrave.com/cgi-bin/fg.cgi?page=gr&GRid=8732240>, by Candice Konopacky [aka Candice xo], 8 MAY 2004, [memorial #8732240], printout dated 12 Mar 2010.

[34] This family has not been researched by the author.

[35] Death Certificate, George W. M. Green, filed 2 Sep. 1898, registration no. 641, file number 32030; New York State Department of Health, Vital Records Section, Genealogy Unit, P.O. Box 2602, Albany, NY 12220. Copy in possession of author.

[36] Principal Frank L. Greene, *Descendants of Joseph Greene, of Westerly, R. I.; also Other Branches of the Greenes of Quidnesset, or Kingston, R.I., And Other lines of Greenes in America,* (Albany, N.Y. by Joel Musell's Sons, pub. 1894) p.432-435.

[37] Death Certificate, Persis V. Greene, filed 27 Dec 1933, registration no.43-33, file number 111237; Division of Vital Records, 101 South Mercer St., P.O. Box 1528, New Castle, Pa 16103. Copy in possession of author.

[38] Photograph of Geo. M Greene headstone, Spafford Cemetery, Spafford, New York; Taken by author, 12 Jul 2008. Copy printed.

[39] Cemetery Record, Arthur F. Greene, Rose Hill Cemetery, Hallstead, Pennsylvania. [cemetery record transcribed by Jan Myers and headstone photo taken].

[40] Photograph of Persis V. Greene headstone, Rose Hill Cemetery, Spafford, New York; Taken by author, 8 Jul 2008. Copy printed.

[41] Susan Kresge, grand-daughter of Elizabeth (Greene) Mason, Oral Interview, AUG 2008 by author via multiple in personal visits. [Susan is currently 73 and with full mental capacity.]. Notes taken by author.

[42] Petition of John L. Hazard, Probate for Edward A Hazard; Index to Wills and Proceedings 1806-1916, Broome County Surrogate Court, Binghamton, Broome, NY. Copy in possession of author.

[43] Photo of Edward A Hazard headstone, Riverside Cemetery, Kirkwood, Broome, New York; Taken by author, 25 Jul 2008. Copy printed.

[44] Deed of Sale from Lydia Brooks to George M. Green, 4 Apr 1883 (filed 12 Apr 1883), Susquehanna County Courthouse, *11 Maple St.,,* Montrose, *PA* 18801. [Author forgot to record the deed book and page number]. Copy in possession of author.

[45] Sandra Button, great grand-daughter of Arthur Greene, Oral Interview, AUG 2008 by Jan Myers. [Sandra did not have very much information other than stated here.]. Notes taken by author.

[46] Death Certificate, Elizabeth V. Mason, [Transcribed by Gladys Kresge], filed 16 Nov. 1931, Located at Broome County Historical Society, 185 Court Street Binghamton, NY 13901; Greene Family Files. Copy in possession of author.

[47] Certificate of Marriage, M. M. Mason and Libbie V. Greene, License No. 104, Issued 12 Jun 1895, Susquehanna County Courthouse, 11 Maple St., Montrose, *PA* 18801. [Author forgot to record the deed book and page number]. Copy in possession of author.

[48] Death Certificate, Merton M. Mason, [Transcribed by Glady Kresge], filed 16 Jun 1949, Located at Broome County Historical Society, 185 Court Street Binghamton, NY 13901; Greene Family Files. Copy in possession of author.

Harley Edward Greene

---

[49] Cemetery Record, Merton M. Mason, dated 16 Jun 1949, Chenango Valley Cemetery, Binghamton, New York. [Headstone photo taken by author] Copy in possession of author.

[50] Death Certificate, Arthur Greene, registration no.244; Division of Vital Records, 101 South Mercer St., P.O. Box 1528, New Castle, Pa 16103. Copy in possession of author.

[51] Obituary, Sgt. Max A. Greene, undated clipping from Binghamton Press, Binghamton, NY, in family papers of Glady Kresge, Binghamton, NY; inherited 1974 by her daughter Susan Kresge, Conklin, NY and in her possession as of 2008. Scanned at Conklin, NY, 13 Jun 2009 by author [Image has been digitally retouched by Jan Myers to remove artifacts and for clarity. Data has not been changed.] Copy printed.

[52] Death Certificate, Cora B. Greene, filed 1932, registration no30-32, file no. 78098; Division of Vital Records, 101 South Mercer St., P.O. Box 1528, New Castle, Pa 16103. Copy in possession of author.

[53] Arthur Greene, Lawsuit, Syracuse, NY, The Syracuse Journal, 14 May 1903, p. 6, col. 7.

[54] George Knapp Collins, Mortuary Records with Genealogical Notes of The Town of Spafford, Onondaga County, New York. (Onondaga Historical Association, Dehler Press; 1917) [Guernsey Memorial Library, Norwich, New York.]p.110-112.

[55] Rhoda Green, Obituary, Syracuse, New York, The Syracuse Journal, 20 Feb 1905. pg 6 col. 3.

[56] "Whigs of 1776 and 1843" clipping from an unidentified newspaper handwritten date 7-8-43, Trib., in greene family file of Onondaga Historical Association, Syracuse, New York; [Lists Revolutionary War soldiers on their subscription list, reads: John Greene, ("father of one of the publishers of this paper, and son of Christopher Greene, of Revolutionary memory") of Onondaga Co. John Greene's son owned the Black River Journal in 1843, this may be the newspaper.] Photo taken by author and printed.

[57] Rev. Joel Greene, Biosketch, [online http://www.rootsweb.ancestry.com/~papastor/2j/joel_green.htm] Directory of Crawford County, Pa 1879-1880 pg 292. [Reads: "Joel Greene is a son of John Greene and grandson of Col. Christopher Greene, of revolutionary memory." In the original 1843 newspaper clipping nothing is stated that Christopher Greene was a Colonel.] Printout dated 15 Jun 2010.

[58] Revolutionary War Pension Application, John Green, [online footnote.com] Service State: Conn. No. S23659. Copy in possession of author.

[59] Andrew R. Myers, SAR Application, NSSAR # 159887, register date 2 Feb 2009. [death date had been entered incorrectly, and it was corrected with an actual date during the review process by a member of SAR.] Copy printed.

[60] Caroline Edith Hall, [Member of Onondaga Chapter, U.S.D. of 1812] A Partial List of Soldiers of The War of 1812 Who Are Buried in Onondaga County, New York. (Baldwinsville, New York, by the author, 1935) pg. 49.

[61] Birth Certificate, Mary Ellen Spotts, Local registration no. 4360, file number 1165; State of California, Department of Public Health, Bureau of Vital Statistics. [Since person is living this documentation is not provided.] Copy in possession of author.

[62] Marriage Certificate, Dale L. Myers to Mary E. Spotts, 20 Aug 1964, Portland, Oregon. [Since person is living this documentation is not provided.] Copy in possession of author.

[63] Birth Certificate, Dale Lawrence Myers, State registration no. 513, Local registration no. 218; Oregon State Board of Health, Vital Statistics Section. [Since person is living this documentation is not provided.] Copy in possession of author.

[64] Andrew Jackson Hicks, Obituary, undated clipping from an unidentified newspaper, located in the Pioneer Obituary Books at the Fossil Museum, Fossil, Oregon; [States he is survived by five children, one being Dale Hicks Myers. My father has always known he was adopted and Grandpa Andy as I called him growing up, lived with us before he died.] Photo taken by author and printed.

[65] Helen A. Spotts, Memorial Obituary, mailed to Andrew Myers by Mary Myers, daughter of Helen Spotts, along with photos of the casket; [Grandma, Helen, died shortly after I moved to New York and I was unable to attend her funeral.] Copy in possession of author.

[66] Marriage Certificate, Roland E. Spotts to Helen A. Wehunt, 19 Apr 1940, Los Angeles County, California. [This document was provided to me, the author by my mother, Mary (Spotts) Myers.] Copy in possession of author.

[67] Death Certificate, Roland E. Spotts, [This document was provided to me (author) by my Uncle Raleigh Dale Carothers] Oregon State Board of Health, Vital Statistics Section. Copy in possession of author.

Dear Debby …

By Debra Slater Garner, Researcher

Debra Garner

U. S. Army

It has been a busy year as Corresponding Secretary and Researcher for the Melting Pot Genealogical Society. During the first six months of the year, we have had more than one hundred requests for obituaries alone. Thanks to the efforts of our volunteers, we are updating our archived files of obituaries from various newspapers, as well as those that are sent to us to archive. The index for these obituaries is also updated daily by our web-host, Patti Hays on the Melting Pot website:

http://www.rootsweb.ancestry.com/~armpgs/.

We appreciate the dedication of all of those that help with this project to archive these obituaries for our researchers. An obituary can be a vital link in researching a family history.

Below I am listing a few of the interesting requests for information and for help with research that The Melting Pot received during the past several months.

Ms. Alsup had her fathers Army Service number. She was referred to the Veteran's Affairs office where she could obtain a record of his service during WWII. We were able to find general information on his service history at http://aad.archives.gov/aad/. Further research on this family led to the discovery that Ms. Alsup is a direct descendant of three men who served in the Revolutionary War: Capt. Archibald Wiggins, Thomas Christian, and John J. Amburgery, Jr. This information entitled her to membership in the Daughters of the American Revolution.

•

Dear Debby,
I am a petroleum land man who works with SEECO, INC. I am looking for descendants of Odum Augustus Pepper whose Van Buren County, AR land lease was notarized in Garland County, AR. Mr. Pepper died in 1954.
R. Haynes

Dear Debby,
My father died when I was 7 years old, and I know little about his family or history. I want to know about his time in the service and his ancestors.
Can you help me?   *D. Alsup*

Dear Debby ...

We were able to locate four children of Mr. Pepper's from census records and old telephone books. Mr. Pepper had a son living in Keene, TX at the time of his death. The telephone and address information of the Pepper families still living in the Keene, TX area was given to Mr. Haynes. Mr. Haynes needed to contact the family members concerning mineral rights.

•

Dear Debby,
I have some information on my Rucker family, but need to have it organized and researched further.
    C. Rucker

We were able to take Mr. Rucker's information and start the research for his Rucker Family. In doing do, we discovered a copy of a rare family book published in 1927. This book was a family history compiled by Edith Rucker Whitley which is out of print. We were able to get a copy of the book and it is now available at the Melting Pot Library. This research project was very successful by being able to take the Rucker family history back to the time of their arrival in the New World.

Dear Debby,
My great-great grandfather was Christian Jacob Fries. He was eight years old when he came to this country in 1880. I would like for you to check the passenger lists of ships that came into New York in 1880.
    J. Fries

Fries is a common surname for passengers coming from Germany. In checking more than 6,000 Fries, using various spellings, we were not able to determine which ship brought them to shore. However, we did locate the Naturalization papers of Christian Jacob Fries, who listed his address as Boston, MA. Later we found him in the 1900 and 1910 census records of St. Louis County, MO.

•

Dear Debby,
I am searching for the burial place of my grandparents, Herbert and Lou Ella Hasty Seay. They died in Hot Springs, AR. My mother is very ill, and has searched for almost sixty years in hopes of having a marker placed on their graves.   *A. Rockwell*

In researching the funeral home records by Lewis Stephens, we were able to find the names of both of the Seays. They were buried in Greenwood Cemetery.

Dear Debby ...

Ms. Rockwell was referred to Selected Cemetery Company so that they could locate the plots, and they could be marked with tombstones.

Greenwood Cemetery Entrance

•

Dear Debby,
Why does the Melting Pot list graves of people who are not deceased in the cemetery readings?
        G. Oldfather

When a volunteer is transcribing the tombstones at cemeteries, we often find markers with two names on them. Some of these markers have dates of birth, but no dates of death. This type marker is usually placed by the owner of the plot when the second person named is to be buried beside the first person. This is especially true in rural cemeteries to mark the plot as being reserved for the living person. We do not know if the person is deceased or not, so everything on the tombstone is listed so that we do not overlook an actual burial.

•

Dear Debby,
Please send me the death certificates for Elbrige and Hannah Smith who are buried in Morning Star Cemetery.
        S. Timblin

Morning Star Cemetery Entrance

Due to privacy laws, we are not allowed to request the death certificates of non-family members. Ms. Timblin was referred to the Vital Records office in Little Rock, AR. She was also given the online address below to request these certificates:
http://www.healthy.arkansas.gov/progra msServices/certificatesVitalRecords/Pag es/DeathRecords.aspx The Melting Pot Genealogical Society does not archive death certificates, unless a family requests that we do so.

•

Dear Debby,
I am searching for information on my great grandmother Elinor McGarth Lake who died in Hot Springs, AR.
        T. McGarth

For historical reasons, this request was among the most interesting to research. I was able to find the burial place of Dr. Elinor McGarth Lake in Greenwood Cemetery. Her grave is not marked.
Dr. Elinor McGarth was a 1910 graduate of Chicago Veterinary College. She is remembered as a pioneer, not just because she was a woman, but because of the type of veterinary practice which she chose. She was a small animal veterinarian in a time when most practices were tied to the farming industry and horses.

Dear Debby ...

Building a practice around pets was highly unusual. Dr. McGarth later married, but retained her maiden name. She was recently honored by the American Veterinary Medical Association on the hundredth anniversary of her graduation.
http://www.avma.org/onlnews/javma/jun07/070615d.asp

These are only a sample of the many requests that come our way during the year, and even as I write this article, there are still several months of adventures to come before the year is over. Several family histories are still being worked on and will be completed as time allows.

It has been a privilege to have a part in the creating of these family histories. I hope that the MPGS has been of help to those seeking answers about their ancestors. There have been occasions when, unfortunately, the 'brick walls" we run into in research are still standing, even after we have tried all avenues available.

If you have a family that you would like research data for, please let us know. Thanks to all of you that have helped in the preservation of the stories about the lives of your wonderful ancestors.

**Rebecca House Thornton
(Mother of Thomas Pascal Thornton)**

**Thomas Pascal Thornton and Annie Graham
(Ancestors of Debra Slater Garner)**

In Remembrance

Donald Brown

Jesse V. Clardy

Donald "D.A." Brown, 83, of Hot Springs, died Dec. 22, 2009. He was born to Andy and Janice (Morris) Brown. He was a member of New Salem United Methodist Church. He was a former Hot Springs fireman and policeman. He was a member of Texas VFW where he served as state judge advocate, district commander and district quartermaster. He was a retired electrician for Mary Kay Cosmetics in Dallas, TX.

Survivors include his wife of 59 years, Alma Nell Soward Brown; two sons, Gerald D. Brown and wife Vicky of Coppell, TX, and John G. Brown and wife Tracy, of Hot Springs; daughter, Elizabeth D. Miller and husband Mike, of Irving, TX; brother, Kenneth Brown and wife Dean , of Danville; two sisters-in-law, Patricia Brown, of Hot Springs, and Ramona Brown, of Ocean Springs, MS.

Funeral services are at Caruth-Hale Funeral Home with Pastor Don Robinson officiating. Burial is in Godwin Cemetery.

Jesse V. Clardy, 80, of Warrensburg, Missouri passed away Thursday, 24 December 2009 at the Western Missouri Medical Center in Warrensburg.

Jesse was born 15 February 1929 in Olney, Texas, son of Jesse Ellis and Tina Faye (Pringle) Clardy. He graduated from high school in Levelland, Texas and later served in the U. S. Army in Korea and Germany. He married Betty Sue (Powell) Cogburn on 6 August 1964 in Fayetteville, Arkansas. Jesse received his B.A. and M.A. at Texas A & I and his Ph.D in Russian History at the University of Michigan. He was a history professor at the University of Missouri for 45 years. He published several books and articles on Russian history and had six sabbaticals in Russia. He retired from teaching in 1999.

Survivors include his wife, Betty; two daughters: Kathy Prenger of Atco, New Jersey and Nita Cogburn of Overland Part, Kansas; two sisters: Gloria Heatherington of Louisville, Kentucky and Donna Luginbyhl of Mill Creek, Oklahoma; a brother; Dick Clardy of Lubbock, Texas; three grandchildren and several nieces and nephews.

In Remembrance

Willie Vance

Willie Doyle Vance, 83, died at his home in Owensville on July 15, 2010.

Born October 28, 1926, in Owensville to Reyburn Peay and Roxie Jane Caldwell Vance, he was a member of Owensville Baptist Church.. He attended Owensville and Paron Schools where he graduated in 1945. After high school graduation, he entered into the United States Army and was transferred to the Army Air Corps where he served in Japan and the Philippines. After being discharged from the service, he returned to Saline County and began working for Saline County Motors in Benton where he served as sales manager. He then worked for Thomas Auto Company in Benton where he served as general manager and worked there until retirement in 1990. After retirement, he returned to his family's farm raising livestock.

He was predeceased by his parents; brother, Gerald Vance and granddaughter Denise Denison.

Survivors include his wife of 60 years, Jimmie Wilson Vance; daughter, Patti Vance Hays, and husband, Dave, of Hot Springs; son, John Vance, and wife, Dorcas, of Owensville; grandchildren Lauri Denison McAdory and husband, Scott, of Benton and Justin Vance of Conway; great-grandchildren Olivia "Libby" Rosenthal and Drew McAdory; niece, Brenda Vance Richardson, and her husband, Larry; and sister-in-law, Jacqueline Dyer Vance.

Pallbearers are Justin Vance, Scott McAdory, Larrry Richardson, Andy Weise, Jerry Carden, and Gerald Wilson. Honorary pallbearers are Leonard Cathcart, Raymond Thomas, Lyndolf Ziegler, and Sonny Smith.

Funeral services will be July 19, at the Ashby Funeral Home Chapel with burial at Owensville Cemetery with the Rev. Gary Gipson and Rusty Keltner officiating.

☩

Willie's daughter, Patti Vance Hays, is the webmaster for The Melting Pot Genealogical Society.

Audrey Ann (Peters) Wilson Atherton

Family History
(Arkansas)

Although there are few dates in this narrative, some of the family background information may be interesting to the reader.

Henry Peters and his family lived on a small island off the coast of Schleswig - Holstein in northern Germany. Henry was the father of Leonard I and August I Peters. August I was the father of August Peters II, Leonard II, Mary, Rosa, Louisa, and Metz. All of these Peters' children were born in Germany, but dates are unknown except for August II, who was born in 1841.

The family set sail for America, and during the trip, Metz died aboard the ship. The family apparently settled in Missouri, where August II served in the Union Army during the Civil War. After the war, he married Sarah Wenzel who was born in Vichy Springs, Missouri, on January 3, 1851. She died in Hot Springs, Arkansas, on May 13, 1921.

About Sarah Wenzel: In 1664, the Tatum family left England for Virginia. The ship ran into a hurricane, and the passengers were shipwrecked near Bermuda. They were rescued and stayed in Bermuda until King Charles I sent another ship and gave the family a land grant of 300 acres in Westmoreland County, Virginia. This land adjoined the Washington family land. Nancy (Ball) Tatum and Mary (Ball) Washington were sisters, and their children Nancy Tatum and George Washington played together. Nancy Tatum married Mr. Barrow, and they had a daughter, Hannah Barrow. Hannah married Dr. John Leonard Roy, a Revolutionary War surgeon.

Hannah and Dr. John Roy had a daughter Mahalia, who married Mr. Wenzel. Mahalia was the mother of Sarah Louise, who married August Peters II.

Sarah and August II had five children, who were all born in Union, Missouri. Their children were Walter L., Oscar, Albert, Robert Leslie, and Mabel Eloise. Following the Civil War, August II sold his property in Missouri. He moved his family to Hot Springs in 1884 or 1885 for the thermal baths, as he was crippled with rheumatism and was in a wheelchair for twenty years. He bought the lumber company on Grand Avenue later known as Valley Lumber Co. August II died in Hot Springs on February 13, 1898, and was buried in Missouri. His parents, who were living in Washington, D.C., at the time, were too ill to attend the funeral.

Robert Leslie Peters

Audrey Ann (Peters) Wilson Atherton

Robert Leslie Peters was the fourth son of Sarah and August II. He was born June 3, 1880, in Union, Missouri. He married Corinne Nichols, who was born April 4, 1880. Robert was the founder of Peters Paint Company in 1906. Peters Paint was owned and operated on Ouachita Avenue by Robert, and later by his son, Bernard, until 1965, when it was sold to Richard Clem and moved to Malvern Avenue.

Robert Leslie and Corinne Nichols Peters had three children: Robert Bernard, Constance Arline, and John Leonard. Robert Leslie died February 1, 1953, and Corinne died December 19, 1970. Robert and Corinne are both buried at Greenwood Cemetery in Hot Springs, Garland County, Arkansas.

Robert's eldest child, Robert Bernard, was born June 15, 1904, in Hot Springs. He married Ann Marie Raible, who was born May 5, 1902. Bernard and Ann had one daughter, Audrey Ann. Bernard died August 12, 1967, while on a trip in Belgrade, Yugoslavia. Ann Marie died December 5, 2000. Both are buried at Greenwood Cemetery in Hot Springs.

Robert Bernard Peters

Ann Marie Raible Peters

Audrey Ann Peters married Gordon Balch Wilson, and they had two daughters, Suzanne Beall and Evelyn Peters. Evelyn married Hal Landrith, and they had two children, Graham and Audrey Ann.

Audrey Peters Wilson later married Dr. Lee Atherton.

Audrey Ann Peters Wilson Atherton

PEDIGREE CHART
of
JAMES CLARENCE BROWN

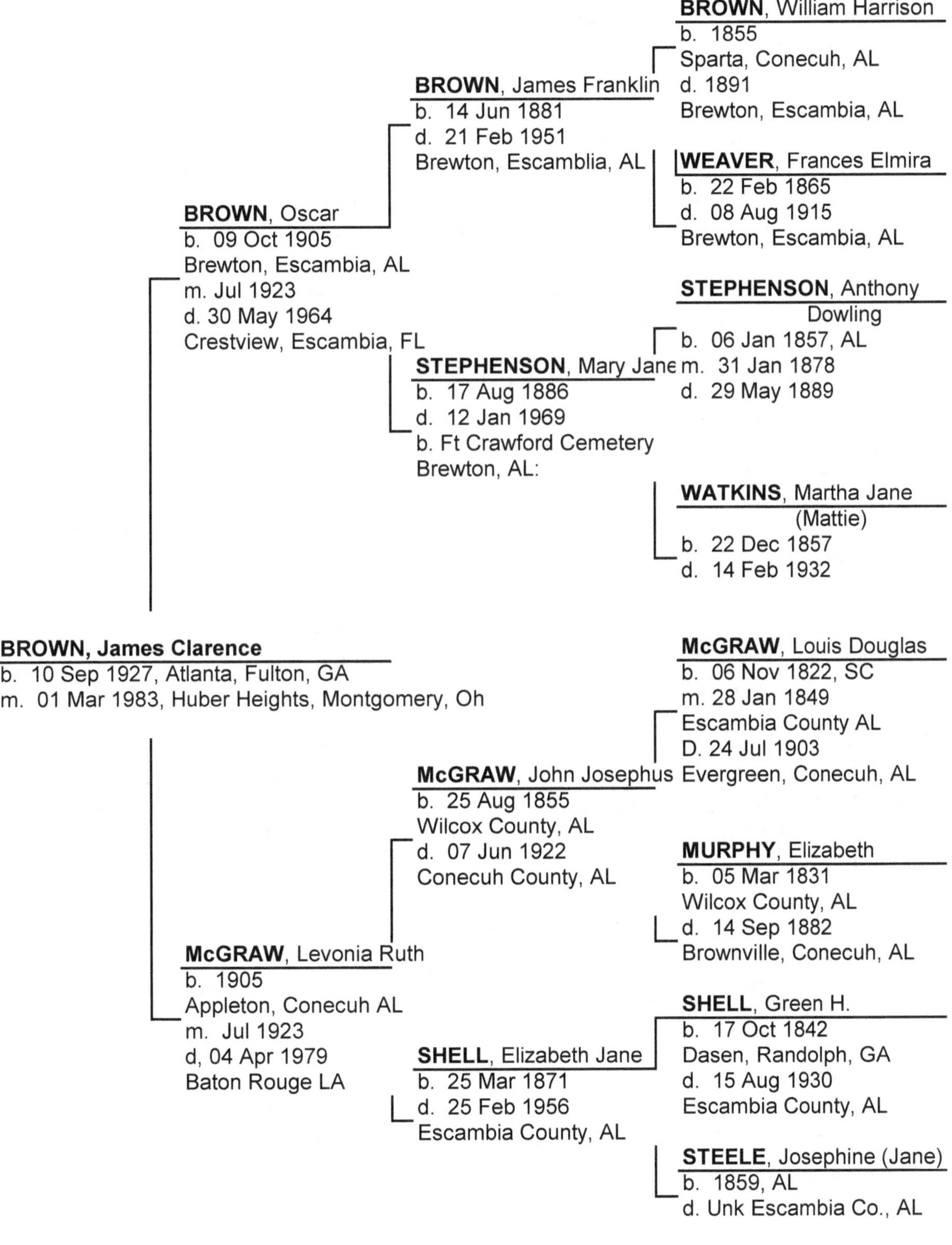

LINEAGE OF TWILA MARIE ACKLEY BROWN
SURNAME "ACKLEY"
(Ackley/Akly/Acly/Hagley/Atcherley/Hackley/Hackluite/deHackluite)

GENERATION 1. Twila Marie Ackley was born on 31 Dec 1934 on a farm east of Milton, Sumner County, Kansas to John Henry Ackley and Bertha Marie Whitmarsh Ackley. In 1943 the family moved to Wichita, Sedgwick, KS. She worked as a civilian with the Department of the Air Force, serving in Kansas, Arkansas, Ohio, Maryland, and Virginia. Upon retirement she moved to Hot Springs, Garland County, AR with her husband James C. Brown.

GENERATION 2. John Henry Ackley was born on 14 Nov 1903 in Sheffield, Jackson, Missouri. In 1920 he was living in Pratt County, KS with his grandparents, Allen and Sophie Ackley. He married Bertha Marie Whitmarsh (daughter of Julious Whitmarsh) in Macksville, Stafford, KS on 7 Jun 1933. They had two daughters. In 1960 John and Marie moved to a farm in Ozark County, MO. He died 1 Apr 1973 at Baxter Memorial Hospital, Mountain Home, AR, and was buried at Smith's Chapel Cemetery just north of Zanoni, in Ozark County, MO on 3 April 1973. Marie died 30 Mar 1985.

GENERATION 3. Marvin Edward Ackley was born on 27 Feb 1879 in Fairport, DeKalb, MO. He worked at a farm laborer in the Kansas City, Jackson County, MO area.
He married Mary Ellen Cunningham on 21 November 1900 in Sheffield, Jackson, Missouri, and they had three children - - Ethel Sophie Jane, John Henry, and Frances Elisabeth. Marvin and Mary Ellen separated in 1907-08 and he worked in Kansas and later as a ranch hand in South Dakota. He died in 1942, a homicide victim, near Deadwood, Lawrence, SD.

GENERATION 4. Allen Sylvester Ackley was born 13 Oct 1850 in Amherst, Erie, New York. He was a farmer in June 1880 at Grant, DeKalb County, Missouri and in 1920 in Pratt County, KS. He married Sophie Elizabeth Tucker on 6 Oct 1872 in Maysville, DeKalb, MO, and they had eight children. He died on 18 May 1943 in Macksville, Stafford, KS and was buried in Naron Cemetery, Byers, Pratt, KS.

GENERATION 5. Salmon C. Ackley was born on 4 Dec 1811 in Clarence, Erie, NY.
On 30 Jan 1842 he married Elizabeth Halter in Williamsville, Erie, NY. During the 1850s he moved with his wife and family to LaPorte, Indiana.   He died on 3 Sep 1869 in Fairport, DeKalb, MO and is buried in Woods Cemetery at Fairport.

GENERATION 6. Zebulon S. Ackley was born about 1774. He purchased land about 1804 in Western New York. He was involved in the war of 1812. He was living in Clarence, Erie, New York and died there in Jan 1813 during a cholera epidemic that swept the area during the winter in 1812-1813, leaving 4 small children and his wife Esther Kelsey Ackley who died on 6 Jul 1813.

GENERATION 7. Jeremiah Ackley was born on 26 Sep 1742 in Colchester, New London, CT. He died about 1817 in Lancaster, Erie, NY when struck by a falling tree. He served in the French

LINEAGE OF TWILA MARIE ACKLEY BROWN
SURNAME "ACKLEY"

and Indian Wars in Connecticut Second Regiment in 1760. Jeremiah was a Loyalist. He married Sarah W. Woodson.

GENERATION 8. Nicholas Ackley was born 16 Dec 1708 in East Haddam, Middlesex, CT and was baptized on 6 Mar 1709. He served in the military French and Indian Wars in Colchester, New London, CT in Lyman's regiment, Col Phineas Lyman commanding, 11th Company Capt Edmund Welles, commanding campaign of 1757, and the Connecticut Second Regiment in 1762. He married Jerusha ?. He died about 1763.

GENERATION 9. James Ackley Sr. was born abt 1677 in East Haddam, Middlesex, CT. He was baptized on 29 March 1707. He died on 19 Sep 1746 and was buried in Cove Cemetery, East Haddam, Middlesex, CT.   He married Elizabeth Comedy about 1706 in East Haddam. She was born abt 1689 and died on 19 Sep 1755.

GENERATION 10. Nicholas Ackley, son of John and Elizabeth, was born in 1635 in Shalford, Essex, England; died 29 April 1695 in East Haddam, Middlesex, CT. He married Hannah Ford Mitchell abt 1656 in Hartford, Hartford, CT. He married Miriam Moore after 1687.
Notes for Nicholas Ackley: Nicholas may have been one of several young men brought over to America by William Wadsworth on the good ship "Mary and John" from Plymouth, England to Nantucket MA. His address in 1655 was on Turnbull Street in Hartford, CT. Nicholas had two pieces of land recorded to him in Hartford.   He was one of 28 young men, pioneers of Haddam, who bought land in 1662 at "30 Mile Island" later called Haddam. He moved his family to this land in 1667. Nicholas owned in Haddam a 14 acre home lot as well as the "little island at the lower end of the cove" and a "6 acre lot towards Saybrook." This cove is where the Salmon River enters the Connecticut River.

GENERATION 11. John Hackley/Ackley was born in 1621 and was baptized on 16 September 1625 in Hopton Castle, Shropshire, England, and died in England. He married Elizabeth Bailey in St. Anselm, daughter of Peter Bailey. He married his second wife, Jane on Feb 2 1659. She was buried at Hampton Castle on Mar 16, 1680. John was buried in October 1684.

GENERATION 12.   John Hackley was born 24 Mar 1581/82 in England, and married Mary Gates, daughter of Peter Gates and Mary Joselyn, on 3 May 1603.

GENERATION 13. William Ackley was born 11 Jan 1550/51 in Hopton Castle, which is a few miles south of Acton, England and died in England. He was a Grocer in London, E. On 9 Jun 1581, he married Joanna Chattfield in St. Andrew Hubbard.

GENERATION 14. Richard Hagley was born 4 May 1503 in Acton, Shropshire, E. He married Mathilda (Maud) Wall, daughter of Richard Wall, on 29 October 1548 in Hopton Castle. He died and was buried on 17 June 1591. His widow Matilda Hagley was buried on 22 Sept 1593.

LINEAGE OF TWILA MARIE ACKLEY BROWN
SURNAME "ACKLEY"

GENERATION 15. Roger Hackley was born between 1452-1482 in Stanwardine, Shropshire, E, and died in England. He married Margaret Wythem, daughter of Richard Wythem, on 17 March 1499/00,

GENERATION 16. Rogeris Hackley/Atcherley was born in England and died between 1471-1533 in England. In 1466, he married Anne Hadley.

GENERATION 17. Richard Hackluite was born between 1456-1489 in England, and died in England. He married Sybill (Sibill) Maylborne, daughter of Symonde Maylborne, about 1500. Richard owned property in Yetton County, Hereford (Eaton in Leominster).

GENERATION 18. Henry Hackluite was born between 1448-1480 in England and died between 1505-1567. He married ? Cassey about 1500 in Whitefield, East.

GENERATION 19. Richard Hackluite was born between 1391-1420 in England and died in England. He married Maulde Vaughn, daughter of Roger Vaughn, between 1412-1480.

GENERATION 20.   Walter Hackluite was born Abt 1370 in England, and died in England. He married Elizabeth Oldcassell, daughter of Thomas Oldcassell, abt 1390. .

GENERATION 21. Hughe De Hackluite, Sheriff of Hereford, was born Abt. 1340 in Easton Roster, Leominster County, Hereford, England and died in England.

Ackley Family

Back: Marvin Edward (3), George Lee, Thomas Corwin, Martha Mariah,
Front: Arthur William, Allen Sylvester (4), Harvey Allen,
Sophie Elizabeth (Tucker), Roy Sylvester

John Henry, Ethel Sophie,
Marvin, Frances Elisabeth Ackley

ARKANSAS MAP 1819
Donated by Twila Ackley Brown

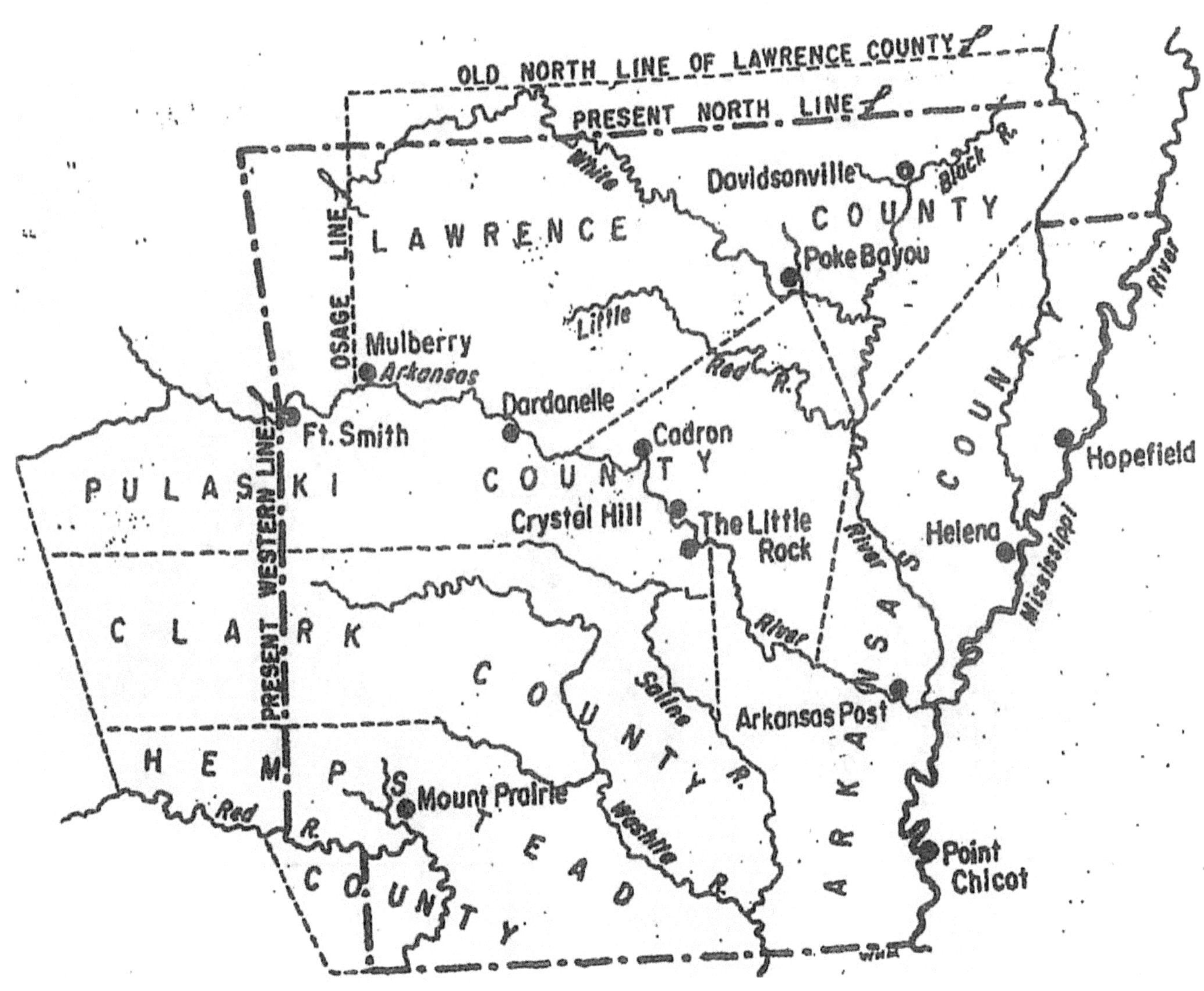

Oak Street School
6th Grade, 1944

Oak Street School was located on Olive Street in the lower three story section of the Hot Springs High School, Hot Springs Junior High, and Oak Street School complex of buildings. The large lot across the alley from Oak Street School was the playground.

Ms. Robbie Allen was the Principal of the elementary school, and this was the 6th grade class that she taught in 1944.

6th Grade Class of Robbie Allen's, Principal

(Left to right)
<u>bottom row</u>: Dorothy Ann Pyle, Mary Jane Maus, Mary Ann Grantham
2nd <u>row</u>: (unknown), Mary Angela Clinton, Catherine Anderson, Burnell Owens, Robin Dale Wilson, Anna Jean Pappas, Betty Mann?, Jack Panzer, James Harmon
3rd <u>row</u>: (unknown), Betty Lou Taylor, Theresa McCammond, Marjorie Searcy, (unknown), Barbara DeBolt, Gregory Fotioo
4th <u>row</u>: (unknown), Sue Fleming, Opal Morgan, Margaret Cannon, Argie Slates, Jo Ann Honeycutt
5th <u>row</u>: (unknown), Jerry Collins, Sally Harmon, Owen Overton, J. D. Anderson
<u>Top</u>: Clifford Ledbetter

DISCOVERING MAXINE …

By Pamela Tremé
(Florida)

Every genealogist I know has brick walls and I'm no different. The twist for me is that my brick walls usually start with a name in a will that has no match in my records. And so it was with one Mrs. Maxine **OWEN**, nee **GREEN** of Vega, Texas. Maxine is mentioned as an heir in an Executor's Notice in the will of Robert **McKINLEY**[i]. Unfortunately, the will makes no mention of Maxine's relationship to Robert.

Robert **McKINLEY** had a large family—eight children—and I have tracked down a considerable number of family members from cradle to grave. Still no **GREEN** or **OWEN** appear in any of my research.

THE ROBERT McKINLEY FAMILY

Front row from left: Robert Charles, Lemuel Ransom

Second row from left: Samuel Gilmore, **Robert**, **Sarah**, and Ella Jane

Back row from left: John William, Nancy Harriet, Mary Susan, and James Henry.

The wall calendar is turned to October 1897.

(Visit the following website to learn more about this family:
http://freepages.family.rootsweb.ancestry.com/~amckee/index files/Page 624.htm)

I am nothing if not a methodical researcher. One rainy afternoon while doing a survey of missing records, I realized I was missing a 1900 census entry for Robert's oldest daughter, Ella Jane **McKINLEY** (Mrs. William **STEWART**). The **STEWART** family wasn't in Randolph County, Illinois, where I expected to find them. So I widened my search to include St. Clair County. From experience, I knew that my family members frequently moved to Marissa, Illinois. The record for the **STEWART** family popped right up[ii].

DISCOVERING MAXINE ...

The 1900 census entry revealed that I had been missing a child, one Ruana **STEWART**. I had traced two other **STEWART** children to Deaf Smith and Oldham counties in Texas. Vega, Texas, the home of Mrs. Maxine **OWEN**, is in Oldham County. Therefore, it seemed logical to search for the names **GREEN** and **OWEN** in Oldham County. Using Google, I immediately hit a cemetery entry: (Note: The correct name is Ruana rather than Ruey as spelled on the cemetery entry.)

> **GREEN**, Ruey (correct spelling): April 8, 1882 - March 6, 1915; "Wife of H.G. **Green**" (Section 5, Row 2) [iii]

The website also included a corresponding entry for her husband Herbert Glenn **GREEN**, b. 27 February 1876, and died 23 February 1949. This line of research looked promising.

A quick check of the 1910 census shows Ruey and Herbert **GREEN** living in Deaf Smith County, Texas. The census reveals that Ruey and Herbert have one child, Maxine **GREEN**[iv]. Ruana's sister, Ella Ethel **STEWART**, is also shown in the household and Ruana's brother, William Melvin **STEWART**, appears on the same page—a few lines above the **GREEN** family.

My next step was to contact Kay **JETTON** of the Marissa Historical and Genealogical Society, and she found a marriage record for Ruana **STEWART** and Herbert **GREEN**. They married 5 September 1901, in St. Clair County, Illinois.

Ruana Stewart Green

Herbert Glenn Green

Ruana died in 1915 in Vega, Oldham County, Texas. Raising a daughter on his own in Texas must have been problematic for Herbert, because in the 1920 census, I find Maxine **GREEN** living with an aunt and uncle in St. Clair County, Illinois[v].

By the 1930 census, Maxine would be 27 years old and most likely married. If Maxine married someone named **OWEN**, she would be Maxine **OWEN** on the 1930 census. A check of the 1930 census has Maxine married to Joplin Garrett **OWEN**, living in Vega, Oldham County, Texas, with the following children[vi]:

DISCOVERING MAXINE …

- James Herbert Owen, b. 27 March 1923, Vega, Oldham County, Texas
- Evelyn Maxine Owen, b. 1 March 1925, Vega, Oldham County, Texas

     Checking the Texas Birth Index and Social Security Death Index confirms the birth dates of the children.

Maxine Green Owen   Joplin Garrett Owen

     The Texas Death Index provides another lead in that it lists the death of Joplin Garrett **OWEN** on 2 October 1933, Vega, Oldham County, Texas. Using NewspaperArchive.com, I was able to find an obituary for Joplin. (Note: this obituary lists the last name as Owens rather than as Owen.)

The *Amarillo Globe*, Amarillo, Texas, 2 Oct 1933, Page 2

VEGA NEWSMAN DIES SUDDENLY HEART ATTACK CLOSES
CAREER OF SENTINEL EDITOR EARLY TODAY

Joplin Garrett **OWENS**, 33, editor and owner of the Vega Sentinel, died suddenly at 12:30 o'clock Monday morning at his home in Vega. Death resulted from a heart attack. **OWENS** apparently had been in excellent health. He spent most of last week attending the Tri-State Fair in Amarillo.

A resident of Vega for 25 years, **OWENS** had been associated with the Vega Sentinel for the last 15 years. He attended Wayland College and was a World War veteran. He also was a member of the Masonic Lodge.

Surviving are his wife (Maxine) and two children, Jimmie and Evelyn; his father and mother, Col. and Mrs. J. T. **OWENS**, all of Vega.

Funeral arrangements had not been announced Monday afternoon. The body is in charge of the N. S. Griggs & Sons Funeral Home.

     My next hint for family members comes from the 1949 obituary of Ruana's husband, Herbert Glenn **GREEN**.

Amarillo Daily News, Amarillo, Texas, 24 Feb 1949, Page 19

DISCOVERING MAXINE ...

GREEN

Herbert **GREEN**, 73, Vega, husband of Lillian **GREEN**, father of Mrs. Richard **CARTER**; Mrs. Maxine **GIRARD**; also survived by three grandchildren. Services 2 PM Friday, Vega Methodist Church.

This obituary gave me my first hint that Maxine **(GREEN) OWEN** was Mrs. Maxine **GIRARD** by at least 1949 but probably earlier. The Social Security Death Index shows Mrs. Maxine **GIRARD**, b. 17 September 1903, d. February 1992 in Arkansas. Where in Arkansas was another question.

Hank and Maxine (Green) Owen Girard

A little bit of hacking around on Google led me to a Find A Grave entry for Jimmie Herbert **OWEN**. The entry has Jimmie b. 27 Mar 1923; d. 25 May 1987, (U.S. Navy WWII) married to Helen **SPENCER**. Jimmie is buried in Oakhill Cemetery, Fountain Lake, Garland County, Arkansas.

After failing to find an obituary using my usual sources, I checked the Random Acts of Genealogy Kindness website for a volunteer. The very gracious Linda **MILLER** (genealogist and president of The Melting Pot Genealogical Society) looked up Jimmie's obituary.

Sentinel Record, Hot Springs, AR, Wednesday, 27 May 1987, Page 18

Jimmie H. **OWEN**

Jimmie Herbert **OWEN**, 64, died Monday, May 25, at a local hospital.

He had been a resident of Hot Springs since 1940. He was retired from Reynolds Metals Co., a naval veteran, and a Methodist.

Survivors included his wife Helen **OWEN** of Hot Springs, two sons, Michael **OWEN** and Randy **OWEN**, both of Hot Springs; one daughter, Barbara **MELUGIN** of Little Rock; his mother, Maxine **GIRARD** of Hot Springs; one sister, Evelyn **SARGO** of Hot Springs, and two grandchildren, Missy **MELUGIN** and Dax **MELUGIN**.

DISCOVERING MAXINE ...

Services will be held at 10:30 a.m. Thursday at Hot Springs Funeral Home Chapel with the Rev. James **NEWMAN** officiating.

Pallbearers will be Rocky **SMITH**, Ron **HARRIS**, Sam **SARGO**, Doyle **LEE**, Scotty **DODD** and Glen **WARREN**.

Honorary pallbearers are Ernest **BRESHEARS**, Joe **DODD**, Alfred **WILLIAMS**, Charles **WELCHMAN**, Wayne **BERKEY**, Earl **DAVIS**, Dr. **REDDY**, Dr. **CRABTREE**, Dr. **JAYARAMAN**, and the Heart Clinic Oncology Unit staff of St. Joseph's Regional Health Center. Burial will be in Oak Hill Cemetery under the direction of Hot Springs Funeral Home.

Jimmie's obituary proves that Maxine **(GREEN) OWEN GIRARD** was still living as late as 1987, probably in Hot Springs, Arkansas.

Book presentation at Garland County Library in honor of Maxine Girard,

(sitting lower left). Maxine's knowledge of Art Glasses resulted in people from all over the country sending pictures to her for identification. Her collection of resource books formed the foundation for the library's antique glassware section.

After some more searching on Google, I found the Rockdale Cemetery list with the following entry[vii]:

Girard, Henry B. 09/08/1899-02/19/1974 with Maxine 09/17/1903-02/15/1992

With a date of death, I was able to ask Linda Miller to look for this additional obituary.

Sentinel Record, Hot Springs, Arkansas

Maxine **GIRARD**

Maxine **GIRARD**, 88, of Hot Springs, died Saturday, Feb. 15, 1992, at her home.

DISCOVERING MAXINE ...

She was a resident of Hot Springs for 50 years, the retired owner of **GIRARD**'s Antiques, founder and member of Hot Springs and Arkansas State Antiques Dealers Association, a past worthy matron of The Order of the Eastern Star and a member of the Arkansas Iris Society.

Survivors include, one daughter, Evelyn **SARGO** of Hot Springs; five grandchildren, six great grandchildren and one great-great-grandchild.

Services for Maxine **GIRARD**, 88, of Hot Springs, who died Saturday, Feb 15, will be at 10 a.m. Thursday in Rockdale Cemetery.

The Rev. James W. **MOSLEY** will officiate.

Friends may call at the **SARGO** residence, 3822 Park Ave.

With this obituary, I had gathered a body of evidence that has allowed me to track down many pieces of additional information. And thus I discovered exactly who **Maxine (GREEN) OWEN GIRARD** was along with lots of other relatives I would never have otherwise known about. Because of many finds like this one, I've learned to embrace my brick walls as opportunities to flex my research muscles and test my search instincts.

McKinley Family Line to Maxine and Her Children:

Robert **MCKINLEY**; b. 20 Jul 1941, Lakewood, Cuyahoga Co., OH; d. 20 Dec 1923, Tilden, Randolph Co., IL, married 10 Oct 1861, Randolph Co., IL
Sarah **MCKEE**; b. 1841 New York City, NY; d. 18 OCT 1909, Tilden, Randolph Co., IL

Ella Jane **MCKINLEY**; b. 12 Apr 1863, Randolph Co., IL; d. 10 Jan 1910, in Iola, Allen County, Kansas. Married
William **STEWART**; b. Aug 1854 Ireland; d. between 1900 and 1910 probably in Texas
At the time of her death, Ella is living with her youngest son, Wesley James Stewart, Ruana's younger brother.

Ruana **STEWART**; b. 8 Apr 1882, Perry Co., IL; d. 6 Mar 1915, Vega, Oldham Co., TX, married 5 Sep 1901, St. Clair Co., IL

DISCOVERING MAXINE …

Herbert Glenn **GREEN**; b 27 Feb 1876, St. Clair Co., IL; d. 23 Feb 1949, Vega, Oldham County, TX

Maxine **GREEN**; b. 17 Sep 1903, Marissa, St. Clair Co., IL; d. 15 Feb 1992, Hot Springs, Garland Co., AR, married
Joplin Garrett **OWEN**; b. 11 Nov 1899, Joplin, Jasper Co., MO; d. 2 Oct 1933, Vega, Oldham Co., TX   (Thus, Maxine is the great-granddaughter of Robert **McKinley**).

Child #1:
James Herbert **OWEN**; b. 27 mar 1923, Vega, Oldham Co., TX; d. 25 May 1987, Hot Springs, Garland Co., AR, married
Helen Leona **SPENCER**; b. 20 Jul 1928, Hot Springs, Garland Co., AR

Child #2:
Evelyn Maxine **OWEN**; 1 Mar 1925, Vega, Oldham Co., TX; d. 28 Jan 2003, Hot Springs, Garland Co., AR, married Burton Otis Samuel **SARGO** b. 25 Jan 1925, Hot Springs, Garland Co., AR, d. 17 Oct. 2004, Hot Springs, Garland Co., AR

---

[i] Will of Robert MCKINLEY, Randolph County Court House, Chester, Illinois, 1924, Box 213, Page 110; See also http://genealogytrails.com/ill/randolph/willofmckinley.htm

[ii] 1900 United States Federal Census, Illinois, St. Clair County, Marissa, SD 15, ED 115, Sheet 14 B (8007)

[iii] USGENWEB Website: Memorial Park Cemetery in Vega, Oldham County, Texas; last accessed 12 September 2009 at the following address:
ftp.rootsweb.ancestry.com/pub/usgenweb/tx/oldham/cemetery/vega.txt

[iv] 1910 United States Federal Census, Texas, Deaf Smith County, Justice Precinct 4, District 76, SD 13, ED 76, Sheet 22 B (1921) (Marine)

[v] 1920 United States Federal Census, Illinois, St. Clair County, Marissa, SD 14, ED 197, Sheet 14 A (9122) living with Charles and Della Morganthaler

[vi] 1930 United States Federal Census, Texas, Oldham County, Vega, ED 180-3, SD 1, Sheet 4 A (65, 9737)

[vii] Garland County, Arkansas Website; Rockdale Cemetery List; last accessed 12 September 2009 at the following address: www.argenweb.net/garland/rockdale.html

Pictures of Stewart, Green, Owen, Girard family members provided by Jan Sargo Thomason, daughter of Evelyn Owen Sargo and granddaughter of Maxine Green Owen Girard.

About the Author: Pamela Ann Tremé was born and raised in New Orleans where she developed a natural affinity for old things – including old long-forgotten relatives. Pam has been researching her Scots-Irish family for many years. She currently lives in the Tampa Bay area and works as a technical writer for a large telecommunication firm. She is a member of a number of genealogical societies and a regular contributor of articles to society quarterlies and newsletters. She serves as editor of the Florida State Genealogical Society newsletter. Pam is one half of a team that presents for genealogical societies in the Tampa Bay area. She has two books in the works at the moment, and she hopes to finish and publish them soon. She plans to publish a series of books about her Scots-Irish family and the times in which they lived.

ROCKDALE CEMETERY

Transcribed by
Patti Vance Hays and Charleen Cook Nobles
February 2010

GPS coordinates: Latitude: 34.58257 Longitude: -93.98216

Directions from Hot Springs, Arkansas: Take Park Avenue (Highway 5/7 North) from Central Avenue; go about 100 yards past where Highway 7 veers off Park Avenue staying on Highway 5 instead of taking the left on Highway 7. (You will have driven about 6.2 miles after entering Park Avenue from Central Avenue.) Turn left on Rockdale Road (sign says Rockdale Baptist Church); then turn left on a dirt road past 215 Rockdale Road and before the church.

Rockdale Cemetery was read by Patti Vance Hays in February 2010. Charleen Cook Nobles assisted in listing the parents and spouses of those resting in the cemetery. There are numerous unmarked graves in this cemetery, and it is believed that the cemetery is actually much older than the markers indicate. The name on the marker, with the dates of birth and death are as shown on the marker. Information in parenthesis is additional information that was found through research.

Abbreviations: LNU (last name unknown)

Billy Don Sargo (11/16/1932-02/01/1993) was buried in Rockdale Cemetery but was moved to Hollywood Cemetery in Hot Springs.

ROCKDALE CEMETERY

Name on Marker	Date of Birth	Date of Death	Parents	Spouse
Bashor, Florence P.	01/22/1867	04/17/1937	Jasper Pugh and Emily Ingersoll[1]	John L. Bashor
Bashor, John L.	06/22/1858	09/06/1940	Joseph Bashor and Margaret DeLauder[1]	Florence Pugh
Bierman, Charles W. C.	08/20/1874	08/27/1880	R. C. and J. W.	
Bierman, Sidney Daniel	06/26/1889	06/06/1890	J. W. and R. C.	
Biermon, John E. G.[a]	02/07/1876	04/10/1901		
Brown, Elizabeth Sargo	03/07/1905	01/06/1983	Simon Sargo and Mary Cates	Jesse F. Brown
Brown, Jesse F(red)[2]	04/24/1877	12/14/1960	George Brown and Lucinda Church[2]	Elizabeth Sargo
Caldwell, Fletcher W.	06/03/1908	06/27/1980	Walter Samuel Caldwell and Dora Moore	Ollie Brown; Thelma L. (LNU)
Caldwell, Kenneth Jack	01/29/1937	11/04/1995	Fletcher W. Caldwell and Ollie Brown	Patsy Graves
Caldwell, Ollie M.	03/02/1902	04/10/1975	Will Brown and Daisy Dickson	Joseph A. Moore; Walter S. Caldwell
Caldwell, Patsy N. "Pat"	03/30/1941	01/27/1995	Bert Graves and Sylvania Breshears	Kenneth Jack Caldwell
Cook, Donald Eugene	05/06/1922	11/02/1969	John Roland Cook and Edna Leake	
Cook, Edna Leake	01/30/1897	06/19/1994		John R. Cook[3]
Cook, Harry G(erome)[1]	10/09/1901	06/13/1956	John Cook and Margaret (LNU)[1]	

---

[a] His tombstone is spelled Biermon.

ROCKDALE CEMETERY

Name on Marker	Date of Birth	Date of Death	Parents	Spouse
Cook, John Roland	12/03/1896	07/13/1981	John F. Cook and Margaret Jane Purtle[4]	Edna Leake[1]
Cook, Margaurite J.[b] (Margaret Reynolds)[1]	08/11/1871	12/04/1949	Jack Pirtle and Mary Ann Bucks[1]	
Cowan, Carl B.	04/17/1917	07/03/1979		Mary[2] or Bertha (LNU)[7]
Cowan, Mary Etta Hinkle	08/07/1921	12/17/2000	John Hinkle and Emma Sargo	Carl B. Cowan
Disheroon, Andrew T.	1869 09/06/1869[5]	1933 11/10/1933[5]	S. Disheroon[5]	Laura (LNU)[5]
Dodson, Arthur[c]	09/03/1876	08/16/1891	Thomas M. Dodson and Cora Cooksey[6]	
Dodson, Claudy[c]	04/17/1878	08/16/1891	Thomas M. Dodson and Cora Cooksey[6]	
Dodson, William M. Sr.	1874 (05/28/1873)[2]	1959 (04/29/1959)[2]	Thomas Milton Dodson and Cora Cooksey[2]	Rose M. (LNU[2]
Downen, Violet Ann Cockrell[9]	09/20/1958	11/15/2006	Glenn T. Cockrell[7] and Beatrice Phillips[3]	Edward Downen[7]
Edwards, Sylvia Sargo	11/16/1895	04/09/1979	Simon Sargo and Mary Cates	Will David Edwards
Edwards, Will David	06/11/1886	06/01/1965	Young Edwards and Sarah Jane Allen[2]	Sylvia Sargo[3]
Edwards, William A.	10/23/1921	06/24/1977	Will David Edwards and Sylvia Sargo	Freda Burgess; Katherine (LNU)

---

[b] Her surname is shown as Reynolds in Arkansas Death Index.

[c] His date of birth was very hard to read.

ROCKDALE CEMETERY

Name on Marker	Date of Birth	Date of Death	Parents	Spouse
Garner, Newton E(zekiel[7])	03/02/1921	04/24/2001	Newton H. Garner and Mary A. Shafer	Aline (LNU); Velma (LNU)
Girard, Henry B(ryan)[2]	09/08/1899	02/19/1974		Maxine Green Owen
Girard, Maxine	09/17/1903	02/15/1992	Herbert Glenn Green and Ruana Stewart	Joplin Garrett Owen; Henry B. Girard
Hanson, Christine	1905 (07/26/1905)[4]	1984 (01/28/1984)[4]		Leo Hansen[4]
Hanson, Leo	1896			
Hinkle, Emma Sargo	05/07/1899	11/26/1963	Simon Sargo and Mary Cates	John Hinkle[3]
Kay, Dr. John H.	11/15/1882	10/27/1949	John Harvey Kay and Martha Ann Shanberger[1]	Lena (LNU)[1]
Kay, Lena	12/23/1889	03/10/1986	C. H. Colbert and Rosabel Davis[4]	John H. Kay
Kilgore, Barry I.	1881	1919		
Kinniell, W. E. "Bill"	06/30/1869	01/05/1917		
Kitchens, Charlie M.	05/20/1917	12/18/1970	Frank Kitchens and Cora Boyd[1]	
LeCroy, Fannie Sargo	02/12/1903	01/05/1959	Simon Sargo and Mary Cates	Curtis Grady LeCroy[10]
Lent, Clyde L.	11/02/1899	11/29/1964	Robinson Lent and Tempy Belle West[2]	Ora Lewis
Lent, Ora L.	11/08/1906	11/02/2001[7]	William L. Lewis and Ida Ferguson	Edward Furr; Clyde L. Lent
Lewis, Ida	1878	1950	Andrew Ferguson and Nancy Lanier	William Lewis

ROCKDALE CEMETERY

Name on Marker	Date of Birth	Date of Death	Parents	Spouse
Lewis, William	1867	1916	William H. Lewis and Mary Jane Futrell	Nettie Keller; Ida Ferguson
Loy, John Paris[8]	1884	1962		
Mr. Doc (E. L. Baggett)[1]	04/22/1878[1]	08/23/1950[1]		
Newkirk, Gracie G.		12/18/1898	T. M. and A. J. Newkirk	
Newman, Joseph H.	1920		Wiley Newman and Catherine Sargo	Margaret Jean Dillard; Ann (LNU)[10]
Phillips, Freeman Lyman	02/16/1885	04/28/1973	Henry Phillips and Rose Ella Scott[4]	
Phillips, Mary Susan	01/14/1895	05/26/1949	Gus Swenson and Martha Rasberry[1]	F. L. Phillips[1]
Phillips, Randy DeWayne	02/11/1964	02/12/1964	Zenas Phillips and Edythe Marie Phillips[1]	
Rasberry, Cassie Jane	06/01/1871	06/28/1937	J. J. Hurst and Matilda Short	J. W. Rasberry
Rasberry, J. W.	09/12/1869	06/20/1917		Cassie Jane Hurst
Rasberry, Mrs. Temperance[1] [no marker]		07/06/1929 age 88[1]		J. T. Rasberry[1]
Rasberry, W. G.[5] [no marker]	03/23/1868	06/07/1934	John Rasberry and Susan Gassey	
Sargo, Annette	1907	1936 (07/29/1936)[5]	Simon Sargo and Mary Cates	
Sargo, Burton (Otis) Samuel[9]	01/25/1925	10/17/2004	Samuel A. Sargo and Vay Bashor	Evelyn Maxine Owen

ROCKDALE CEMETERY

Name on Marker	Date of Birth	Date of Death	Parents	Spouse
Sargo, Evelyn Maxine	03/01/1925	01/28/2003	Joplin Garrett Owen and Maxine Green	Burton Otis Samuel Sargo
Sargo, Mary	1868 (03/03/1868)[5]	1953 (02/17/1953)[5]	Joseph Cates[5]	Simon Sargo
Sargo, Samuel	02/14/1901	06/28/1960	Simon Sargo and Mary Cates	Vay Bashor[10]
Sargo, Samuel Jr.	09/25/1927	06/10/1928	Samuel Sargo and Vay Bashor[5]	
Sargo, Simon	1860	1932 (06/28/1932)[1]	Lorenz Sargo (Sorgo) and Gertraud Krabina[10]	Mary Cates
Sargo, Vay B.	02/09/1895	02/12/1980	John Lee Bashor and Florence Idella Pugh[10]	Samuel A. Sargo
Shafer, Ada D.	06/10/1875	11/07/1918		George W. Shafer[3]
Shafer, George W.	02/22/1850	06/22/1929		Ada Miller[3]
Shafer, Infant Daughter	07/15/1911	07/15/1911	George W. Shafer and Ada Miller	
Shafer, Mary Alice	06/17/1896	02/11/1972	George W. Shafer and Ada Miller	N. H. Garner
Shafer, Sara Jane	1891	1893		
Stacy, Andrew Sr.	1875	1948	Shelby Stacy[5]	Huldah Mae Stone
Stacy, Andrew J. "Jack"	12/27/1929	01/16/2002	Andrew Jackson Stacy and Huldah Mae Stone	Mary (LNU)
Stacy, Huldah Mae	1901	1993 (09/16/1993)[7]	Unk Stone and Elizabeth (LNU)	Andrew Stacy
Stone, S(urept)[5] C.	1859	1931 (03/12/1932)[5]	Mr. Mankel[5]	

ROCKDALE CEMETERY

Name on Marker	Date of Birth	Date of Death	Parents	Spouse
Stone, W. C.	1855	1919		
Swenson, Mrs. Martha	67y8m8d (12/02/1872)[1]	08/10/1940	John T. Rasberry and Temperance Wood[1]	
Thomason, Cecile (Gwendolyn) Moore	12/12/1918	05/31/1988	Franklin Moore and Ola Retherford	Thomas M. Thomason[10]
Van Dorn, Ethel	01/30/1899	10/02/1977	George Shafer and Ada Miller[5]	M. K. Reedy; James Van Dorn
Warner, Mattie Swenson	01/28/1907	04/23/1995		
Williams, Catherine S.	0/29/1897	04/15/1972	Simon Sargo and Mary Cates	Wiley Newman; Emmett W. Williams
Williams, Earl "Bud"	09/12/1925	03/24/2007	Emmett Williams and Catherine Sargo	Dahlia Albright; Nancy (LNU)
Williams, Emmett W(illis)[5]	12/15/1888	11/21/1945	John Williams[5]	Catherine E. Sargo
Williams, Junie	06/07/1928	11/30/1928	Emmett Williams and Catherine Sargo	

---

[1] Lewis Stephens. *Caruth Funeral Home Records 14 July 1909 to 31 Dec. 1970* (Hot Springs, AR: n.p., 1989).

[2] Lewis Stephens. *Gross Funeral Home Records Hot Springs, AR 16,435 Records from January 1, 1958 to December 31, 1992* (Hot Springs, AR; n.p., 1989).

[3] Garland County marriage license

[4] Lewis Stephens. *Caruth Funeral Home Records 1 Jan. 1971 to 31 Dec. 1990* (Hot Springs, AR: n.p., 1989).

[5] Lewis Stephens. *Gross Funeral Home Records Hot Springs, AR 12,362 Records from June 1, 1921 to December 31, 1957* (Hot Springs, AR; n.p.).

[6] Paul B. Dotson

[7] *Sentinel-Record* obituary

[8] His marker in Rockdale Cemetery is a funeral home marker and is set under a tree. He has a full granite marker at Fourche Loupe Cemetery.

[9] The Melting Pot Genealogical Society has obituary in their library.

[10] Jan Sargo Thomason

The Sargos of Garland County

By: Jan Sargo Thomason

(janthomason@cablelynx.com)

Simon "Sorgo" Sargo

The first Sargo in Hot Springs, Arkansas, was Simon, but his surname was spelled Sorgo. Simon was born August 15, 1861. His birth was registered at the Parish St. Thomas at Zeiselberg, Austria. His line of Sorgos in that area goes back several hundred years. Allegedly, the first Sorgo in Carinthian, Austria, came from the former Austrian province of Venetian (present day Italy). That Sorgo was a priest; however, he abandoned his status as a priest and married the owner of the local castle. Out of this connection, and over the course of time, two lines were formed, i.e. an Upper Carinthian line, with 15 or more royal family members in your lineage, Lower Carinthian line with 14½ or fewer royal family members. Simon "Sorgo" Sargo was undoubtedly from the Lower Carinthian line. This explanation was written by Josef Sorgo from Klagenfurt, Siebenhuegelstr, on August 1, 1954, to Alfred Williams, one of Simon Sorgo's grandsons, in answer to Alfred's inquiries about Simon's Austrian relatives. Alfred received another letter from Frieda Sorgo Scheuerwenk. She made an unusual statement in the opening sentence when she wrote, "I am in possession of Aryan proof, dating back to 1650 for the Sorgo family." This response was written in answer to the question, "Was Simon Sorgo a relative of yours?" Instead of first answering the question, she wanted to convey the important message that she was in "possession of Aryan proof." Maybe in 1954, with World War II less than ten years ended and World War I still a vivid memory, this opening statement, when placed in the context of time and place, makes more sense. To an American in the year 2010, it sounds off the mark. However, she had just lived through a time period where family lineage decided whether a person lived or died under Hitler's regimen.

Austria had been ravaged by multiple wars in the 1860s and had become devastated by the consuming poverty that almost always follows any war. In one twenty-year span, Germany went to war at least seven times, taking on neighboring countries such as Austria, France, Belgium and Russia. As a result of those devastating times, Simon had to resort to traveling from town to town in search of work in order to make a living. He was armed with a letter from the Bourger Meister (similar to a town mayor in America). The letter stated that Simon was an honest, hard-working man, and it recommended him for employment. Several other letters were in his possession also, and we believe they, too, stated he was a good worker. Austrian documents show that Simon was still in Austria in 1884. The exact time of and reason for Simon leaving Austria to come to America are lost to his American descendants. Given the economic hardships Austrians (particularly Simon) had been facing, Simon must have felt that he could find a solution to his problem in America.

The Sargos of Garland County

Most stories of his traveling to America and landing in New York are lost except for one family history. That family story tells of Simon landing in New York and finding a job with a construction crew. Apparently the foreman fired Simon every day, but Simon spoke no English so he just worked harder. When payday came, everyone was paid except Simon. Simon received one of his first American lessons. Simon was a big, brawny man standing 6'7"; one can only wonder at the sight it must have been when Simon confronted that foreman.

It is a matter of record that German immigrants left New York as quickly as possible because of the hostile laws and attitudes that were designed to make the German-speaking immigrants move on. Many of the immigrants had families who picked them up, enabling them to leave New York quickly. Simon wasn't that fortunate. He had no family, but leave New York he did. He worked his way from town to town as he had done in Austria. When he got to Springfield, Missouri, he purchased twenty-five goats and a pocketful of watercress seeds and joined a caravan headed to Arkansas. Simon's goats provided at least two benefits to the caravan. First, the goats were staked out at night around the outside of the camp. If wolves, which were numerous at the time, approached the camp, the goats would sound the alarm. Secondly, mosquitoes were attracted to the goats instead of the humans.

Stories have been told of Simon in Hot Springs, Arkansas, in 1892 regarding the occasion of his marriage to Mary Catherine Cates. She was born in 1868 in Missouri, and the Cates family was said to have been in the same caravan coming to Arkansas as was Simon, although that statement has not been verified. Mary Catherine was over 6 feet tall herself and was a fitting partner for Simon's 6'7" frame. The story goes that while in Springfield, Simon attended a revival where he first saw Mary Catherine. It was told that, after the service, he went up to her and proposed on the spot. This scenario was played out every night of the revival. He spoke only German; she spoke only English, but apparently he managed to communicate his intentions, and eventually he got the answer he wanted.

The couple obtained acreage off Highway 7 North on the opposite side of the road from Coleman Crystal Shop. They farmed their land, raised goats, and planted the free-flowing, spring-fed stream on the property with watercress. The sale of the watercress provided cash for things they could not raise themselves. The tradition of selling watercress was passed down through the generations. Simon's son, Samuel Sargo, and Samuel's sons, Burton and Bill Sargo, sold watercress to the Arlington and Majestic Hotels and to other eateries in town. Simon and Mary Catherine lived at the Highway 7 North location until the railroad came through and bought all but forty acres of their land. They moved to Mountain Valley Cut-Off, now known as 737 Fox Pass. They built the house and barn shown in the pictures and cleared the land for planting. The house and barn are long gone, the only remaining feature is the well. They owned the valley that begins at the house and goes to Hwy 5 and 7 by Belvedere Country Club. They planted the valley with fruit trees.   Someone set the trees on fire, and while battling the fire Simon suffered a stroke. He survived the stroke but battled the blaze in his head until his end.

The Sargos of Garland County

This picture was taken in front of the Sargo home on Fox Pass.
Pictured from left to right are Samuel, Mary Catherine Cates,
Annette, Elizabeth, Fannie, Emma, Catherine and Sylvia Sargo.

This picture was taken in front of the barn at what is now Fox Pass. From left to right: Emma, Catherine, Sylvia, Elizabeth, Fannie, and Mary Catherine holding Annette with Sam on the mule. All the children had dark hair and dancing blue eyes, a trait that was passed down.

Mary Catherine and Simon Sargo had seven children who lived to adulthood. Each of these children stood over 6' tall, with the only son, Sam, turning out to be 6'5". It is believed they had more children who did not survive. Behind Simon and Mary Catherine's graves at Rockdale Cemetery are five little graves marked only with stones. One can only speculate whose babies those were and the circumstances of their deaths.

The Sargos of Garland County

Sylvia, Zeke, Bill, and William Edwards

Of the living children, the first born was Sylvia Sargo, 1895. Sylvia Sargo married William David Edwards, and they had two sons: William "Bill" Allen Edwards born in 1922, followed by Samuel Ezekiel "Zeke" Edwards in 1923. They built their house upon a hill with a beautiful view of the orchard valley. Their house was dug into the ground about 3 feet. This act saved on timber to frame the house as well as insulated it from the heat and cold. They were a God-fearing family and went to church as often as the doors were open. William and Sylvia are buried at Rockdale Cemetery.

William "Bill" Allen Edwards was born in 1922. He married Freda Burgess, and they had a daughter, Linda Edwards. Bill and Freda later divorced. Bill then married Katherine Garner. They had two children, Janet Edwards and Allen Edwards. Bill died in 1977 and is buried at Rockdale Cemetery alongside his parents.

In the picture on left, from left to right: Joe Newman, Alfred Williams, Bill Edwards (center) Bud Williams and Burton Sargo. These five boys were first cousins. This picture was taken in front of Catherine Sargo Williams' house on Quarry Mountain Road.

Zeke Edwards, Alfred Williams, Joe Newman, Burton Sargo, Jess Brown, Sam Sargo, Grady LeCroy, Emmett Williams; children are Grady Joe Newman and Jan Sargo.

The Sargos of Garland County

The man by the car is William Edwards, Sr., next is Alfred Williams, Zeke Edwards is the man in the hat, Burton Sargo, Bill Sargo (turning), and Grady LeCroy.

Samuel Ezekiel "Zeke" Edwards, born in 1924, married Evelyn Gossett. They had no children. A veteran of WW II, Zeke, spent three years in the Air Force and saw service in India and the South Pacific. He was a former Garland County Deputy Sheriff. Zeke was killed in an accident at the airport in Russellville, Arkansas, at the age of 28. He had been employed as a pilot for the Farmers Agricultural Service at West Memphis. He was killed July 4, 1951, when the cotton-dusting plane he was flying crashed and burned after failing to gain altitude on takeoff. He was buried at Memorial Gardens Cemetery.

Catherine Sargo was born in 1897. She married Wiley Newman in 1919, and they had one son, Joseph Harvey Newman. Family history relates that Wiley was a mean-tempered man who beat Catherine. It is unknown if the beating happened only once or if it was repeated several times. Family history says that Simon sent Catherine and her sister to town on the street bus while he paid a call on Wiley. The story goes that Simon located Wiley at the top of the hill and thrashed Wiley and then tossed him to the bottom of the hill. As the story goes, "they" say the divorce was final when Wiley hit the valley floor. The truth of the story cannot be verified, however. Wiley never darkened Catherine's door again. A family will tolerate many things, but abuse was not tolerated, at least not by Simon. Records indicate that Wiley married two more times and had a total of nine additional children.

◄

1918
Catherine and
Sister Sylvia Sargo

►

1950's
Central Avenue
Catherine Williams

The Sargos of Garland County

Catherine's second marriage was to Emmett Williams, who had two sons and a daughter by a previous marriage. The children were Velmer "Buster," Curtis and Gertrude. Buster entered the Air Corp in March 1944. Curtis entered the Seabees in July 1943. Emmett was a Dairyman for 23 years. From Catherine and Emmett's marriage they had eight children, with only three surviving to adulthood. The babies included three sets of twins; two sets of twins died shortly after birth. Another boy, named Junie, died at five months of age from a virus that was running rampant through the community. The three who survived are Alfred and the surviving twins, Earl "Bud" and Pearl. Catherine's life was dedicated to her children. She raised Garry Gene Newman, her grandson. Her work outside the home was caring for children. She gave wonderful care as well as her heart to each little soul in her charge. Catherine was a strong woman and the "go to" person to get things done in the family. Later, she shared this position with her brother Samuel. Emmett and Catherine are buried at Rockdale Cemetery.

Along with the three surviving children from the marriage to Emmett was Catherine's son, Joseph Newman. At age 24 Joe entered the Quartermasters Corps in January 1942.

Joseph H. Newman   **Margaret Dillard & Joe Newman**   **Joe Newman and Anne Bell Farr**

Catherine and Wiley Newman's son Cpl. Joseph "Joe" Harvey Newman had five children of his own: Joseph Grady and Garry Gene with his first wife Margaret Jean Dillard; Elizabeth Ann, Barbara Kay, and Catherine Lynn by his second wife Anne Bell Farr. Additionally, they adopted a son, Joseph Wesley Newman. Anne Bell Farr had a son by a previous marriage, Bobby Ray Chambers. Joseph H. Newman is stilling living, although his headstone is in place at Rockdale.

Lt. Col. Alfred Williams is buried beside his wife, Doris Watson Williams, at Owensville Cemetery. They had two daughters, Kathy Lynn and Allison Sue. Alfred was the one responsible for writing the letters while he was stationed overseas, and he was the sole reason we know as much as we do about our Sorgo's relatives in Austria. Alfred's military service began in March 1944. After retiring as a Lt. Col. from active service, he taught ROTC at Lakeside High School for twenty plus years.

The Sargos of Garland County

The only set of Catherine's twins who survived to adulthood was Earl "Bud" Williams and Pearl Williams.

Earl "Bud" Williams graduated in 1942 from Fountain Lake High School. He entered military service in December 1943, and by age 18 he was a corporal. He married Dahlia Albright, and they had one daughter, Johnnie Sue Williams. Bud was a grocery store owner in the Lakeside area and a home builder. He served as Garland County Judge for many years. He was buried at Rockdale Cemetery between his parents.

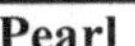

Pearl

Pearl Williams

Pearl

Bud's twin sister, Pearl Williams, graduated in 1942. She married Roy B. Coleman, an army major. Pearl was an army nurse and retired as a major. She entered training with the Army Nursing Corp at St. Joseph's Infirmary April 1944. Upon retirement from the service, they moved to Lakeland, Florida, where they raised their two daughters, Beth and Renee. Pearl is still living (2010).

John Hinkle, Mary Etta, and Emma (Sargo) Hinkle

Carl B. Cowan and Mary Etta (Hinkle) Cowan

Sue Jane (Cowan) and Logan Brown taken at Rockdale Cemetery

The Sargos of Garland County

Emma Sargo, the third child of Simon and Mary Catherine, was born in 1899. She married John Hinkle, a railroad man, and they moved to Oklahoma. The family kept in touch, and Emma brought her family back as often as possible for the holidays. Mary Etta Hinkle, John and Emma's daughter, married Carl B. Cowan, and they had one daughter, Sue Jane, who is married to Logan Brown. Emma Hinkle and Carl and Mary Etta Cowan are buried at Rockdale Cemetery.

Sam, Burton (standing), Billy Don, and Vay Sargo

Samuel "Sam" A. Sargo was born in 1901. He was a large baby and a big hard-working man like his father. He married Vay Bashor, who once remarked she married Sam because he was strong enough to lift her into the wagon seat with ease. They were married Christmas Eve morning in 1920 at the First Presbyterian Church on Whittington across from the old St. Joseph's Hospital. Their first son, Samuel, died at age three from the red measles. The second son was Burton Otis Samuel Sargo, born in 1925, and the youngest son was Victor Billy Don Sargo, born in 1933. You rarely saw Sam that he didn't have a grin on his face. I remember one evening when the whole family was leaving the rodeo at the Garland County fair. (Sam was on the board of directors for the fair.) A group of rowdy boys was tugging and pulling on a young horse, trying to load him into their trailer, all the while beating the wild-eyed creature with a whip. Sam hollered and asked if they would like to sell that horse. They retorted, "No, we wanted to kill him." As Sam and his son, Burton, neared the horse, they grabbed an arm lock with each other and lifted the backside of the horse to the point he had to move his front legs and jump in the trailer. Sam then told the boys to have a good evening, and he and Burton walked away. Neither Sam nor Burton could abide cruelty, and they were smart enough to have more than one answer to a problem. Like Simon before them, there were some things they were not going to tolerate.

Sam was a builder. He helped in the construction of the Arlington and Eastman Hotels and worked on the building of Belvedere Country Club. Sam was foreman for W. S. "Mr. Jake" Jacobs for years at Belvedere. Also he helped each of his sisters build homes and gave them land if needed. He loved that the basement of his and Vay's home was used as a meeting place for the fledgling Fountain Lake Methodist Church. He donated the land for the church to be built and

The Sargos of Garland County

helped with its construction. He started Snow Springs Park, which Fountain Lake residents, tourists, and town people remember as the coldest swimming pool they had ever experienced. It was cold and pure because it was fed by seven natural springs.

Fountain Lake Methodist Church

Snow Springs Park late 1950s

Sam amassed hundreds of acres before his death from a heart attack in 1960 at age 59. Oftentimes, his need for more land left Vay, his wife, to lament "Sam, you just want everything in the county." "No," he said, "only the piece of ground that touches mine." He accomplished all of this success with only a third-grade education. Vay was everything Sam was not, formal education-wise. She was a school teacher/music teacher. She taught at Howard School before it became Fountain Lake and was the first woman to be on the Fountain Lake School Board. She was president of the local chapter of the Iris Society, and she was a charter member of the Garland County Historical Society. The day the charter for GCHS was signed, April 19, 1960, Vay signed in as member 31 out of 58. Sam and Vay made a formidable team based on hard work, self-reliance and Christian values. Sam and Vay are buried at Rockdale Cemetery.

Burton Sargo, 1942

Evelyn Owen

Burton and Evelyn March 3, 1945

The Sargos of Garland County

Sam and Vay's son Burton Otis Samuel Sargo was born in 1925. He married Evelyn Maxine Owen, also born in 1925. They were the first couple married at Fountain Lake Methodist Church, even though the church's interior had not been completed at the time of their wedding on March 3, 1945. They had two daughters, Rebecca Ann Sargo born in 1947 and Janice Vay Sargo born in 1948. They were named "Arkansas Farm Family of the Year" in 1947. Burton raised Duroc hogs and had a dairy herd. Also he ran a one-man concrete block-making operation and was the distributor for Gravely Tractors. Evelyn, like most young brides across America at the time, tended to the home and children. Evelyn was active in her local Home Demonstration Club and later became president of the Garland County Association. At the time of her presidency, the need arose for a new kitchen at the county fairgrounds. Evelyn marched into the bank and signed a loan so the club could build the kitchen, not thinking to mention her intentions to Burton. The banker called Burton and asked what he wanted to do. Burton replied, "If she wants money, I guess you had better give it to her." Needless to say, the club was able to

pay the loan back in a timely manner. Eventually, Evelyn joined her mother, Maxine Girard, in the antique business and invested forty-three happy years buying and selling antiques with a relish.

Burton worked at Reynolds Aluminum for thirty years. When he got laid off during a shut-down, he became a Hot Springs Police Officer. One Christmas Eve he was working swing shift and pulled over a speeding car just before he got off work. The woman cried and told him she was working two jobs to buy Christmas presents for her children. Being a dutiful officer, he wrote her a ticket. When he got home and went to bed, he couldn't sleep. So he got up, dressed, went to the lady's house, tore up the ticket, came home, and had a Merry Christmas.

Burton and Evelyn are buried under the hickory tree at Rockdale.

Burton Sargo

Victor Billy Don Sargo was born in 1933. He married Lillian Byrdie DeVane January 27, 1956. They had two children, Delia Mary Sargo born in 1956 and Samuel Hiram Sargo born in 1959. Bill went to college to become a minister, but during his time there, he changed his degree to teaching.

Billy Don Sargo and Lillian Byrdie DeVane

Wedding, January 27, 1956.

The Sargos of Garland County

Bill Sargo studying at Hendrix College

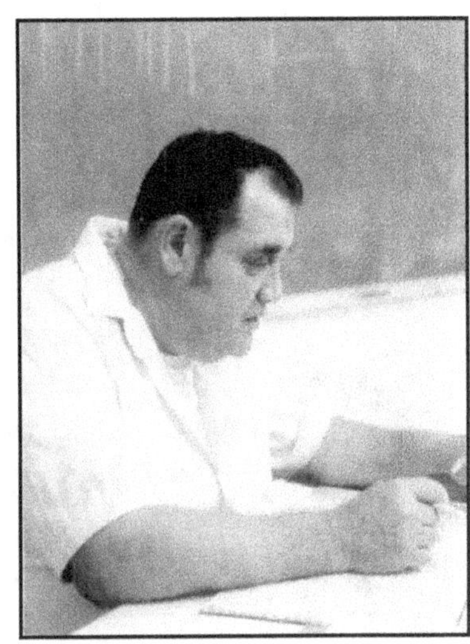

Bill Sargo at Fountain Lake

Bill taught at Fountain Lake School for thirty-two years. He also ran a dairy herd with the help of his wife and family. Later he branched into landscaping in Hot Springs Village. He was everyone's friend, students and adults alike. In 2010 his daughter, Mary, completed her thirty-fourth year of teaching at Fountain Lake. Following in her Grandmother Vay's footsteps, she was the music teacher. She and her husband, Jay Schapiro, have no children. The kids at school fill that spot. Mary's brother, Sam. also did not have children, so, the father-to-son line of Simon Sargo in America ends with him. There are plenty of other Sargo descendants but none will bear the surname. Bill was buried at Rockdale Cemetery beside his parents but has since been moved to join Byrdie's mother, Lillian DeVane, at Hollywood Cemetery in Hot Springs.

Fannie Sargo was born in 1903. She married Curtis Grady LeCroy. They did not have children. They owned and operated the Carrier Heat and Air Conditioning distributors in Hot Springs, and they were Charter members of Fountain Lake Methodist Church. Fannie baked a wonderful pound cake. She was always beautifully groomed and had the warmest smile. Fannie died from cancer and was buried at Rockdale Cemetery. Grady re-married and is buried with his wife, Betty Baggett LeCroy, at Memorial Gardens Cemetery.

Fannie Sargo and Curtis Grady LeCroy

Elizabeth Sargo was born in 1905. She married Jesse Brown who had served in the military in World War I with the Ohio 329th Infantry. He was a first lieutenant and was awarded a purple heart for injuries received. He wrote poetry, played the fiddle and carved wooden items. Elizabeth worked for years at Stewart Grocery Store and as a bookkeeper for Carrier Heat and Air Conditioning. She was dedicated to her family. Elizabeth and Jesse had no children of their own, but they raised Joseph Grady "Grady Joe" Newman. Elizabeth and Jesse are buried at Rockdale.

The Sargos of Garland County

Picture taken in 1950:
Back row from the left:
Elizabeth Sargo Brown wearing a skirt with buttons down the side, Catherine Sargo Williams, Burton Sargo, Bill Sargo, Bill Edwards, Zeke Edwards, Jesse Brown, Emmett Williams. 2nd row from the left: Evelyn Owen Sargo, Evelyn Gossett Edwards, Grady LeCroy, Fannie Sargo LeCroy, Doris Watson Williams, Vay Bashor Sargo and Mary Catherine, Grady Joe Newman, Alfred Williams, Garry Newman, Jan Sargo and Becky   Sargo

Annette Sargo was the baby of the family, born in 1907. She had not married before her untimely death at the age of twenty-nine. Annette was traveling in a car with Mrs. M. O. McKeller, returning from a visit to the Centennial Central Exposition in Dallas, Texas. A car turned left in front of them, and they plowed into the car's side. Annette was thrown through the windshield and was rushed to Baylor Hospital but died from her injuries within an hour. She was a sales person for Southern Bakery on Central Avenue. Her mother, Mary Sargo, was one of the operators of the Dinner Bell roadside café located on the Little Rock highway. Annette was well-known and loved in the area. She is buried at Rockdale Cemetery.

Annette Sargo

A few more family relations have a place in the Sargo portion of the Rockdale Cemetery's story, beginning with Vay Bashor Sargo's parents.

John L. and Florence Bashor had four children other than Vay: Mark, Harley, Iva, and Cora.

Florence, their mother, was an artist. She painted, sculpted animals, and made pottery. Her art is still treasured in the family. John L. and Florence are buried at Rockdale Cemetery. It is likely that Florence's mother, Emily Anna Engersoll Pugh VanDeVanter is buried at Rockdale.

The Sargos of Garland County

Maxine Green Owen Girard, the mother of Evelyn Owen Sargo, was married to Henry Bryan Girard, who died in 1974. Henry was a skilled furniture maker, a wonderful husband to Maxine, and a great stepfather to Evelyn Owen Sargo and her brother, James Hubert Owen. Henry was the best friend of Maxine's first husband, Joplin Garrett Owen, who died suddenly from a heart attack in Vega, Texas, in 1933, leaving Maxine with two small children.

Henry and Maxine Girard with Evelyn Owen (and Buster)

Henry and Maxine married and eventually moved to Arkansas. Henry and James came ahead to build the log house and antique/work shop at the intersection of Hwy 7 North and Walnut Valley. During their visits with Maxine and Evelyn, Henry and James told stories about the big strong men who brought them logs for the house and shop. The men turned out to be Sam, Burton and Bill Sargo. Once the house and shop were built, Maxine and Evelyn moved to Arkansas. It was Evelyn's senior year, and she met Burton Sargo at Fountain Lake. The rest is history. As for Henry, he raised beef cattle and made furniture while Maxine ran a small antique shop that became known for the delicate art glass she loved. Later, they moved Girard Antiques to Airport Road in Hot Springs. Maxine Green Owen Girard was much revered for her textbook knowledge of antiques. After leading a full life, she died in 1992. Maxine loved English bulldogs, and the dog in the picture was named "Buster." Henry and Maxine are buried at Rockdale Cemetery.

Cecile and Frank Thomason, 1947

Cecile and Frank Thomason, 1949

The Sargos of Garland County

Cecile Gwendolyn Moore was born to Franklin and Ola Retherford Moore. They lived in Magnet Cove, where she graduated from high school. Cecile was the youngest of four children: Francis, Maurice, Katherine and Cecile. After high school, Cecile moved to San Antonio, Texas,

to attend beauty school. Upon graduation, she returned to Hot Springs and opened her first beauty shop in the old Rockafellow Hotel. Cecile Moore married Thomas Marshal Thomason, and they had one child, Thomas Franklin Thomason. The couple divorced shortly after his birth, and Cecile never remarried. She moved her beauty shop in the early 1950s to the Velda Rose Hotel, where she operated the shop for forty-three years until she retired. She collected dear friends and silver and was loved by all who knew her. Her son, Thomas Franklin Thomason, married Janice Sargo Knox on August 7, 1971. Cecile is buried at Rockdale Cemetery.

A previously unknown burial in Rockdale Cemetery, along with the Sargo Family, is "Mr. Doc." Sadly, we do not have a picture of Mr. Doc. When this story was started, we did not have his true name. But Charleen Cook Nobles, who is relentless when handed a genealogy puzzle, was determined to solve the mystery. Once Charleen got the name, Patti Vance Hays, quickly found the newspaper article telling of the fatal accident. Mr. Doc's true name is E. L. Baggett (1878 – 1950). He lived in a one-room house by the creek behind Sam and Vay Sargo's home and was killed crossing Highway 7 from Cave Springs while going home. He was called Mr. Doc because he had some medical training. He gave up medicine in search of a simpler life, which he found by being a general fix-it man and a great story-teller for little boys like Bill Sargo, who wanted to while away the evening hours listening to Mr. Doc's tall tales.

Thus ends the story of the adventures of Simon "Sorgo" Sargo and his prodigy in Garland County. Rockdale Cemetery has been closed to all but those who have family buried there. Not many are left to be added to the Rockdale roster, and fewer still that will have the Sargo name. However, with a little bit of searching, the Sargo connection will continue at the old site.

Whatever the future may hold for the Sargos and the cemetery, remember one thing: Close the gate on the way out; it may be a while before someone comes back.

Sources (1 – 8) are among family held documents:

1. "German Immigration to the Midwest" 123HelpMe.com 17 May 2010
   http://www.123HelpMe.com/view.asp?id=23205
2. Letter written by Joseph Sorgo, 1, August 1954 Klagenfurt, Siebenhuegelstr 80/25. To Alfred Williams
3. Letter written by Fried Sorgo, Scheverwenk, St. Margarenten I. Ros. Karaten, Telefon Feriach 5/1954. To Alfred Williams
4. Birth Certificate from St. Thomas, Zeiselberg, Tom. 8, Page. 81, Nr 48, 1861, Simon Sorgo
5. Three Letters of introduction from the mayors of different towns in Austria.
6. "Christmas Eve in the Morning" A Fantasy, by Vay Bashor Sargo, 1971, Found on Ancestry.com Sargos of Garland County.
7. Selected pictures and family stories provided by: Joseph Grady Newman, Garry Gene Newman, Elizabeth Newman Fryar, Byrdie DeVane Sargo Mooney.
8. Obituaries, factual details and research provided in part by Charleen Cook Nobles, Patti Vance Hays and Pat Humphrey Tillery.
9. Editing help given by Nancy Gibson Pinkston, Priscilla Teague Minor, and Caroline Seiz Campbell.

The Arkansas Flag
Everything Has A Meaning

The United States built a battleship in 1912 and named it *Arkansas*. The Pine Bluff Chapter of the Daughters of the American Revolution voted to present the new battleship with a stand of colors which would include the United States flag, the naval battalion flag, and the Arkansas state flag. Upon investigation, however, they found that Arkansas, from 1836 to 1911, had no state flag. The group then published articles in leading newspapers appealing to artists to submit designs for an official state flag. The flag adopted by the Legislature on February 18, 1913, was designed by Miss Willie K. Hocker of Pine Bluff.

In the flag adopted, the national colors of red, white, and blue were chosen because Arkansas is one of the United States. The background is <u>red</u>; the large diamond in the center is <u>white</u> and signified that Arkansas is the only state that has diamond mines. The word "Arkansas" in bold <u>blue</u> letters across the white diamond proclaims that this is the flag of Arkansas. The three stars in the diamond below the word Arkansas stand for the three nations that have ruled Arkansas: France, Spain and the United States, as well as the fact that Arkansas was the third state carved out of the Louisiana Purchase. The two stars nearest Arkansas stand for Michigan and Arkansas as sister states. The single star in the diamond above the word Arkansas is placed there in memory of the Confederacy. The twenty-five stars in the <u>blue band</u> surrounding the diamond show that Arkansas was the twenty-fifth state admitted to the Union.

You can see that everything in the Arkansas flag has a meaning.

Last Veteran of Gen. George Custer's Civil War Brigade

The Sentinel Record, Hot Springs, Arkansas
June 9 and June 12, 1948

Last Veteran of Custer's Brigade Dies Here at 104

JULIAN RANSIER

Julian Ransier, 104-year-old last surviving member of Gen. George Custer's Civil War brigade, died yesterday at his home, 800 Prospect, and his wife, Mrs. Cora Ransier, in her 90's is seriously ill and not expected to live more than a few days. Both have been in ill health for the past several years.

The couple celebrated their Golden Wedding anniversary on September 27 of this year.

Mr. Ransier, a native of Manlius, N. Y., came to Hot Springs more than 20 years ago. He is probably the oldest white resident of Garland county and is one of the last 15 surviving members of the Grand Army of the Republic.

Mrs. Ransier's son, Col. R. V. Ladd, of San Diego, Cal., has been here with the couple since last

He said yesterday that his step-father's body would be returned to Manlius, N. Y., for funeral services and burial, but no date for the last trip has been set, pending the outcome of Mrs. Ransier's condition. In event of her death, he said, the two will be taken together for burial to lie side by side. Lots and grave stones were purchased some time ago by the Ransier's, Colonel Ladd said, their wish being that they be buried together.

It was disclosed at Manlius, according to the Associated Press, that Ransier will be buried in Manlius Cemetery beneath his father's 600-pound limestone washbasin which Ransier had converted into a tombstone.

He made arrangements for the "washbasin monument" on a visit to Manlius in 1933. He had a stone cutter polish the stone, carve his father's and mother's names and his own on it. Then it was erected over their grave.

Records at Syracuse, N. Y., show that Ransier's father, James M. Ransier, operated a farm and quarry at Eagle Village, near Manlius, in 1837.

The elder Ransier noticed that the wash basin was constantly being misplaced by workmen on his farm and quarry.

"He stuck upon the idea of a basin that couldn't be carried away and went to his quarry and hauled out a 600-pound block of limestone," historical association records state, adding:

"Two deep depressions were carefully chiseled out of the stone and for the remainder of his life the elder Ransier had no fear of anyone stealing his washbowl."

Ransier fought in seven major battles of the civil war, the Syracuse records show. His grandfather George Ransier, fought in the Revolutionary War and was a pioneer settler of Manlius.

OBITUARIES

Double Funeral Service Today For Aged Couple

The bodies of Mrs. Cora Getty Ransier, 89, who died here yesterday, and of her husband, Julian M. Ransier, 104-year-old GAR member and last survivor of Gen. George Custer's Brigade, who died Monday, will be sent to Thompson Brothers Mortuary in Memphis today for cremation.

Both will eventually lie under the same tombstone in Ransier's native Manlius, N. Y., where some years ago the aged veteran made arrangements for conversion of his father's 600-pound limestone wash basin into the head stone. Final arrangements at Manlius will be made by Mrs. Clara Reals, of 148 Washington street, in that city, a friend of the family.

Funeral services for both will be held here today at 10 a. m. at Gross Chapel with the Rev. Roland Moncure, pastor of St. Luke's Episcopal church, officiating.

Mrs. Ransier died early yesterday morning at her home in Hot Springs where she has lived for the past 20 years. She and her husband had been in ill health for some time prior to death.

She is survived by her son, Col. R. V. Ladd of San Diego, Calif., who has been here with the couple since last June and who will accompany the bodies to New York.

Mrs. Ransier, in past years, was a talented musicain and was organist in one of the leading churches in Minnesota before coming to Hot Springs. She was a composer and has had many songs and poems published.

Editor's note:
Further research at *christchurchmanlius.org/index.php?id=125* *shows that these records for Ransier burials listed as #41, 44, 91, and 92 have information for and about (1) Georg Friderich Ranzieur, (2) George Ransier, (3) George Ransier, Jr, (4) James M and Frederick G. Ransier, and (5) Julian M Ransier – five generations. Also, this site suggests Julian M. Ransier was born in 1846, making him 102 years old instead of 104 as stated in his obituary.*

Last Veteran of Gen. George Custer's Civil War Brigade

Tuesday Morning, November 9, 1948
The Sentinel Record, Hot Springs National Park
Obituary
Transcribed by Linda Miller

JULIAN RANSIER

Julian Ransier, 104-year-old last surviving member of Gen. George Custer's Civil War Brigade, died yesterday at his home, 806 Prospect, and his wife, Mrs. Cora Ransier, in her 90's is seriously ill and not expected to live more than a few days. Both have been in ill health for the past several years.

The couple celebrated their Golden Wedding anniversary on September 27 of this year.

Mr. Ransier, a native of Manlius, N. Y. came to Hot Springs more than 20 years ago. He is probably the oldest white resident of Garland County and is one of the last 100 surviving members of the Grand Army of the Republic.

Mrs. Ransier's son, Col. R. V. Ladd, of San Diego, Cal., has been here with the couple since last June.

He said yesterday that his step-father's body would be returned to Manlius, N. Y. for funeral services and burial, but no date for the long trip has been set, pending the outcome of Mrs. Ransier's condition. In event of her death, he said the two will be taken together for final resting side by side. Lots and grave stones were purchased some time ago by the Ransier's. Colonel Ladd said, their wish being that they be buried together.

It was disclosed at Manlius; according to the Associated Press that Ransier will be buried in Manlius Cemetery beneath his father's 600-pound limestone washbasin, which Ransier had reverted into a tombstone.

He made arrangements for the "washbasin monument" on a visit to Manlius in 1933. He had a stone cutter polish the stone, carve his father's and mother's names and his own on it. Then it was erected over their grave.

Records at Syracuse, N. Y., show that Ransier's father, James M. Ransier, operated a farm and quarry at Eagle Village, near Manlius, in 1837.

The elder Ransier noticed that the wash basin was constantly being misplaced by workmen on his farm and quarry.

Last Veteran of Gen. George Custer's Civil War Brigade

"He struck upon the idea of a basin that couldn't be carried away and went to his quarry and hauled out a 600 pound block of limestone", Historical Association Records state, adding:

"Two deep depressions were carefully chiseled out of the stone and for the remainder of his life the elder Ransier had no fear of anyone stealing his washbowl."

Ransier fought in seven major battles of the civil war, The Syracuse records show. His grandfather, George Ransier, fought in the Revolutionary War and was a pioneer settler of Manlius.

Friday Morning, November 12, 1948
The Sentinel Record, Hot Springs National Park
Obituary
Transcribed by Caroline Seiz Campbell

Double Funeral Service Today For Aged Couple

The bodies of Mrs. Cora Getty Ransier, 89, who died here yesterday, and of her husband, Julian M. Ransier, 104-year-old GAR member and last survivor of Gen. George Custer's Brigade, who died Monday, will be sent to Thompson Brothers Mortuary in Memphis today for cremation.

Both will eventually lie under the same tombstone in Ransier's native Manlius, N. Y., where some years ago the aged veteran made arrangements for conversion of his father's 600-pound limestone washbasin into the head stone. Final arrangements at Manlius will be made by Mrs. Clara Reals, of 148 Washington Street in that city, a friend of the family.

Funeral services for both will be held here today at 10 a.m. at Gross Chapel with the Rev. Roland Moncure, pastor of St. Luke's Episcopal Church officiating.

Mrs. Ransier died early yesterday morning at her home in Hot Springs where she has lived for the past 20 years. She and her husband had been in ill health for some time prior to death.

She is survived by her son, Co. R. V. Ladd of San Diego, Calif., who has been here with the couple since last June and who will accompany the bodies to New York.

Mrs. Ransier, in past years, was a talented musician (sic) and was organist in one of the leading churches in Minnesota before coming to Hot Springs. She was a composer and has had many songs and poems published.

Civil War Soldiers
Buried in Garland County

(Not a complete listing)
Information and Pictures furnished by
Debra Slater Garner

Avery Cemetery
    Slaten, James C. 1842-1909
        Co. E. 3rd Ill Cal.

Bain Cemetery
    Bain, Henry D. 1815-1897
        3rd Sgt. Perry Adcock's Co. 16th Reg TN ARMY
    Bain, William U. 1847-1917
        Perry Adcock's Co. 16th Reg. TN ARMY

Briggs Cemetery
    Bird, James (C68)
        CO I 57 USC COL'D INF

Buckville Cemetery
    Boone, Columbus S. 1848-1905
        8th GA Inf. Div. I
    Robbins, William R. 1840-1892
        Co. A. 1st TN INF.

Cosby
    Cash, Hugh b.18 Jul 1829, d. 29 Jan 1916
        Co. F, 11th Arkansas Infantry
    Cozby, Joseph Crawford
        Co. H, 4 Alabama Cavalry, CSA

Crossroads Cemetery
    Priddy, J. R.
        Co. H. S. MO Cal

Cunningham Cemetery
    Arman, Geo. W. 1840-1920
        Art. Sgt. Co. F 33 Regt. ILL
    Gillham, John C
        Co. C 3rd MO CAL
    Kallanblink, Herman C. 1835-1919
        Pvt. Co. C 1st MO CAL
    Kizziar, James H. 1841-1913
        4th AR CAL. Co. D
    Cunningham, R. M.
        Owens Btry. AR Arty CSA
    Wheeler, William Perry 1840-1906
        Co. F 2nd GA Inf.
    Wright, James W.
        Co. A 6th TN CAL

Henry D. Bain
Bain Cemetery

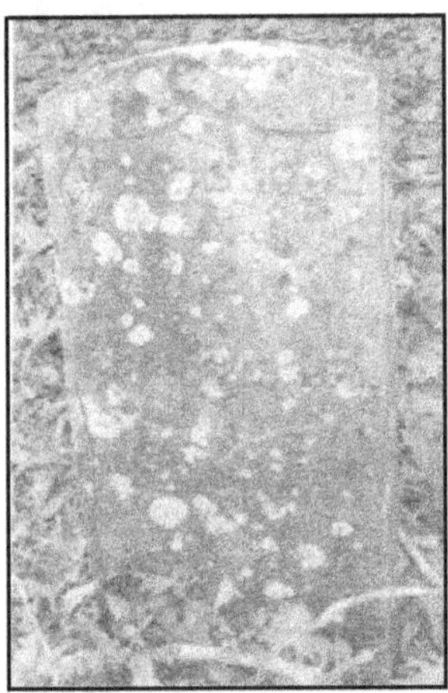

James Bird (marker)
Briggs Cemetery

Civil War Soldiers
Buried in Garland County

Greenwood Cemetery
Bain, John Knox 1827-1915 Perry Adcock's Co., 16th Reg TN ARMY

Columbus Boone
Buckville Cemetery

Wm. R. Robbins
Buckville Cemetery

John Knox Bain
Greenwood Cemetery

Godwin Cemetery
Echols, James
  Co. G 4th ARK CAL
Heller, Phillip J.
  Co. K 193 OHIO Inf.
Woods, Charles C. 1841-1927
  K 11th OHIO CAL

Glazier Peau Cemetery
Jennings, Silvanus
  Co. G 1st MO L.A.

Green Cemetery
Dickson, Pvt. William Graham   b. 11 Oct 1832, d. 28 Dec 1913
  Co. E, 32nd NC Infantry
New Kirk, Sgt. Hiram Crabtree   b. 11 may 1837, d. 9 May 1921
  Co. H, 1st Arkansas Cavalry

Hollywood Cemetery   *(This information for Hollywood Cemetery was furnished by Jimmie Caton Jones, United Daughters of the Confederacy)*
Brown, Henry
  1st Missouri Infantry d. 13 Feb. 1899
Brown, Henry
  d. 21 Apr. 1895 – age 67
Cochran, H. J.
  d. 8 Aug. 1905 – age 67
Coker, Tom
  d. 14 Dec. 1900 – age 60
Creel, (Mr.)   (No dates)

Civil War Soldiers
Buried in Garland County

Dale, Thomas
    Member Gen. Pillow's staff, CSA
    d. 9 May 1895 – age 75
Graham, Walter S.
    No dates
Harrell, Col. John Mortimer
    b. Gatesville, NC 14 Dec. 1828
    d. San Antonio, TX 4 Jul 1907
Hill, George W.
    b. 19 Jul 1841; d, 7 Dec. 1908
Jacobs, J. H.
    b. Lexington, KY, 17 Feb. 1839, d. 22 Apr 1892
McGoldrick, William H.
    d. 28 May 1900
Morris, James T.
    b. 10 Jun. 1840, d. 8 Aug. 1907
Rankin, W. H.
    b. 14 Aug. 1840, d. 2 Jun. 1906
Ripley, Martin
    No dates
Robinette, Stephen C.
    b. May 1845, d. Jul 1928
Ruffin, M.
    d. 28 Jan. 1912
Ryan, David Stone
    b. 8 Sep.1839, d. 8 Aug. 1907
Sloan, N. M.   General Shelby's Brigade
    d. 22 Apr. 1899 – age 62
Smith, T. H. S.
    d. 18 Mar. 1902 – age 70
Starr, C.
    d. Jun. 1903 – age 66
Thornton, Clay
    d. 3 Jan. 1905 – age 57
Toffier, Col. W. A.
    2nd LA. Cavalry, New Roads, LA
Walker, Benjamin F.
    b. 15 Jul. 1844, d. 8 Mar. 1913
Williams, Robert Andrew, Wirt Adams Cavalry with Forest's Command
    b. 17 Oct. 1845, d. 18 Jun. 1916
Williams, William S.
    b. 12 Feb. 1840, d. 24 Dec. 1932
Wilson, William H.   (No dates)
Wood, Thomas H.   C TX Cavalry
    d. 17 Mar. 1895 – age 68

**Monument and Burial Sites
Donated to UDC in 1919
By David Stone Ryan
Added to National Register
of Historic Places 6 Dec. 1996**

Civil War Soldiers
Buried in Garland County

(There are also several unmarked graves. "Unknown Soldiers" rest here.)

Lowe Cemetery
  Cearley, Clement
      Co. H. 3rd MO Cal.
  Lavender, John 1843-1919
      Co. G. 4th ARK Cal.
  Mackey, Andrew J.
      Co. G. 6th KANSAS Cal.
  Pate, Allen P.
      Co. F. 4th ARK Cal.
  Rawls, John 1838-1913
      Co. G. 4th ARK Cal.
      Pvt. Co. G. 60th NC
  Edge, John 1828-1864
      Co. D. 4th AR Cal.

Mt. Valley Cemetery
  Bishop, Wm. P. 1840-1902

Newkirk Cemetery
  Glenn, Sgt. Calvin Thompson b. 20 Oct 1836, d. 3 May 1911
      Co. F, 3rd Arkansas Infantry
  Howard, Abraham   b. 13 Nov 1849, d. 3 May 1937
      Woods Battalion, Arkansas Cavalry
  Johnson, Pvt. William   b. 26 Nov 1824, d. 3 Dec. 1879
      Co. H, 1st Arkansas Cavalry
  Merriott, James Wesly b. Aug 1823, d. 22 Mar 1906
      10th Arkansas Cavalry   CSA
  Merriott, John Westley   b. 21 Jan 1845, d. 1 Dec 1903
      10th Arkansas Cavalry CSA

Oakgrove Cemetery
  Burden, James F.
      Co. B 4th MS Inf. CSA
  Ketchum, Jesse Carroll 1843-1890
      Co. C 4th ARK Inf.
  Mathews, Elisha W. 1841-1913
      Pvt. Co. H. 40th GA Inf.
  Richards, Dewitt C. 1839-1901
      Co. A 3rd MO SM CAL

Pleasant Hill Cemetery
  Smith, John A. 1847-1924
      Co. G 45th Missouri Infantry

Talley Cemetery
  Akin, Samuel L.   b. 19 Dec 1838, d. 16 Jul 1864
      Sgt. Co. F, 3rd Arkansas Infantry

John Rawls
Lowe Cemetery

Civil War Soldiers
Buried in Garland County

Baldwin, Elihu A.   b. 1845, d. 1921
    Pvt. Co. B, 10th Arkansas Infantry
Baldwin, Thomas A.   d. 20 Nov 1880
    Pvt. Co. H, 1st Arkansas Cavalry
Baldwin, William M. b. 1841, d. 1871
    Pvt. Co. F., 11th and 17th Consolidated Infantry
Smith, Daniel H.   b. 1842, d. 10 Jul 1910
    Pvt. Co. E, 19th Arkansas Infantry

Civil War Soldiers
Buried in Garland County

CONFEDRATE MEMORIAL

COMO SQUARE

(Note: Graphic design work of removing Landmark Building from background for The Kettle was done by Matt Wiese, Seiz Sign Company)

Civil War Soldiers
Buried in Garland County

CONFEDERATE MEMORIAL
COMO SQUARE
Information furnished by Jimmie Caton Jones

In 1922, the United Daughters of the Confederacy (UDC), Hot Springs #80 was asked to put a Confederate Memorial statue in Hot Springs. The UDC asked the Hot Springs city officials to help establish a fund to purchase a monument. There were many ice cream socials, tea parties, and any entertainment that could be put together for a benefit to purchase the statue.

In 1931, by City Ordinance of Hot Springs, the UDC was given what was then called Como Square, which was a triangle left from closing the water tank from "bygone" days, to erect a Confederate Monument.

In 1934, the UDC Chapter 80 erected the city's only memorial monument. The George Granite Company made plans for building this statue of a Confederate soldier. The Monument stands at the beginning of the downtown business area of Hot Springs, and it has been maintained over many years by the UDC, with the help of many people.

1953, the first Parks & Play Ground Department of the city was organized with Prosecuting Attorney H. A. Tucker as President and Ray Owens, Sr. as Secretary. The UDC was presented a deed to the triangle that held the Confederate Monument.

The Confederate Monument was placed on the National Historic Register on 26 April 1996, and it is part of the Arkansas Historic Preservation Program (AHPP).

The park has been improved over time with help from the Master Gardeners, Grow and Show Garden Club Members, and the City. The UDC and Sons of Confederate Veterans (SCV) met and designed the walkway of concrete and bricks with the same design as the Arkansas flag. The Confederate Memorial Park is a beautiful place to visit, and it is the gateway to the downtown business area of Hot Springs.

Ancestors of Joyce Ann Witherell Walker

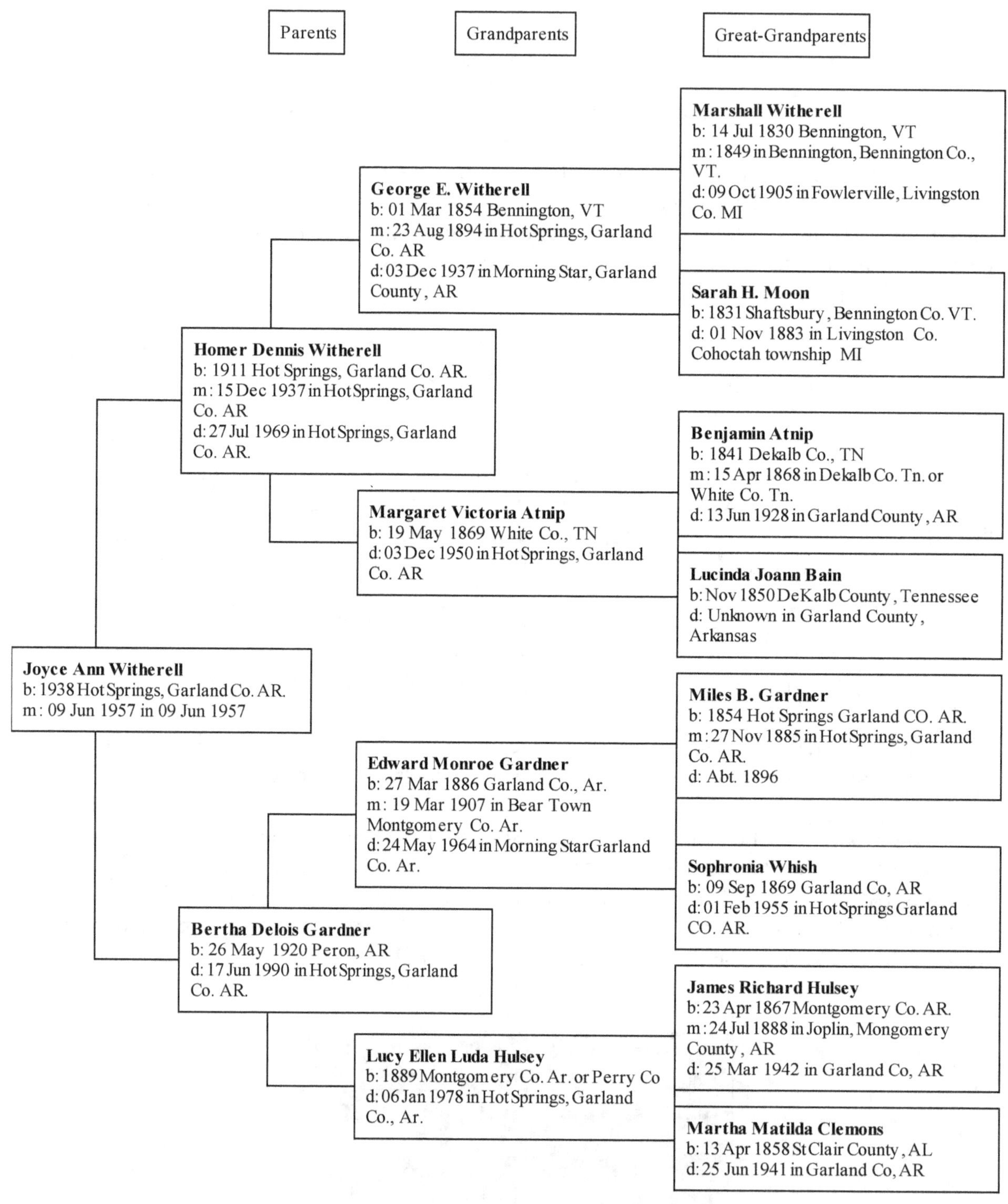

Ancestors of John Franklin Walker, Jr.

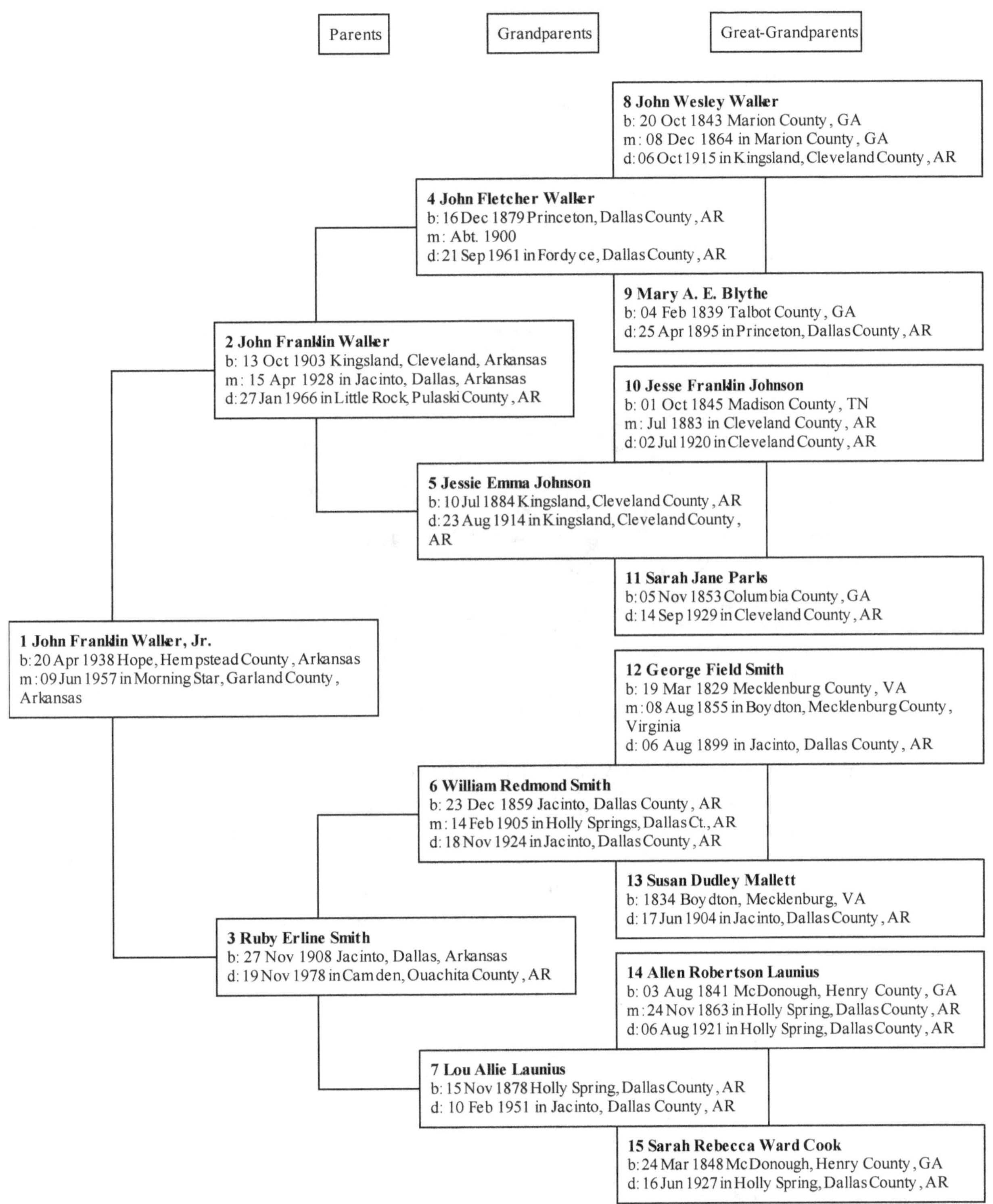

Prepared by John F. Walker, Jr.
Phone 501-760-7559

The Stroope and Kea Families

By Kathy Stroope Veasey
(Washington)

In the late 1930's, looking for work, dad (John Vernon Stroope) took up with an old couple by the name of Ma and Pa McCraven (Roland and Loretta). And just like the "Grapes of Wrath", he drove their truck from Arkansas to Wallowa County, Oregon. Once there, dad drove a logging truck. The McCravens were logging camp cooks at Maxville, Oregon. One day, to buy potatoes for the camp, dad drove to the Walter Carper farm for a load. Carper grew plenty of potatoes for sale (and the rest were for his still under the front porch). It was there dad first caught sight of our mother, (Elsie Mae Evelyn Carper), a young pretty girl, peering around the barn house at this handsome young logger.

Walter Carper Farm

As a young single man, John Vernon lived at a boarding house run by Sadie and Gib Lyon in Wallowa. Coincidentally, Sadie was one of mother's older sisters. After mom had finished school at Maxville (the 8th grade), she went to live with Sadie to help with her young children and the boarding house chores. There she and John Vernon were reacquainted and began their courtship. On September 7, 1940 they drove to Walla Walla, Washington and were married. She was 16 and he was 26. They returned to Wallowa County to set up housekeeping and start their family.

Elsie Carper and John Vernon Stroope

The Stroope and Kea Families

John Vernon and Elsie Stroope had six children. They are Constance Joan (Connie Brooks), 1941; Linda Janette (Warnock) and twin Jettie Lynette (Jones), 1943; Kathaleen Ann (Kathy Veasey), 1945; John Vernon, Jr., 1949 and Waverly Christine (Roan), 1954. During their thirty six years together they lived in Oregon, California, New Mexico and Alaska. Dad died on September 11, 1976, and mom on June 22, 2006. Their remains rest in Juneau, Alaska.

John Vernon's parents were John Ceborn Stroope and Bertha Zula Kea. Johnnie and Bertha were married December 13, 1908 in Montgomery County, Arkansas. During their courtship Johnnie adventured off to Oklahoma Territory.

"Darling, you ask me if I was going to or had decided to get any land here now. It will be a long time before land can be bought here. This territory will become a state on the 4th day March, then the Indians will get their allotment of land. There is a large hunting reserve in the NW part of the territory. And after all is settled and it becomes a state then what is left can be bought by white people from the government. I think after staying here a while and I continue to like it, I will buy a town lot here. I like to live here and I think you will, too."

Johnnie ande Bertha (Kea) Stroope

The Stroope and Kea Families

We're not sure how long Johnnie stayed in Oklahoma or how lonely he was for his family and especially his "darling Bertha". Fortunately for us he returned to Arkansas and on December 13, 1908, John C. Stroope and Miss Bertha Kea married. To this union were born Edrie Jeanette (married Freeman C. Knight), Jettie Virginia (married George Anderson Souter), John Vernon (married our mom), Clarence Julian (married Bonnie Estelle Winter), Winfred Leon (married Mary Ellen McKaskle).

In the fall of 1921 a fever touched the Pearcy community. Both Bertha and Johnnie were ill, as were their children. Bertha passed first on October 5th and on October 9th Johnnie Stroope joined his "darling Bertha".

Edrie and Virginia went to live with grandparents Lou and Ginny Kea and later with Bertha's brother Gordon Kea.   Gordon took in Clarence and Winfred in 1921 and John Vernon went to live with Bertha's sister Elaine Rowell. By the early 1930's both Edrie and Virginia had married and the three Stroope boys lived with Jim and Annie Stroope, Johnnie's brother.

Dad would attend school, work a year, and then return to school, finally graduating from Caddo Gap High School in the Class of 1935 at the ripe age of 21.

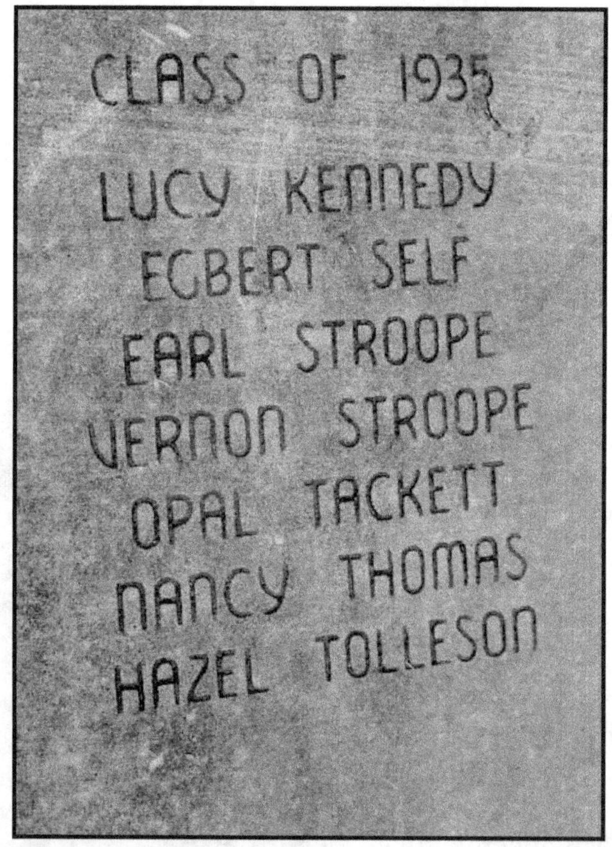

The Stroope and Kea Families

Caddo Gap High School Students
(Left to right, top row: Earl Stroope, Harold Diffee, Egbert Self, Vernon Stroope, Willard Bassinger
Bottom row: Opal Tackett, Lucy Kennedy, Alta Phillips, Hazel Tolleson, Nancy Thomas)

After graduation there were few jobs for young men. Dad joined the CCC, (Civilian Conservation Corps) a work relief program providing unskilled manual labor. During the time of the CCC, volunteers planted nearly 3 billion trees to help reforest America, constructed more than 800 parks nationwide that would become the start of most state parks, forest fire fighting methods were developed and a network of thousands of miles of public roadways and buildings were constructed connecting the nation's public lands.

John Vernon Stroope

The Stroope and Kea Families

John Vernon Stroope, was born October 20, 1913 at Pearcy, Garland County, Arkansas. His parents were John Ceborn Stroope and Bertha Zula Kea.

1930's   John Vernon Stroope   1940's

The Stroope and Kea Families

Dad's Stroope grandparents were Albert J. Stroope and Mary Jane (Molly) Pitts. Albert was born October 6, 1843 in Greenville Township, Clark County, Arkansas. Albert first married Julia Ann Measles, January 10, 1872. They had two children, a girl and a boy. During their short marriage they lived in McKinney, Collin County, Texas. By the 1880 census, Julia and the children are still at McKinney. At this writing, we don't know what became of Julia and the little Stroope children. However, we do know that Albert returned to Clark County, divorced Julia and on 8 February 1881 at Hollywood, Clark County, Arkansas he married our great grandmother, Molly Pitts. Born to this union were James Martin (married Alice Annie Moore), Tabitha Theodosia (married Lewis Harmon Hammonds), John Ceborn (our grandfather), Lillian Lenora (married Pleas M Powell), Eathel Mary (married John Taylor Wacaster) and Roxie (married Tom Biddle). Albert died September 6, 1928 at Anderson Township, Clark County and Molly died at Mazarn, Montgomery County.

Albert and Molly (Pitts) Stroope

Annie and Jim Stroope

Stroope Sisters
(Eathel, Roxie, Theodosia, Lillie)

The Stroope and Kea Families

Albert's parents were William H. Stroope and Delphia Trammel. Delphia was born May 9, 1810 in Georgia and died December 24, 1890 in Clark County. Her parents were Lucretia Caroline and David Trammel. William was born August 27, 1807 at Bayou Bartholomew, Ouachita Parish, Louisiana and died February 4, 1861 at Greenville Township, Clark County, Arkansas. William and Delphia were married at Caddo Township, Clark County, December 12, 1824.

William & Delphia's children were: Mary Ann, David Trammel, Elizabeth H, Eliza Edna, Jacob Stroud, Lucretia Caroline, William Hill Miller, Nancy Melissa, Martha M., Albert (our great grandfather), Delphia Julia, John Hampton and Margaret Lane Isabel.

William's parents were Elizabeth and Jacob Stroope, and his grandparents were Anna Maria Troutman and Jacob Stroope. His great grandparents and our immigrant ancestors were Mary Elizabeth and Wilhelm Strupp of the Palatinate, now Germany.

For years we researched our roots and in the early 1990's we published "Stroope/Stroop Family History", a three volume set of books featuring our family line of about 12 generations. We included lots of history, photos, documentation, including court records, censuses and information on many, many allied families.

Bertha's parents were Virginia Belle Howton and Vincent Louis Kea. Virginia (Ginny) Howton was born at Bucksnort, Caldwell County, Kentucky on July 27, 1866 and died May 2, 1941 at Little Rock, Pulaski County, Arkansas. Her parents were Eliza Jane Hopper and David Harrison Howton, both from Kentucky. Ginny was first married to Jonas Byars Mullings. They had two children: Dovie Henrietta (married Richard Monroe Johnson) and Edward Julian (married Cora Dell Cozart). Jonas died February 28, 1888 at Camden, Montgomery County.

Ginny and Lou Kea

The Stroope and Kea Families

Louis Kea was born August 3, 1861 at Benela, Calhoun County, Mississippi to Permelia A. Thedford and Ephraim A. Kea. Ephraim was born 1837, Greene County, Alabama. Ephraim and Permelia were married 24 September 1860 in Calhoun County, Mississippi. Lou Kea was first married in Calhoun County, Mississippi to Isabella Parker, born 1866 in Calhoun County. To this union was born Sarah Isabelle Kea on August 18, 1883 (she first married Donald A. Freeman and second Tom M. Duncan).

Ephraim enlisted as a Private in the 42nd Regiment, Mississippi Infantry, Company G, CSA. He was an ambulance driver (picture from www.civilwarhome.com). Unfortunately he lost his life May 5, 1864 at the Battle of the Wilderness.

"The May 5-6, 1864 Battle of the Wilderness began a six week campaign that was reported to be the bloodiest campaign in American History. On May 8, 1864 the Union army seized initiative by moving from Wilderness to Spotsylvania Court House. That shift changed the course of the war as the armies began the road to Lee's surrender at Appomattox Court House." (from National Park Service)

In regards to our great-great-grandfather, Ephraim A. Kea, we have no photos of him or Permelia but found the following: From *The Calhoun Monitor*, Pittsboro, Calhoun County, Mississippi, May 14, 1903.

"An Incident of the War by an Old Reb..."

Editor of the Monitor - In order to show your readers what a kind man we had for a division commander in the Virginia army. I will relate a little story of an occurrence with my old comrade, E. A. Kea. Kea was promoted from the ranks of my company to be Ambulance Sergeant and one starlight night while on march through a low muddy country Capt. Woods' Mississippi Battery which was just in front of Sergeant Kea's team stuck up in the mud, as they had an almost broken down, weak team. Of course every thing behind this Caisson and gun had to check up and wait till the way was made clear. Sergeant Kea was away back in the rear of his own

The Stroope and Kea Families

team trying to keep them closed up and hurrying them on.   Finding every thing tied up he put spurs to his horse and went to the front, to ascertain the cause of delay.

Just before reaching them Gen. Heath rode up to the stalled team to look on, leaving his staff a few paces to the rear. When Kea rode up he mistook General Heath for a corporal of the battery and ordered him to dismount and take hold of a wheel and roll that piece out so that his own train could move up.

The General quickly and politely got off his horse and waded into the mud and got hold of a wheel, and looking up at Sergeant Kea said: 'Who are you?' the reply was 'I am Sergeant Kea, roll that piece out of there, I want my train to move up." Well said the General, "I am General Heath, Sergeant, you dismount and take hold of this other wheel." Sergeant Kea, Ephraim, didn't wait to get off his horse he just fell off and waded into the mud and got hold of the wheel, then the word was given, the team started and out rolled the piece.

 "Well done" said General Heath, "this should be a lesson to us, you see what a Sergeant and a General can do." Now Sergeant you can move your train on up, is your feet wet? "Yes, sir. Is yours wet, General? "Oh! no I have on boots, Sergeant."

Kea afterwards went back to our ranks and fell in the Battle of the Wilderness on the 5th day of May, early in the battle. On the 7th I helped to dig a hole and put him, with several other young men in it, in a lonely spot in the wilderness, near which place, doubtless, the weird song of the whippoorwill and mocking bird as "full many a time and oft" made the woods ring with their melody, yet unheeded by the brave boys whose bones molder near them.

Bentley, May 11, 1903.

At the close of the Civil War, amongst the surviving soldiers of Calhoun County, Mississippi, returned one David Lee. Before the war he and his family had lived in the Benela community as well, no doubt he and Ephraim were friends and had gone off to war together. About 1866, David married Ephraim's widow, our great great grandmother, Permelia. They appear on the 1880 census with daughters Martha and Mary. So our great grandfather, Vincent Louis Kea had two step sisters and a step father.

Ephraim's parents were Francis and Joab Kea of South Carolina. Ephraim's siblings were James, Nancy, Arthur, Martha, Josiah and Sarah.

Joab Kea's parents were Elizabeth Ferguson and James Kea of Chester District, South Carolina. Joab's known siblings are Ferguson and Eliza.

Through our research we have learned much of Stroope and Kea ancestors but as with all family lines the search goes on. Aldrich/Aldridge Cemetery in Garland County, Arkansas is the resting place of Johnnie and Bertha Stroope and Bertha's parents Lou and Ginny Kea.

GARLAND COUNTY JAIL MINISTRIES

24 Years of God's Work in Our Local Jail

By Marguerite Holzer Robbins

Chaplain Lanny S. Robbins

What is now the Garland County Jail Ministries, Inc., began in August 1986 as Arkansas Jail Ministries under the corporate cover of CrossRoad Ministries, Inc., in Des Moines, Iowa, but it sprang from an earlier vision of Hot Springs native Lanny S. Robbins for reaching the incarcerated in his hometown.

Army Chaplain Lt. Colonel Lanny S. Robbins had been a jail ministry volunteer in Fairfax, Virginia, in 1972 while working as Deputy Commander of the Armed Forces Courier Service after 3 years with the Defense Intelligence Agency at the Pentagon. Lanny had come to faith in Jesus August 19, 1972, and in February 1973 felt called to leave active army duty and enroll in Southwestern Baptist Theological Seminary at Fort Worth, Texas, to pursue a Master of Divinity degree and become a full-time pastor or chaplain. After his graduation in July 1976, Chaplain Robbins worked with the Good News Jail & Prison Ministries of Arlington, Virginia, to organize its first chaplaincy ministry in the Polk County Jail in Des Moines, Iowa. In 1980, God led Lanny to establish CrossRoad Ministries, Inc., an independent work in the Ft. Des Moines Correctional Facility. Both ministries are still thriving under other chaplains.

As early as 1977, with the approval of Sheriff Clay White, Chaplain Robbins began ministering in the Garland County Jail when visiting family in Hot Springs. Shortly before returning from a pastorate in Kearney, Nebraska, in July 1986, Lanny met with a group of Christian men in Little Rock to pray and plan for establishing a full-time chaplaincy ministry in Garland County similar to the ones he had begun in Iowa. In August 1986, Arkansas Jail Ministries became the first full-time chaplaincy jail

GARLAND COUNTY JAIL MINISTRIES

ministry in the state of Arkansas. A local executive board created to oversee the ministry included Clay White, Roy Helms, Jay Holsted, Tom Hunter, Clarence Jordan, John B. Robbins, J. E. Sanders, and Darrell Short, with Warren Campbell as Chairman. Lanny served as full-time Chaplain 1986-88 without pay while continuing his active reserve chaplaincy duties with the 95th Training Command in Little Rock. Funds for ministry expenses were sought through contact with individuals, churches, and civic organizations. Office space was provided in the basement of the Meyer Building 1986-87, and in April 1988 Chaplain Robbins was given a small office in the secure (locked) part of the jail so that he could counsel inmates and be available to deputies as needed. Captain Carl Lacey, then the Jail Administrator, was especially helpful and supportive of Lanny and his ministry in the jail.

A jail chaplain's ministry is much like that of the pastor of a church with a diverse and ever-changing congregation. The jail chaplain's flock includes not only the incarcerated but also law enforcement personnel and families of both. The chaplain, like the pastor, is called upon to officiate at funerals and weddings and is expected to visit those in hospitals. He is responsible for encouraging and comforting his people as well as teaching moral values and biblical truth. Just as much work within the church is done by volunteers, so it is with the jail ministry, and the chaplain is ultimately responsible for selecting and training those volunteers. While the pastor

encourages his congregation to support the church financially, the chaplain must depend upon support from those outside his "congregation" who believe in the importance of his ministry.

In January 1988 Arkansas Jail Ministries became the Garland County affiliate of the Virginia-based Good News Jail & Prison Ministries, whose president then was Harry Greene, an associate of Chuck Colson. Chaplain Bob Potter of Omaha, Nebraska, became our Regional Director and came to speak at our first fund-raising banquet, held at the Royal Vista Inn in 1988 with 155 in attendance and music by Gene and Rheta and their Weston Family Singers from Lockhaven Nazarene Church. Also in 1988, the First Baptist Church of Hot Springs presented its first annual Volunteer Mission Service Award to Lanny and Marguerite Robbins for chaplaincy service with the Garland County Sheriff's Department 1986-88. In 1996 Lanny received their John and Jewel Abernathy Home Mission Service Award.

By 1989 our board, then called the President's Council, consisted of 17 members: Chairman Warren Campbell, Chaplain Lanny Robbins, Dan Abernathy, Scott Allison, H. C. Croslin, Gene Ellis, Betty Emerson [now Mrs. Roland Graves], Earl Henson, Sam Hunt, Clarence Jordan, Glenn Pettus, John B. Robbins, J. E. Sanders, Darrel Short, James Swedenburg, Clay White, and Jimmy Young. Our second ministry banquet was held in October 1989 at 2nd Baptist Church with Good News President Harry Greene as keynote speaker

GARLAND COUNTY JAIL MINISTRIES

and the Weston Family Singers again providing music.

By 1989, ministry included 3 Sunday evening worship services inside the jail, Bible studies, and Chaplain's ministry to staff and patrol personnel as well as prisoners and family members. The Good News headquarters provided a New Testament Bible study 36-lesson series with true/false, multiple choice, and short answer items followed by "thought" questions asking what a passage meant and how it applied or what was important to the individual personally, and each person completing all 36 lessons received an Award Bible. Ministry volunteers graded the lessons and added encouraging comments. Our earliest volunteer graders, led by Traci Thrash at Grace Bible Church, included Becky Pawelzak and Betty Herrmann; other early volunteers included Pauline Kemp and Helen Baird Wilson.

Mark and Traci (Nevill) Thrash

The same lessons are still being used, and

records show that more than 3000 lessons have been completed in a single year. Personal answers are often printed in our newsletters without individual names. In the late 1990's our most frequent lesson grader was Arlee Blankenship.

Volunteer Arlee Blankenship

The Chaplain was on call 24/7, often riding with deputies on patrol and counseling in suicide and other stressful situations. Christian films and videos were shown, and Bibles and educational materials were provided. Outside the jail Chaplain Robbins screened and trained volunteers to work with inmates under his supervision. Early volunteers for worship services and one-on one visits included Jimmy Young, Mark Thrash, Phil and Myra Cox, Larry Brown, Don Henry, Dick Herrmann, Gary Egleston, Bob Edwards, Marvin Oliver, Grover Heard, David Dahl, David Crane, Betty Emerson, Carolyn Robertson, Cyndi Miller, Sarita Cox [later Mrs. Morris Meacham], Jackie Guinn, Melba Haynes, Sandra Huffman, Beverly Torgerson, and Dee Michau.

GARLAND COUNTY JAIL MINISTRIES

Volunteers Henry Frazier and Larry Brown

Volunteers E. W. Poe and Sandra Huffman

Banquet attendance continued to grow. Our purpose for banquets was, in Lanny's words, "not just to raise funds but to show appreciation for ministry support and to raise public awareness of ministry functions and accomplishments." In 1990 the focus was on interviewing a panel of inmates and volunteers; the next year Chaplain Robbins gave his personal testimony of how God had changed his life and called him to jail ministry. Our speaker in 1992 was Chaplain Michael Dunker from Chicago, and Judy McEarl brought 4 members of The Witness cast to provide music. Banquets were held at 2nd Baptist Bayless Hall until 1996, featuring twice each Chaplain Bobby Shurden and CrossCountry, a Christian comedy team of Boyd Tweedy and R. L. Hullum from Mississippi. Early volunteers who helped with the banquets and Christmas

activities included Pearl Dahl, Betty Lee Hill, Ann Marshall, Drew Terry, and Nina White. In separate years Traci Thrash, Linda Harris, and Melba Haynes were banquet coordinators.

Banquet Coordinator Linda Harris

Our first banquet held at the Assemblies of God Mountain Valley Retreat Center was in 1997 with Rev. Scott Murrish as speaker and musician. CrossCountry returned in 1998, and Beth Anne Rankin with testimony and special music in 1999 received a standing ovation from 550 guests who had come through a downpour of rain to attend. In 2000 we hosted musicians Dan and Bonnie Utter, and 2001 brought back CrossCountry with 600+ attending the last year the Retreat Center was available for a banquet.

Sheriff Larry Selig and Barbara Selig

GARLAND COUNTY JAIL MINISTRIES

Caterers in 1997-98 were Mickey's BBQ and in 1999-2001 Bob & Mary Goodman. The next 3 years we hosted Gospel Night concerts at Music Mountain Jamboree with a variety of Christian groups, and in 2005 met at the Church at Crossgate Center with CrossCountry, DeWayne Hodges, and 4-Given.

In 1990-91 the President's Council included Warren Campbell, Gene Ellis, James Swedenburg, Joe Wilkerson, and Chairman Jerry Mixson, who led in planning a golf tournament fund-raiser in June 1991. In December 1991, after much consideration, Council members chose to remain an affiliate of the Good News Jail and Prison Ministries but to incorporate independently in Arkansas as the Garland County Jail Ministries, Inc., effective December 31, 1991. Attorney Philip M. Clay donated his services to prepare our Articles of Incorporation and By-Laws, and we received IRS conditional approval as a 501(c)(3) organization to become permanent after 5 years. 1991 Council members who signed the incorporation papers were Bob Edwards, John B. Robbins, Carl Russell, Darrel Short (treasurer), Mark Thrash (vice president), Sheriff Clay White, Jimmy Young, and Chaplain Lanny Robbins (president). Marguerite Robbins was elected to join the new Board as secretary at the first meeting in January 1992. Other Board members added in 1992-93 were Grover Heard, Merlyn Weeks, and new Sheriff Larry Selig.

In 1992, with Sheriff White's cooperation, Chaplain Robbins hosted a seminar for pastors and others who were visiting county jail prisoners and/or wanted to initiate a regular chaplain's influence in their county jails. About 12 counties were represented and formed the nucleus of what later became the Fellowship of Arkansas Jail Chaplains in partnership with the Arkansas Sheriffs' Association by the official recommendation of then Sheriff Larry Selig. A September 28, 1992, letter from Chaplain Robbins expressed appreciation for Sheriff Clay White, Chief Deputy James Holt, Captains Carl Lacey and Ed Smith, Sergeants Steve Michau and Roy Lee Elliott, and Deputies Jim Ericksen, George Merriott, Lynn Bennett, and Gregg Youngblood for their help "in the planning and execution of the conference." Our first official training conference was held at the DownTowner Inn in Hot Springs in 1998. Chaplain Marion Reynolds of the Arkansas State Baptist Convention joined Lanny in encouraging volunteer chaplains to participate in training and providing ministry in cooperation with their local sheriffs. In the beginning Chaplain Robbins served as FAJC president, and later Chaplain Ed Losey held the same office.

In 1992-93 Myra Cox and Jerry Daniels kept records in the jail office on a part-time paid basis, and Danella Grant worked with Chaplain Robbins there for several months in 1994. In May 1994, our son-in-law, Rev. Scott Murrish, spent 3 weeks working primarily with juveniles under Lanny's supervision during an interval between youth ministries in Nebraska and Kansas. Volunteers Monette Allen and later Harry

GARLAND COUNTY JAIL MINISTRIES

Moussas came into the jail for Laubach literacy tutoring for a few years.

In August 1994 volunteer Kenneth King became Assistant Chaplain and served until he moved to Cabot, Arkansas, late in 1995. In November 1994 Glynn Brown and Robert Owens were added to the Board of Directors. As members retired or moved, others were added: Carrel Anderson and Cal Campbell (1995); Bob Denbo, Deputy Bill Livingston, Roger Smith, and County Judge Larry Williams (96-97); Roy Henderson and Walter Mays (98-99); J. R. Alexander and John Huffman (2001); and Ted Dahinden and Karen Green [later Mrs. Jim Hogue] in 2002. Through these years Glynn Brown, Roy Henderson, and Richard Boysen were regular volunteers with juveniles in the Detention Center. Special recognition came with Governor Mike Huckabee's proclamation of April 1999 as "Jail Chaplaincy Month."

Lanny's office in the Support Center

In 1995 County Judge Larry Williams offered us the upstairs of an old county-owned building at 223 Hazel Street in return for paying utilities, insurance, and upkeep. Volunteers including George and Betty Beaver helped prepare the building for our use. We maintained an office/support center there until the building was demolished in August 2004, and we moved to our current location at 238 Woodbine. Also in 1995 we hired a part-time office assistant, Cecelia (Suzy) Alexander. She was followed by volunteers Patricia Payton, Linda Harris, and Connie Law as temporary receptionists, and Tena Haynes worked in 1996. Volunteer Mary Kay Litzel, then working at Jay Blumer's Precision Lighting, produced our monthly newsletter in 1997. Volunteer Melba Haynes worked full-time at the center 1998-2000, and Yvonne Frazier was office assistant in 2001.

In 1997 Ed Losey, then a volunteer with men's worship services, became part-time Assistant Chaplain and was ordained by his church to the gospel ministry. He then worked full-time as Chaplain with Lanny in all aspects of this ministry and was elected to the Board in 2000.

Volunteer Glynn Brown installing new sign

at the Ministry Support Center

GARLAND COUNTY JAIL MINISTRIES

Chaplain Ed Losey

Chaplain Robbins retired as Senior Chaplain for health reasons in December 2000 but continued as Board president one more year. Chaplain Losey was then elected Board president to succeed Lanny. In February 2001 Jeryl Johnson became a part-time Assistant Chaplain and served until April 2006. He was then struggling with cancer and died in February 2007. Volunteer Mark West assisted Ed in the jail until Randy Donahue became a part-time Chaplain's Assistant in 2009.

Lanny and Marguerite at his Retirement Service hosted by Emmanuel Baptist Church, Jan. 2002

In January 2003 Carrie Mathis had become our part-time administrative assistant and also volunteered inside the jail.

Carrie Mathis with Bible Study group in the jail

In 2006 God inspired Carrie to plan and coordinate a "Walk for Christ" fund-raiser to be held in Hot Springs Village. It has been repeated each year since then, each time with Barcelona Road Baptist Church providing our starting point and hosting a lunch at our return. In May 2008 Carrie was succeeded by Paula Schwartzmann, who had been a volunteer with women's Bible studies and worship inside the jail for several months. In 2009 Paula also began serving part-time as Assistant Chaplain with the women's Sunday worship volunteers.

Current Board members (2010) are Chaplain Losey, president; Jack Hardin, vice-president; Marguerite Robbins, secretary and treasurer, and directors Cal Campbell, Don Fritz, John Huffman, Sheriff Larry Sanders, Larry Shaw, and Ray Shoptaw. God has greatly blessed this ministry over the past 24 years. He prepared and called Lanny Robbins to establish standards, guidelines and directives for this ministry

GARLAND COUNTY JAIL MINISTRIES

which have made it possible to work with local pastors and churches and hundreds of volunteers to meet the spiritual and emotional needs of law enforcement personnel as well as of the incarcerated and their families. God also prepared and called Ed Losey to serve as Senior Chaplain and direct this ministry to carry on its mission since 2001. He has continued to work with adult inmates and Sheriff's Department personnel and has developed and expanded various areas of ministry including Search and Rescue with deputies as well as crisis intervention. In 2006 he became actively involved in the Juvenile Re-Entry Program assisting F.I.N.S. and delinquent children and their families with behavioral problems and life skills. He also directs volunteer tutoring and mentoring for juveniles.

A ministry of this nature cannot succeed without faithful volunteers who are willing to give their time to help others. It is impossible for me to name all of those who have been part of this ministry during the past 24 years. Hundreds have prayed regularly, given financial support, helped with fund-raising events, and graded Bible lessons. Some have invited the Chaplain or another representative to speak to a church or civic group; some have served as Board members; many have led worship services or Bible studies inside the jail, and in recent years many have taken part in our Walk for Christ. Throughout these 24 years God has continued to change lives. Many of those in jail who once were a threat or a burden to our area are now productive citizens. Volunteers have experienced the joy of

seeing hardened or despairing individuals become excited to learn that God can love and forgive them and give them a new direction for their lives.

This article has focused on the beginning and early years of this ministry. Dates and names are based on written records as well as on my memories of what has been an important part of my life. The real history of this ministry, however, consists of the stories of countless lives impacted and transformed by God throughout these years. One woman who accepted Christ in jail at the age of 35 had been in and out of jails since the age of 13. Formerly a hardened and angry individual, she became a leader of Bible study and prayer with women in her cellblock over several months, and most of them became Christians also. Another young woman who became a Christian in our jail continued contact with us later and became a leader in a local drug rehabilitation program. A young man who had accepted Christ in jail greeted us later in a local church where he was then directing music in Sunday worship. Over the years, Lanny was often approached in a store, a restaurant, a church parking lot, or elsewhere, by someone saying, "Hi, Chap, remember me? I'm working now and doing okay. Just wanted to thank you."

Three months after celebrating our 50th wedding anniversary, my husband, Chaplain Lanny Robbins, died September 4, 2009, but his vision for this ministry is alive and well under the leadership of Chaplain Ed Losey and our Board.

Reflections from Tweedletown

Charles Wagner Smith

Bulldog Beginnings…

Reflections from Tweedletown

Bulldog Beginnings…
By Charles Wagner Smith

The migration from Montgomery County, Arkansas, proved to be a smart move for the Samuels family. Josh and Caldonia, both descendants of slave parents, were excited and eager to begin a new life in Garland County where relatives had found it easier to make ends meet. Their eight children, Louis, Daisy, Joe, Zellie, August, Rachel, and twin boys Caleb and Josh, Jr., were also excited to be moving to a new place.

Later, one of the twins, Caleb Samuels, married Lucille Tweedle, and they settled in a small house in the southwest area of town referred to as "South Hot Springs," although it was actually in the western part of Hot Springs.

Caleb and Lucille (Tweedle) Samuels

Lucille was among the eight children of William and Ida Byrd Tweedle: Robert, Charles, Lewis, Virgil, John L., Ulysses, Rosie, and Lucille. Her grandparents were Austin Tweedle and a Cherokee maiden with the name Adeline. Austin and Adeline had ten children: William, Elbert, Paralee, Dalton, P. C., Zephro, Johnny, Matthew, Marie, and Mary.

Caleb Samuels was a very outgoing and adventurous person who loved music and dancing.

Caleb Samuels performing

Caleb earned his living as a professional boxer throughout the United States and Canada. His opponents believed him to be disadvantaged in the ring due to having only one eye. However, they soon discovered that it belied his ability to fight and win consistently. His livelihood was enhanced by his ability to perform general labor and serve as a maintenance person for the local race track that conducted live horse races. Lucille, most often referred to as "Ms. Lula," would serve as the pianist for the Baptist Church located a block north of her home. Her house would often be filled with the sounds of Gospel and Spiritual songs. Ms. Lula was content to raise her five children, Irene, Louise, Eugene, Ida and Rosalie at home.

Reflections from Tweedletown

Ida, Rosalie, Louise and Irene

Ms. Lula took in washing and ironing from folks in need of these services. Her oldest daughter, Irene Samuels, was my mother. My father's name was Charles Wagner. My mother later married Cleavon Smith in Chicago, Illinois. I lived with my mother and my grandparents in what was called "Tweedletown." Our home was located on the corner of Lacey and Hobson Streets. My brothers and sisters were: Kenneth, Lisa, Russell, and Joseph.

Charles, Irene and Kenneth

My earliest recollection of my childhood is one of the darkest. I remember watching with trepidation and sadness as the casket of my uncle was placed in the living room of our home. It was the custom during the early forties to hold wakes for the departed in the family home to await funeral services the next day. Needless to say, that night as I lay in bed I could not erase the sight of that casket in the next room. My uncle Eugene was a member of the United States Navy and had drowned in Lake Hamilton while home on leave from Pearl Harbor. I have little memory of Uncle Eugene, but I sensed a loss at the time.

Our neighborhood was comprised of a mix of black families and white families, many of which were Tweedles or were Tweedle-related. The community was commonly known as "Tweedletown." Tweedletown is bound on the north by West Grand Avenue, on the east by Summer Street, on the south by Albert Pike, and on the west by an unknown street which at the time was nothing but woods. During my formative years, my days were filled with a series of constant adventures and discoveries. My Aunt Louise would send my brother Kenneth and me to gather clay rocks for her to munch on during the day. Aunt Louise believed, as others did, that the clay held some sort of curative powers and provided nutrients not found in foods. Our nearest neighbors were Aunt Flossie and Miss Indell. Neither was related to us, but we always called one "Aunt" and the other "Miss." Aunt Flossie was the greatest cook in the world. Much to our delight, she would fill her windowsills with pies and cakes each week. I remember a man living with them known as Mr. Harrison. When he passed

Reflections from Tweedletown

away, the pies and cakes disappeared for about three weeks.

Next to Aunt Flossie's house, my grandmother's brother, Uncle Ulysses Tweedle, lived with my Aunt Peach (Alberta) and cousin Pinky (Alberstine) in a patch of land across a narrow branch of water. Uncle Ulysses played several musical instruments and provided great entertainment. He also was the family barber and, much to my dismay, mastered the "bowl haircut." Behind their home was the home of my Aunt Juanita and my cousins Ruby and Callie. Other families in the area included those of Lola Sanders, Miss Coy, Mr. Red, Mr. Ed and Dora; Luther and Arletta Williams with Mrytis Rogers, Ivory T. and Marie; Robert and Hester Crutchfield with Lorraine, Norma Jean, Robert Jr., Georgia Lee (Noonie), Lawrence, Brenda, and Grandma Counts; Janie Stanley Counts with Stella (Estelle) and Marguerite; William and Lena Akins with Christine, Louise, Odessa, and Boycie; Josie Tyson and Mickey, Elizabeth and Maxine; Austin and Blanche Wesson with Betty Jean; Grandma Node with Miss Adeling, Elnora, Dorothy Lee, Mac Jr., Andrew, Johnny, Billy Joe and Irvin; Josh and Bertha Craven with Mary Frances, Shirley, Emma Jean, Mattie Ann, and Eulalia; Mack Duvall with Dorothy, Mary and Stanley; Gladys Rigsby with Mary, Ledell, Annabelle, Sue and Bo; George and Glassie Lee Porter; Randolph and Nannie Lee Crutchfield with Emma, Ronald and Evelyn; Jimmie and Thelma Lemons with Beatchre and Willlye Mable.

One of the most amusing memories of my youth was provided by Grandma

Node. Whenever we misbehaved, she would say, "You kids are so bad, when you were born you were laid by buzzards and hatched by the Devil." The center of the community was Ebenezer Baptist Church. It was here where you learned not only about the Word but also about family. The church provided music, song, food and adventure. Church picnics, hayrides and wiener roasts were eagerly attended. Sunday afternoons offered exciting movie matinees at local theaters; however, to miss the Bible Training Union (BTU) at church was unacceptable, and to do so promised severe consequences.

My best friend, Carl White, and I would often hitchhike to the lakes located on the outskirts of town. If the driver stopped at a service station to purchase tobacco or gas, we would snatch apples and grapes from the fruit stand at the station.

There are various forms of discipline imposed on kids that linger for years and years in their memory. We were warned daily by the words, "Be still before I take this belt to your behind, and you'd better not cry!" or "I brought you into this world, and I'll take you out." The most dreaded form of punishment occurred when seemingly during rain or thunderstorms, someone would begin rapping on our windows after dusk. Alarmed, we would huddle on the sofa and ask our granddad, "What's that noise?" He would answer that because we were bad that day, old "Redhead and Bloody Bones" had come to get us and take us to live in the woods. We began to plead that we would be good and for him to save us. Suddenly, a light would

Reflections from Tweedletown

appear in the window, and we could see the fearsome "Redhead and Bloody Bones" glaring through the glass. He wore a big floppy hat, and his face was black like coal with red rings around his eyes and mouth. All the kids would then run under the beds or hide in the closet. Eventually, the rapping stopped and calm was restored. It was several years before I learned that the demon of the woods was indeed my sweet little grandmother painted with lipstick and soot from a tub.

Among my more enjoyable recollections are of Miss Cook's ice cream parlor and of McClard's Bar-B-Que located on Albert Pike, no more than two blocks from my home. Spending money came easily as there was always people who needed their grass cut or trash raked out from beneath their house so lime could be spread to prevent infestation of mice and other critters.

One Christmas I received a Red Ryder BB gun from Santa. Wow! Now I could really portray Roy Rogers or the Durango Kid, who were my favorite cowboy idols. The BB gun led to another incident for which I must plead temporary insanity. Aunt Flossie was hanging clothes one day as I was pursuing outlaws in our backyard. She was constantly bending over to retrieve clothes from her basket. Well, the sight of her bending over, and the gun in my hands, resulted in my bearing welts on my backside for several days. No, I was not a bad child, just one with an overworked imagination.

When I was seven years old, I contracted typhoid fever from drinking branch water from the creek between Aunt

Flossie's and Uncle Ulysses' houses. I remember lying in bed for weeks, and I remember a special nurse named Mrs. Eden. I hallucinated quite often during the sickness and was later told that if I had been given water during my feverish moments, I would have died. After the sickness, it was determined that I needed to wear eyeglasses. I hated wearing glasses to school and being called "four eyes." Fortunately for me, another life-threatening incident occurred when our home caught fire and I rushed into the burning blaze to retrieve my bike. As I rushed from the house with my bike, I cast my glasses into the fire and never again had to wear glasses to school.

1946 Kindergarten Class at St. Gabriel's

I attended St. Gabriel's Catholic School from kindergarten through the ninth grade. I was baptized as a child in the Baptist church, but again as a Catholic when I began attending college. I remember the strict adherence to my studies demanded by the nuns and discipline throughout the day. When I began the second grade, I noticed a strange looking chair in the school that I had never seen before. I was told it was a chair used to remove a child's tonsils. *I never complained about a sore throat until later after I entered high school.* My English teacher, Mrs. Logan, was an inspiration during my journey through

Reflections from Tweedletown

high school. I delighted in the presentation of school plays and attending literature classes. Shakespeare provided the most memorable cast of characters, and I also enjoyed reading James Weldon Johnson's work, "God's Trombones." I was quite active in sports, especially football and basketball. My friend Carl White and I were competitive in athletics and in attracting girls.

Charles with classmates in high school

My high school days were the most treasured part of my life. My fondest memories were captured in a speech I wrote for a school reunion.

Poets speak in prose, teachers in patterns, politicians in promises, Christians in parables, and I, at this time, would like to speak to you in peculiarities and particulars. I find it most peculiar that few here realize that faith can move mountains, love can open doors and trust can inspire the most adamant of non-believers. That fellowship is a bond stronger than blood and friendship a gift more blessed than the joy of creation.

That the question, are you a good Christian should never be asked, for if you are, the question will never arise.

I find it most peculiar that our youth are bombarded with drugs, seduced by crime, surrounded by violence and misled by their peers. Yet, we come here today, products of another era, in anticipation of a spiritual high, in concert with the Commandments of God and in search of a reflective day. For every man, woman and child who has tasted the forbidden fruit, who has been touched by the shadow of death, who has been a part of life rather than apart from it, who has longed for a kind word and a warm heart, are here to share the peculiarities of brotherhood and memories in particular.

I find it most peculiar that as we wean our way through the Ozark Mountains, as we stare across the lakes of Catherine and Hamilton, as we watch the pine trees point their fingers to the sky, as we cross the intersections of Central and Grand or the corners of Silver and Pleasant, we are reminded of days filled with Homecoming preparations and the smell of Dewey's Bar-B-Q. Hayrides, joyrides, bus rides and carnival rides. History tests, biology pests, lovers nests and recess. Marching bands, assembly stands, graduation plans and Professor Henderson's heavy hand. Pappa meathouse, and Kitty's chicken, sneaking into the moonglow or atmosphere. Rendezvousing at MacKenzie's Courts or Sam Quinn Stadium. Swimming at the businessmen's club and dancing at the Webb Center. Memories of years past, yet vivid as the morning light. Classmates and first dates stir our memories in particular.

With apologies to Dickens...It was the best of times; it was the worst of times. A time when equality meant sharing Rix Stadium. When the chains that were attached to our ankles were removed and attached to our minds. When we had the dream that Dr. King had. When we wanted

Reflections from Tweedletown

to believe that our trials and tribulations were a result of our weaknesses and not of our heritage. To believe that hate was only a misunderstanding of the mind and not conflicts of the heart. That we would be given the opportunity to work at the trades for which we've been trained. We have survived. Not because of freedom, justice, equality, opportunity and human rights. But, because of courage and determination, fortitude and hope. And most of all, because of values instilled in us by our parents, and concern bestowed on us by our teachers. There is only one beautiful child in the world and every mother has it. There is only one home, only one place that we share. Let us not forget, the memories of the past do not relieve the realities of today. We cannot wait for the changes of time, but make today a time of changes. We must pool our resources and reclaim our birthright.

Langston High School

When I became a teenager, I discovered a world of black and white. A world filled with signs and designs. Although I realized Negros (blacks) were unable to access certain facilities or to utilize some public services, the full impact of being regarded as a second-class citizen didn't hit home until I entered high school. My journey through the early years included: riding in the back of the bus and occupying a seat only if no whites were standing; drinking from designated fountains and ordering foods through windows located on the side of

buildings; being unable to sit at department store or café counters; forced to sit only in balconies of theaters; employed only in service industry and laborer jobs; using hand-me-down books and athletic equipment from the white-only schools; and being questioned by authorities if seen in non-minority residential areas.

Graduation at the National Baptist Building

A classmate and I would often try to "catch the hop" at the local theater on weekdays. To "catch the hop" meant to sneak into the balcony area minutes after the ticket booth closed and moments before the last feature began. One such evening after viewing a late movie at the theater, we were picked up near the night life area by the police who wanted to know why we were 'breaking curfew.' They took us to the police station, where the practice was to call your parents to come pick you up, and to wait on a bench until they arrived. While waiting to call our parents, a crazed looking old white woman came in and began shouting, "That's them! Them's the boys that raped me! Them's the ones." The police laughed and asked the woman where she got raped. She responded, "Under my skirt!" When asked "When?" she said, "Every night it rains." Thankfully, the police sent us home without

Reflections from Tweedletown

our parents being called. They warned us to stay away from that crazy old woman.

During my teen years, it was always easy to earn money. I could cut a neighbor's grass, chop wood, work as a bellhop, a busboy or a waiter, and sometimes scrub pots and pans for a bakery located two blocks from my home. I enjoyed working for the bakery because I was allowed to take the stale (day old) doughnuts and cinnamon rolls home to share with my folks.

Football was both an agonizing and rewarding part of my high school days. The practices were long and hard, filled with sprains and hard knocks. During one practice session, I found myself the only tackler between the goal posts and a 230-pound fullback barreling toward me along the sidelines. Now, I weighed 130 pounds when fully dressed in pads, cleats and stuffed uniform pants. My dilemma was to either lie down in front of the onrushing force or to make a frugal attempt to impede his progress. I decided to make a move in one direction and then quickly move to another so as to avoid him altogether. To my dismay, he faked one way and proceeded to advance in the same direction I had decided to move. Well, I regained consciousness about ten minutes later to find my teammates and coaches congratulating me on a terrific tackle. I wept for joy when basketball season finally arrived.

I never considered myself, or any of my race, to be less than someone of another race. I looked with admiration and pride upon the stature and works of those who played an important role in my upbringing. I respected the teachers who

impressed upon me the importance of an education and the businessmen who provided the community with goods and services.

As a college student living in Chicago, I began to think like a man, and I began to anticipate a life filled with challenges, disappointments and successes. One of the most exciting events in my life happened when I was returning one weekend from classes at Western Illinois University in Macomb, Illinois. Awaiting the train I became sleepy, as it was nearly midnight before the train arrived. I boarded quickly and the train was soon on its way. The conductor asked for tickets, and when I presented mine, he asked where I was bound. I grinned and answered, "Chicago," becoming more awake as the realization that I would soon be back in Chi-town began to sink into my thoughts. He replied, "Well, I'm sorry son, but this train is headed to Kansas City." "What do you mean?" I asked. He said that I had boarded the wrong train. The train bound for Chicago arrived thirty minutes later. I asked him what I could do, and he said I could get off at the next stop, which is a flag stop, and flag down the Chicago-bound train. Well, I got off at the next stop and found myself on a depot platform. The nearest structure was about three miles away, and I felt isolated and uncertain. As I looked about the darkness, I visualized blacks alone in rural towns at night being found hanged or severely injured, of blacks being tossed in jail and held for days without being able to reach out to anyone for assistance. Shakily, I tried to enter the depot, but the door was locked. The conductor had instructed me to enter the depot, find a lantern, light it, and flag

Reflections from Tweedletown

down the train. So, I forced open the door and began to look for a lantern. I discovered one on a far wall and found that I didn't know how to light the darned thing. Apparently, there is some special way that the lantern is lit; however, I had no clue. I tried and tried and finally, as my supply of matches dwindled, I lit the lantern and hurried to the platform as the whistle from the oncoming train began to sound. I began waving the lantern, yet the train appeared not to slow. So I jumped on the tracks and waved and waved until I sensed it was time to get back on the platform. Finally the train stopped about 200 yards past the depot, and I boarded-- praising the Lord. <u>I now travel by car, bus or air only.</u>

In August 1963 I was ordered to report for induction into the armed forces of the United States. I was inducted into the Army and reported for duty in Louisville, Kentucky. I arrived at the post with shoes untied, no socks, hair uncombed, bloodshot eyes and a throbbing hangover. Oddly, I was the most coherent of the group.

Charles in the Army

Basic training was all I believed it would be. Upon completion, I was asked if I would like to become an Officer. I agreed and was shipped off to Fort Polk, Louisiana, to complete advanced infantry training. What a dope! I later learned if I had refused, I would have been assigned to an administrative unit in Chicago, Illinois.

I believed that now my life was really going to come alive. The coming years would be filled with sights and experiences I could only dare to imagine!

ABOUT THE AUTHOR

Charles Wagner Smith is a native son of Hot Springs. He served in the U. S. Army during the Vietnam War era, successfully completed courses in Labor Relations at the University of Illinois, secured teaching credentials from the State of California, and became certified as prescribed for Reserve Deputies for the Kern County Sheriff's Department.

Charles is an accomplished playwright whose works have been performed in Chicago, Milwaukee and Los Angeles. With his excellent communication skills, he hosted a weekly television talk show, "Everyday People," on Resort Cable. He serves as a motivational speaker for organizations, agencies, schools and churches throughout the mid-south. He founded the thespian group, Prolific Art Performers, who performed his works in Chicago and Los Angeles. Mr. Smith also worked in the casting department

Reflections from Tweedletown

for the ABC documentary, "Roots," by Alex Haley.

Mr. Smith's many associations and appointments over time will be listed at the end of this story; however, the editor of *The Kettle* wants to stop and recognize the many facets of Charles Wagner Smith's contributions to Hot Springs. Notably, Charles is a board member of Hot Springs National Park Rotary, member of the Lion's Club, the American Legion, past chairman of the Hot Springs Jazz Society, President of the Hot Springs Documentary Film Institute, member of Knights of Columbus, Mentoring Program for Young Minorities, Hot Springs Planning Commission, past executive director of the Emma Elease Webb Community Center (15 years), nominated for Chamber of Commerce Man of The Year, participant in LeadAR, St. Mary's Council, organizer and Project Director of the Friendship Cemetery Preservation Society … and the list goes on!

Business Associations:

- Social Security Administration – 30 years, CA,
- Consultant Mid-South Foundation, MS,
- Winthrop Rockefeller Foundation, grants reviewer,
- Training Community Organizations for Change,
- Univ. of AR Foundation Associate Director
- Training throughout AR, MS, and LA,
- AR Minority Health Commission workshops,
- UofA at Pine Bluff
- AR Rehab Advisory Council,
- State Board of Workforce Education,
- Inspirational speaker,
- Community Development Specialist,
- Department of Human Services,
- AR Minority Health Commission,
- Community Development Advisory Committee,
- Hot Springs Planning Commission
- CWS & Assoc., Business Support Services, Owner

Note: All documentation and other information is on file at The Melting Pot Genealogical Society Library in the Family History Section. (Smith, Charles Wagner)

Family

Stephen Patoc, Charles, Geri (Patoc) Smith, Marilyn and U. S. Reed

Family

Russell, Charles, Irene (mother), Lisa, Kenneth, Joseph

TWEEDLE FAMILY TREE

Adeline (Cherokee) v Austin Tweedle

>>   William v Ida Byrd >>>>>>>

>>   Elbert v Annie Wilson

    Lillie Counts

>> Paralee v Fred Kilbourn

>> Dalton v Emma Crutchfield

    Henry v Viola Bledsoe

        Patricia
        v Joel Purdie
          timothy/Henry/Joel

    Jessie v Marie Connelly

    Elbert v Odessa Strong
    Helen v Butch Wilson
    Ernest v Nadine Hamilton
    Annie v Lyman Page
        Anita
    Raymond v Gladys Baskins

        Anita/Stephen/Gary
        Gregory/Emma

>>   P.C. Elnode Thompson

        Ida

      v Dellie Hence
      v Rachel Crutchfield
      Jack v Minnie
        Allen

>> Zephro v George Sinclair

 >> Johnny/Matthew/Marie

>> Mary v Lem Lemons

    Richard v Rosie Leeks
      Jimmy v Thelma
      Beatchre
      Willye Mable
    v Bud Wesson
    Austin v Blanche Bluenth
    May Eltesia v Clarence D.
    Elvin v Mary Lou Mitchell

    Lewis (snooks) v Nellie
    Irene v Ronald Crutchfeld
      Rhonda
      Michael
      June
    Edward v Alma Beavers
      Eddie Jr
    Wilmer v Frankie Anderson

Middle column

>> Robert

>> Charles

>> Lewis

>> John L v Thelma
    Fannie Mae
    v Minnie B
    John Jr
    Charles

>> Ulysses v Alberta
  Alberstine v Lawrence
    Butch
    Gerald
    Lynn
    Marsha
    Carla
    Ricky
    Donald

>> Virgil v Alberstine
    Virgil Jr.
  v Kitty
    Billy
    Victor
    Jessie
    Shelton
    Harry

>> Rose v ernie sims
    Callie v Leroy
      Bennette
    Curtis
    Cecil
    Myrtle
    Juanita v Herbert
    Ruby
    Cherry/Dexter
    Vega/Marie

Right column

Lucille v Caleb Samuels

>>**Irene** v Charles Wagner

    Charles v Freddye Cobb
        ulysses
    v Geraldine
        stephen
    v Cornelious House
    Kenneth v Emma H
      Ken/Michael/Casey
      v Carolyn Ray
      Jim/Saundra/Kendra
    v Cleavon Smith
      Lisa v Howard Hughes
      Jerrel/Olivia
    Russell v Edna
    Joseph v Marnice
  Joe Jr/Sean/Xavier/Josh/Zoey

>> Louise v Houston Berthia
    Barbara v Daryl
        raisa
    Billy v Janice
        Carmella

>> Ida Mae v Harriel White III
    Harriel v Shirlene
      Jamar/Kaemel
    Anita v Bernard
        jacque
    Diane v Billy
        stephan
    Rita v Gregory
    Susan v Phillip Henry
      Phillip v Nicole
        phillip
      v Rooselvelt B
        brandy
      Inita
      Marvin v Dorothy
        Heather
      Eric

>> Rosalie v William Wilcox
    Larry v Yvonne
    Rodney v Adele

SAMUELS FAMILY TREE

SAMUELS V SANDERS

CALDONIA V JOSH SAMUELS

Kalip (Caleb) V Lucille Tweedle	Josh V Margaret Henderson	Louis V Mattie Brown	Daisy/Joe Zellie Augusta Rachel
Irene v Charles Wagner	Clinton v Shirline	Leroy v Bessie Mae	
Charles	Christine v John	Dora Jean	
v Corneilous House	Eddie v Alberta	Sterling v Rosie Lee	
Kenneth	Nancy v Roger	Diana M	
v Cleavon Smith	Arkie v Leon	Sterling Jr	
Lisa	Jo Ann	Mary v Raymond	
Russell	Bubba	Stacey v Carrie Jean	
Joseph		Stacey Jr.	
Louise v Houston Berthia		Carrie lynn	
Barbara		Janice	
Billy		Steven	
Ida Mae v Harriel White III		Tracey	
Harriel Dean		La Ron	
Anita		Theresa	
Diane		Thelma	
Rita		Rocky v J.B Thompson	
Susan		Dennis Jr.	
Marvin		Katina	
Eric		Brandon	
Eugene		Saundra v Carl Craig	
		Michael	
Rose v William Wilcox			
Larry			
Rodney			

PUBLICATIONS FOR SALE

Crestview Memorial Park Cemetery Book	$20.00
Mt. Carmel and Cunningham Cemeteries Book	10.00
Memorial Gardens Cemetery Book	20.00
Index to Probate Records of Garland County, Ar 1900-1930 Inclusive	12.50
Marriage Records Index of Garland County, Ar 1873-1942 Inclusive	20.00

Grooms are alphabetical, Brides are indexed

Volume 1 – A-G Volume 2 – H-0 Volume 3 – P-Z [set of 3]	50.00
MPGS Members' Pedigree Charts (Indexed)	12.50
Volumes 1, 2, 3 (Each volume contains about 80 charts) [set of 3]	32.50
Oldest Gross Mortuary Records 1874-1889 (Indexed) 126 pages	15.00

Includes the book list, who paid for services and where interred

Garland County 1880 US Census – all thirteen townships including Hot	15.00

Springs, Antioch, Buckville, Cedar Glades, Hale, Lee, Marble, Mill,
Mt. Valley, Ouachita, Phillips, Sulphur, Union

Deed and Mortgage Conveyance Records Grantor and Grantee sorted (each)	10.00

Volume A – 1873-1880;   Volume B – 1880-1884;
Volume C – 1884-1887;   Volume D – 1887-1890;
Volume E – 1890-1893   Volume F – 1893-1896

Saline County Marriages Book A and B	3.25
Research and Writing Tribal History by Duane Hale	19.95
Tracing Indian Family History by Duane Hale	15.00
The Melting Pot Quarterly: (back issues 1978-1987)	1.00
The Melting Pot Biannual: (1988-2000)	2.00
The Melting Pot Biannual: (2001-2006) (each)	5.00
The Melting Pot Annual: 2007	15.00
The Kettle **2008**	15.00
The Kettle **2009**	15.00
The Kettle **2010** (non member cost)	20.00
One copy is included with membership, additional copies for members	10.00

BOOK ORDERS:

Books: Please copy this page and mark the books being ordered.

Total Price all books ordered: _________

Add: Postage and handling – for one: $1.50 for each quarterly or $3.50 for any other book, plus $1.75 for each additional book

Total for all books and postage: ___________

Signature: ____

Address for mailing: _______________________________________

____

Homemade Tombstones
By Debra Slater Garner

During the season of decoration of graves and clean-up of cemeteries, it is a good time to find unmarked graves and give them some sort of marker. Homemade markers are very inexpensive to make (approximately $20 each).

At a local building supply store (e.g. Lowes, Sutherlands, Home Depot) or Wal*Mart get a one-inch flat solid concrete block and a landscape block that when placed upright resembles a tombstone. At a local Awards company you can have a 5" x 7" plaque of stainless steel. (Black with silver or gold embossing looks good.) Glue the plaque with engraving to the front of the landscape block with liquid nail. Attach the block to the flat one-inch concrete block with the liquid nail. These markers are light enough for anyone to place by themselves.

An alternative would be to use black plastic (or get a sheet of black sentra or other substrate from a sign shop), letter with white vinyl letters and laminate for protection, or use paint for information.

These stones/markers are suitable for both marking gravesites and for denoting the location and name of a cemetery which does not have any identifying marker or sign. As time goes by, we are losing the ability to identify unmarked graves as well as the ability to locate specific cemetery locations and names. The Melting Pot Genealogical Society will start a fund specifically to obtain and place cemetery name/location markers in Garland County.

Note: Be sure to check with the cemetery offices or custodian about any restrictions they may have.

ZIEGLER, Norval Finn, Jr.
b. 31 May 1925, Hot Springs, Garland County, AR
m. 18 Dec 1949, Saline County, AR
Mt. Carmel Methodist Church

ZIEGLER, Norval Finn, Sr.
b. 25 Nov. 1897, Saline County, AR
m. 14 Dec. 1921, Hot Springs, AR
d. 25 Sep 1950, Hot Springs, Garland County, AR

ZIEGLER, Robert Michael
b. 06 May 1861, McMinn County, TN
m. 02 Oct 1892, Saline Co, AR
d. 09 Aug 1937, Garland Co. AR

ZIEGLER, Benjamin Tyson
b. 1820, Franklin Co, VA
m. 26 Dec 1838, McMinn Co, TN
d. 08 Oct 1887, Garland Co, AR

MANSELL, Susannah
b. abt. 1823, McMinn Co, TN
d. abt. 1879, Rhea Co, TN

NORMAN, Evaline
b. 09 Nov 1876, Saline Co, AR
d. 22 Jan 1926, Saline Co, AR

NORMAN, James Clinton
b. 09 Dec 1853, McMinn Co, TN
m. 30 Dec 1835, unknown place
d. 08 Oct 1927 Garland Co, AR

GODBEHERE, Sibilas Angelline
b. 07 Feb 1858, TN
d. 27 Jan 1937, Benton, Saline Co, AR

RILEY, Gladys
b. 15 Sep 1900, Hot Springs, Garland County, AR
d. 22 Oct 1991, Benton, Saline County, AR

RILEY, Charles A.
b. 09 Nov 1871, Garland Co, AR
m. 09 Sep 1896, Hot Springs Garland County, AR
d. 06 Sep 1961, Hot Springs Garland County, AR

RILEY, Daniel
b. 09 Jan 1852, Gibson Co, TN
m. abt. 1870, AR
d. 27 Feb 1925, Hot Springs, Garland Co, AR

RUCKER, Anna Elizabeth
b. Nov 1841, TN
d. unknown, AR

RIPPETOE, Mattie
b. 27 Nov 1879, Garland Co. AR
d. 14 Apr 1919, Hot Springs, Garland County, AR

RIPPETOE, Thomas
b. 12 Mar 1853, AR or TN
m. abt. 1876, probably Garland Co AR
d. unknown, Memphis, TN

SNODGRASS, Addie
b. 04 Dec 1859, AR
d. abt 1932, Garland Co, AR

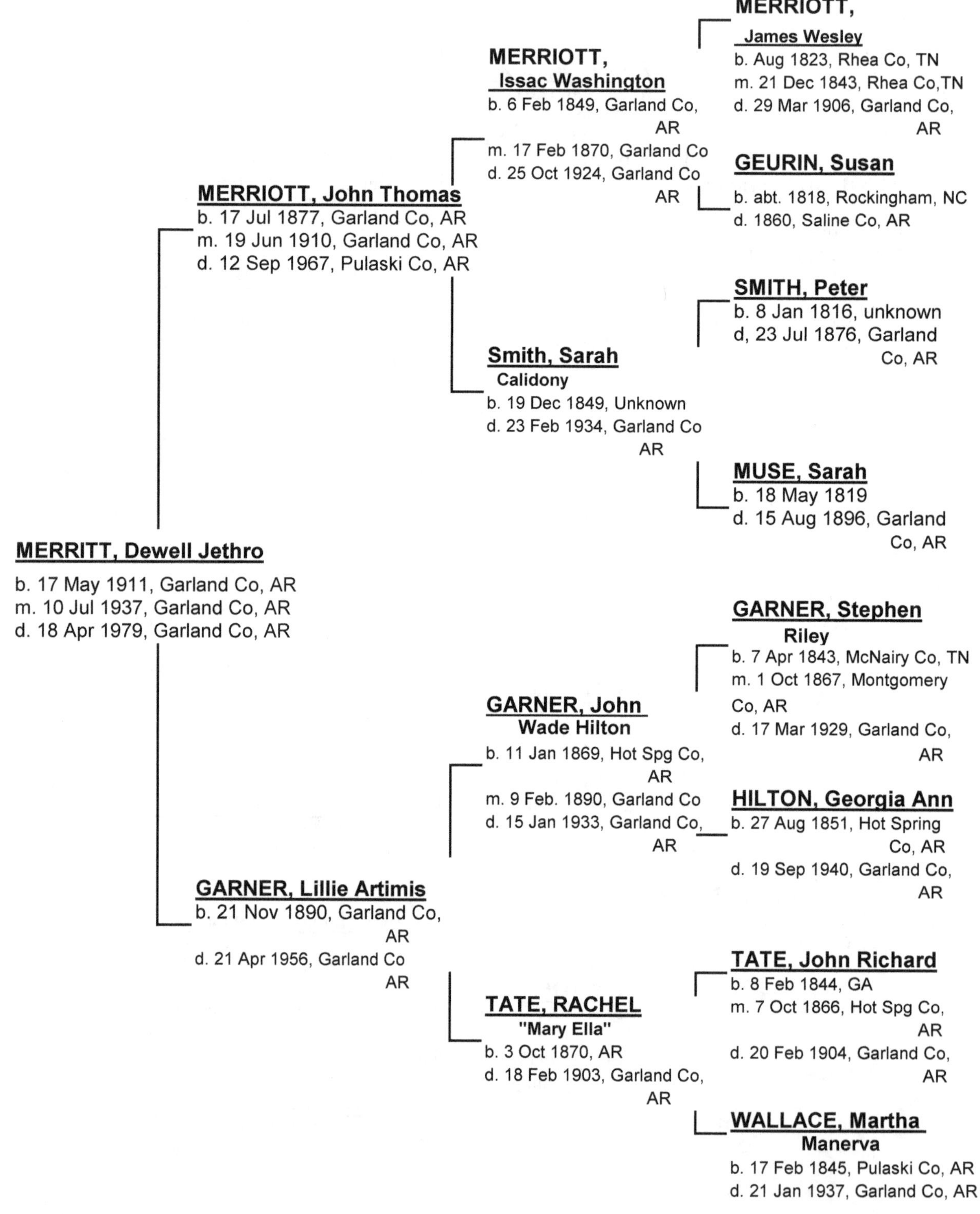
MERRIOTT,
James Wesley
b. Aug 1823, Rhea Co, TN
m. 21 Dec 1843, Rhea Co,TN
d. 29 Mar 1906, Garland Co,
AR

MERRIOTT,
Issac Washington
b. 6 Feb 1849, Garland Co,
AR
m. 17 Feb 1870, Garland Co
d. 25 Oct 1924, Garland Co
AR

GEURIN, Susan
b. abt. 1818, Rockingham, NC
d. 1860, Saline Co, AR

MERRIOTT, John Thomas
b. 17 Jul 1877, Garland Co, AR
m. 19 Jun 1910, Garland Co, AR
d. 12 Sep 1967, Pulaski Co, AR

SMITH, Peter
b. 8 Jan 1816, unknown
d, 23 Jul 1876, Garland
Co, AR

Smith, Sarah
Calidony
b. 19 Dec 1849, Unknown
d. 23 Feb 1934, Garland Co
AR

MUSE, Sarah
b. 18 May 1819
d. 15 Aug 1896, Garland
Co, AR

MERRITT, Dewell Jethro
b. 17 May 1911, Garland Co, AR
m. 10 Jul 1937, Garland Co, AR
d. 18 Apr 1979, Garland Co, AR

GARNER, Stephen
Riley
b. 7 Apr 1843, McNairy Co, TN
m. 1 Oct 1867, Montgomery
Co, AR
d. 17 Mar 1929, Garland Co,
AR

GARNER, John
Wade Hilton
b. 11 Jan 1869, Hot Spg Co,
AR
m. 9 Feb. 1890, Garland Co
d. 15 Jan 1933, Garland Co,
AR

HILTON, Georgia Ann
b. 27 Aug 1851, Hot Spring
Co, AR
d. 19 Sep 1940, Garland Co,
AR

GARNER, Lillie Artimis
b. 21 Nov 1890, Garland Co,
AR
d. 21 Apr 1956, Garland Co
AR

TATE, John Richard
b. 8 Feb 1844, GA
m. 7 Oct 1866, Hot Spg Co,
AR
d. 20 Feb 1904, Garland Co,
AR

TATE, RACHEL
"Mary Ella"
b. 3 Oct 1870, AR
d. 18 Feb 1903, Garland Co,
AR

WALLACE, Martha
Manerva
b. 17 Feb 1845, Pulaski Co, AR
d. 21 Jan 1937, Garland Co, AR

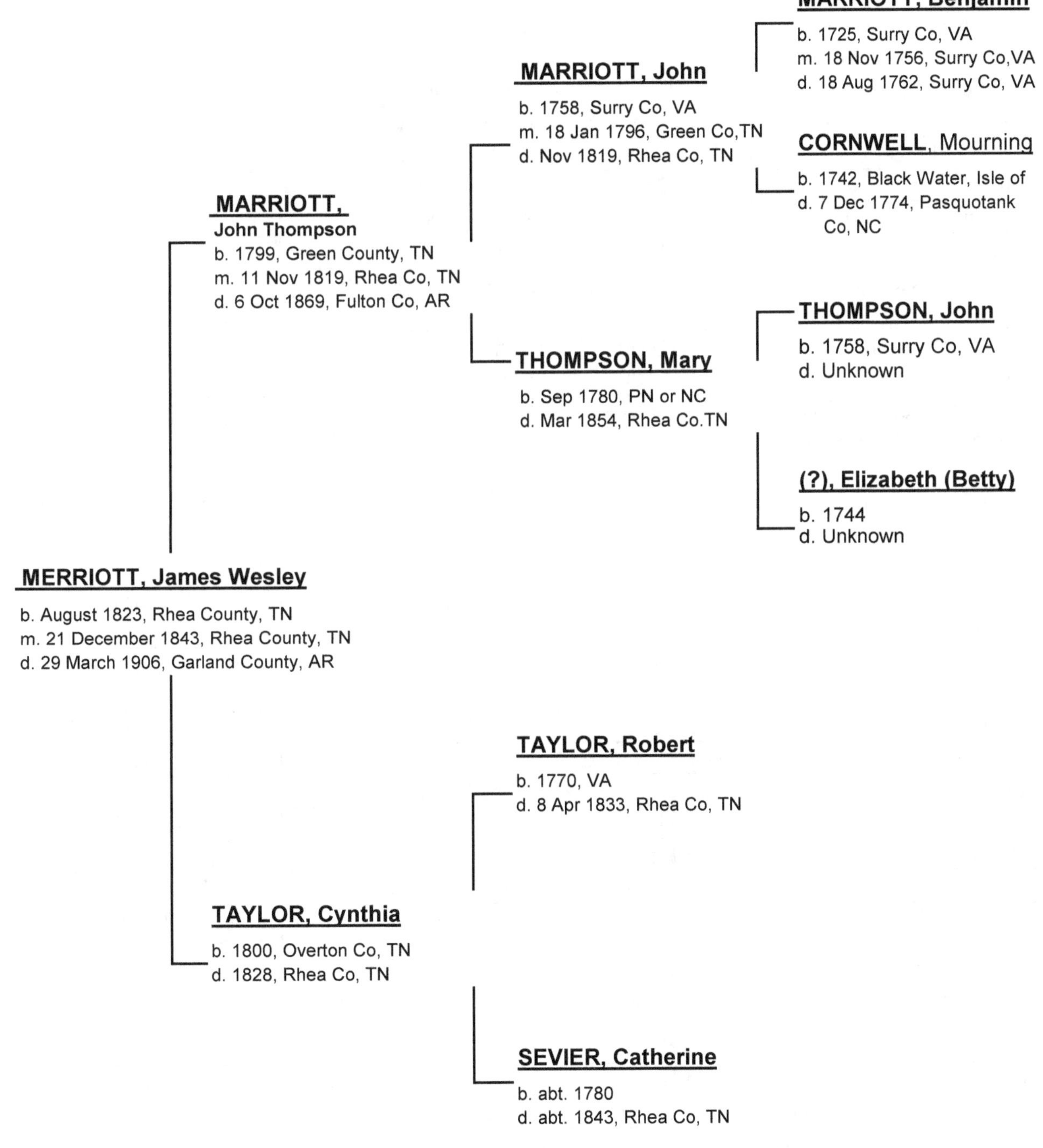
MARRIOTT, Benjamin
b. 1725, Surry Co, VA
m. 18 Nov 1756, Surry Co, VA
d. 18 Aug 1762, Surry Co, VA

MARRIOTT, John
b. 1758, Surry Co, VA
m. 18 Jan 1796, Green Co, TN
d. Nov 1819, Rhea Co, TN

CORNWELL, Mourning
b. 1742, Black Water, Isle of
d. 7 Dec 1774, Pasquotank
Co, NC

MARRIOTT,
John Thompson
b. 1799, Green County, TN
m. 11 Nov 1819, Rhea Co, TN
d. 6 Oct 1869, Fulton Co, AR

THOMPSON, John
b. 1758, Surry Co, VA
d. Unknown

THOMPSON, Mary
b. Sep 1780, PN or NC
d. Mar 1854, Rhea Co.TN

(?), Elizabeth (Betty)
b. 1744
d. Unknown

MERRIOTT, James Wesley
b. August 1823, Rhea County, TN
m. 21 December 1843, Rhea County, TN
d. 29 March 1906, Garland County, AR

TAYLOR, Robert
b. 1770, VA
d. 8 Apr 1833, Rhea Co, TN

TAYLOR, Cynthia
b. 1800, Overton Co, TN
d. 1828, Rhea Co, TN

SEVIER, Catherine
b. abt. 1780
d. abt. 1843, Rhea Co, TN

DONATIONS TO MPGS

Description of Donation	Value	Donated By:	Date Donated
CD with Family Tree Maker	Not given	Doyle Wayne Jackson	9-1-09
Donation for Research	$100.00	Doyle Wayne Jackson	9-4-09
-Copies of Class of 1964 -Old News Paper clippings	Not given	Stephen Merritt	9-4-09
40 OBITS from her research	Not given	Sue Wilson	9-4-09
St Lukes Episcopal Church	Not given	Audry Atherton	9-12-09
Money Order for research	$10.00	Curtis Jones	9-12-09
4 OBITS from her research	Not given	Joyce Walker	9-14-09
Donation to MPGS	$10.00	Stephen Merritt	9-18-09
Donation	$2.00	Carolyn Hill	9-21-09
In Memorium -Lanny Robbins	$20.00	Debra Garner	9-22-09
In Memorium -Lanny Robbins	$20.00	Pat Brown	9-22-09
Yearbooks Lakeview High School –Mich. 68-69-70	Not given	Caroline Campbell	9-22-09
Donation for research	$30.00	David S. Prater	10-15-09
Donation	$20.00	Betty Martin	10-19-09
Donation "The Genie" (70) -"Exploring Your Cherokee Ancestry"	Not given	Dickie Weston	10-26-09
Whisenant Coat of Arms 1974 "Spartan Central Jr. High Yr Bk (1st year made)	Not given	Kathy Irwin	10-27-09
Yearbooks 1970 Cutter Morning Star 1951 Old Gold Book 1953 Old Gold Book	Not given	Linda Miller	10-27-09
"Geurins of Arkansas"	Not given	Rosie J. Morrison	10-27-09
"Born Fighting" by Jim Webb	$15.95 Value	Jane Grebe	10-27-09
Donation	$20.00	Debra Garner	11-4-09
Donation (Mailing Kettle)	$81.42	Debra Garner	11-14-09
3 Old Phone Books	Not given	Patti Hays	11-16-09
Donation	$5.00	Tommy O'Neal	11-16-09
Donation for OBIT	$10.00	Brandenburger & Davis (Olivia Baker)	11-22-09
Donation for research	$25.00	Robin Radford	11-23-09
Donation	$10.00	Linda Miller	12-15-09
Donation	$20.00	Gwin Ary	12-28-09
Donation	$10.00	Anita Bibeau	1-7-10
In Memorium Donald Brown	$25.00	James & Twila Brown	1-7-10
Update on Shady Grove Cem.	Not given	Louis Brodrick	1-12-10
Donation (by check)	$100.00	Janice Holzer	1-8-10
In Memoruim Donald Brown	$25.00	Caroline Campbell	1-20-10
In Memoruim Donald Brown	$20.00	Marguerite Robbins	1-21-10
Donation	$20.00	Stephen Merritt	1-(?)-10

DONATIONS TO MPGS

Description of Donation	Value	Donated By:	Date Donated
Donation (Conley OBIT)	$20.00	Shannon Sylvia	1-23-10
In Memoruim Donald Brown	$20.00	Mary E. Booles	1-25-10
"Nashville Pictorial History" "Down from the hills" Faubus "The Historical News	Not given	Linda Miller	1-25-10
"Bradley Co. AR Cemetery" Volume I "Bradley Co. AR Cemetery" Volume II	$40.00 value $20.00 value	Donald L. Johnson	1-26-10
In Memorium Donald Brown	$20.00	Bob & Martha Gilliam	1-2010
Donation for research	$30.00	Robert Haynes	1-28-10
Donation for research	$100.00	Donald G. Stanford	1-28-10
Donation for OBIT	$10.00	Patty Bowen	2-2-10
Donation of 11 issues of "Crossroad Trails"	Not given	Norma Snider	2-13-10
-1948 "The Old Gold Book"	Not given	Ramona Brown	2-16-10
"I Promise We Will Find The Sheltons" by Evelyn French	$25.00 Value	Janice Holzer	2-19-10
Donation library supplies	$20.00	Gwin Ary	2-19-10
Donation for OBITS	$3.50	Lynnette D. Johnson	2-25-10
IBM Typewriter	Not given	Patricia Brown	2-26-10
Donation for OBIT	$4.00	Cheryl McIntosh	3-8-10
Donation for Buckville Cook Books	$8.00	Debra Garner	March 2010
Donation Bible Info	Not given	Martha Gilliam	3-15-10
Donation Book John Welch	$25.00 value	Jodie Wyatt	3-26-10
Donation	$50.00	Gwin Ary	3-26-10
Donation AR Highway Maps	Not given	Donald L. Johnson	3-26-10
Donation DVD "Silent Storytellers" (from PBS)	$60.00 D –to PBS	Gwin Ary	March 2010
Grant Award to MPGS	$500.00	AR Community Foundation	3-31-10
Donation	$20.00	Curtis & Joyce Craft	3-26-10
Donation	$20.00	Rochelle Cochran	4-7-10
"Emmigrants in Bondage" "The Clan GREGOR" 16 Notebooks 19 FTM Software 8 Magazine holders 16 "Confederate Veteran" mag 1 picture "Grand Lodge" 1916	Not given	Charleen Nobles	4-12-10
Donation File Cabinet	Not given	Marguerite Robbins	April 2010
2 small US Flags 2 small AR Flags	Not given	Debbie Alsup	April 2010

DONATIONS TO MPGS

Description Pot of Donation	Value	Donated By:	Date Donated
Dell printer (used)	Not given	Jean Mann	April 2010
Donation OBITS from ADG	Not given	Betty Parker Martin	2010
"Continental Society Daughters of Indian Wars"	Not given	Rochelle Cochran	4-30-10
"Hezekiah Pennington Malone"	$30.00 value	Caroline Campbell	5-11-10
Donation	$5.00	Sara Berry	5-28-10
Computer Desk File Cabinet Phone Cabinet CD Cabinet	$380.00 value	Janice Holzer	5-28-10
Donation for research	$50.00	Patricia Elsaesser	6-1-10
Donation Yearbooks "The Farmer" Lewisville TX.	Not given	Linda Miller	June 2010
Donation: Yearbooks "The Old Gold Books 1976-82" The Univ of AR. 1962-65	Not given	Pat Muse	July 2010
Donation: Yearbooks "The Old Gold Books" 1975-77-78-79-83 (78-79 are duplicates)	Not given	Margie Hill	July 2010
Donation for OBITS	$10.00	Virginia Furlong	7-12-10
In Memoruim Willie Vance	$50.00	Caroline Campbell	7-19-10
Donation for Research for Blehinger family	$150.00	Virginia Furlong	July 2010
Donation for OBITS	$10.00	Marcel Vallot	July 2010
Donation"50 Anniv –The Visitors Bulletin 1971"	Not given	Stephen Merritt	July 2010
Kettle supplies: 6 Printer ink cartridges, 4 reams of paper, page sleeves, notebook	$225.00	Caroline Campbell	2010
Donation: Watercolor Cover Design for the Kettle 2010	THANKS a million!	Richard Stephens, watercolorist	July 2010

1910 Ford R

PLEASE DON'T FORGET YOUR MPGS DUES!

Hot Springs High School 1924

The Kettle, 2011 will be mailed to those members who include a $3.50 postage/handling fee along with their dues for 2011. All other members are asked to pick up their copy at the library. (A $25 membership covers both a husband and wife.)

MPGS memberships are based on the calendar year. For your 2011 dues, tear out this page (or copy it), complete both sides and mail it with your membership check to MPGS. Your dues are used for the expenses of the library, which is operated entirely by volunteers.

Check one level of membership for 2011 below and mail with your check.

___ Regular Membership $25.00	___ Lifetime Membership $200.00
___ Benefactor $500.00	___ Corporate Membership $1,000.00

All memberships entitle the member to the same benefits. Membership in one of the "higher" categories helps to provide more support to the Society. In addition, <u>any level above the regular membership rate qualifies as a tax-deductible donation.</u>

Please type or print clearly:

Name ____

Street Address ____

City, State and Zip Code ____

Telephone _____________________________ e-mail _______________________________

Mail with your check to:
Melting Pot Genealogical Society
P. O. Box 936
Hot Springs, Arkansas 71902-0936

MELTING POT GENEALOGICAL SOCIETY
QUESTIONNAIRE

The MPGS wants to know what information you want to appear in *The Kettle 2011* and on our website at www.rootsweb.ancestry.com/~armpgs/; therefore, we are asking for your input. We will list your name in *The Kettle 2011* as a member but nothing else without your permission. The website will not contain your name unless permission is given. **Please visit our website**.

The Kettle 2011

	Yes	No
May we publish your address in *The Kettle*?		
May we publish your telephone number in *The Kettle*?		
May we publish your e-mail address in *The Kettle*? If yes, list your e-mail:		
May we publish the surnames that you are researching? If so, what surnames would you wish listed?		
Do you have a personal website that you want listed? If so, what is the URL?		

MPGS WEBSITE

	Yes	No
May we publish your name on the MPGS website?		
May we publish your address on our website?		
May we publish your telephone number on our website?		
May we publish your e-mail address on our website? If yes, list your e-mail address:		
May we publish the surnames that you are researching? If yes, list the surnames you are researching:		
Do you have a personal website that you want listed? If yes, what is the URL?		

Signature (may be typed if sent via e-mail)

____

Date ______________________________
Address, telephone number and e-mail address if permission is given to use them:

____

____

____

MEMBERSHIP LIST

Full Name	Address	Phone and E-mail	SURNAMES RESEARCHING
ALSUP, Debbie R.			ALSUP
ARY, Gwin (Slater)	110 Southern Hills Dr. Hot Springs, AR 71913	gfary@sbcglobal.net	Bain, Boone, Castleberry, Childers, Davis, Fox, Garner, Gross, House, Howell, McCollum, Poor/Poore, Reid, Robbins, Sharp, Slater, Stracener, Strasner, Thornton.
ATHERTON, Audrey Ann (Peters)	201 Trivista Left Hot Springs, AR 71901	501-624-6900	Peters
BASS, W. Bert & Pamela	560 North Wheat Rd. Belton, TX. 76513	bfxrman@aol.com	Bass
BERGMAN, Judith S.	5440 Ashleigh Rd. Fairfax, VA 22030	703-815-2461 jsbergman@verizon.net	Armstrong, Lambert, Murphree, Simpson.
BERRY Sara L. (Johnson)	497 Pitchercane Rd Hot Springs, AR 71909	501-321-9520 slbmlt@hsnp.com	Berry
BLANTON, Norma (Knight)	#8 Grafton Court Hot Springs, AR 71901	321-9878	Blanton, Burton, Knight
BODEMANN, L. C. & Wanda	115 Forest View Cir. Hot Springs, AR 71913	501-609-9630 lcbode@cablelynx.com	Bodemann, Brooks, Casada, Clark, Gantt, Golden, Grenier, Sanders, Straub.
BOOLES, ** *** Mary (Powell) (Librarian)	203 Hyacinth Circle Hot Springs, AR 71913	501-624-5628 mbooles@cablelynx.com	Booles, Dunn, Fowler, Harper, Holloway, Kinsey, McDonald, Moore, Norman, Powell, Tackett, Wacaster, Weston.
BRECKLING, Uva (& Julius)	407 Beachview Cir. Hot Springs, AR 71913		Breckling,
BROADRICK, Louis	110 Broadrick Lane Hot Springs, AR 71901		Sparlin.
BROOKS, Sue (Nooner)	108 Cabe Ct. Hot Springs, AR 71913	501-262-1937 hsnb@sbcglobal.net	Nooner
BROWN, *** Alma Nell (Soward) (Treasurer)	P. O. Box 22483 Hot Springs, AR 71903	501-767-5341 grannynell@cablelynx.com	Brown, Soward, Lavender.
BROWN, Delores (Garner)	5734 Millcreek Rd. Hot Springs, AR 71901	501-623-6096 mawmawdd@aol.com	
BROWN, Don R. & Venita	1943 Highland St. Lebanon, MO 65536	417-532-6905	
BROWN, James, C. & Twila M (Ackley) (Rec. Sec.)	118 Jennison Square Hot Springs, AR 71913	501-525-0196 twila@aristotle.net	Ackley, Brown, Cotton, Cunningham, McGraw, Shell, Steele, Stephenson, Weaver, Whitmarsh, Wilkinson.
BROWN, *** Patricia (Soward) (Registrar)	1966 Cedar Glade Rd. Hot Springs, AR 71913	501-760-1170 granycat@aristotle.net	Armen, Bold, Geffs, Lavender, Polk.
BRUBAKER, Jean A.	45 Arjona Way HSV, AR 71909		
BURROUGH, Don Jerome	211 Bayshore Dr. Hot Springs, AR 71901	501-262-4448 burrough@cablelynx.com	Burrough
CAMPBELL, ** *** Caroline (Seiz) (Editor)	113 Trivista Rt. Hot Springs, AR 71901	501-624-3831 carolinecampbell@cablelynx.com	Seiz
CARTWRIGHT, Ethel (Bradshaw)	500 Pakis St 4-B Hot Springs, AR 71913	501-520-4344 bradshaw1st@sbcglobal.net	Adams, Allen, Bradshaw, Brantley, Cartwright, Caver, Honeycutt, Moore, Peden, Phillips, Powell, Seitz, Shutts, Stricklin, Vaden.
CLARDY, Betty Sue (Powell)			Clardy, Moore, Norman, Powell, Wacaster, Weston
COCHRAN, Rochelle (Evans)	316 Fox Run Cir. Hot Springs, AR 71901	501-623-2257 Rochelle@cablelynx.com	Armstrong, Boone, Braziel, Dromgoole, Evans, Griffin, Howell, Johnson, Snapp, Tilley.

MEMBERSHIP LIST

Full Name	Address	Phone and E-mail	SURNAMES RESEARCHING
CRAFT, Curtis & Joyce	103 Blue Heron Dr. Hot Springs, AR 71913	501-525-4757 craftj@hssd.net	Craft
CREASY, Al & Lena	142 Etta St. Hot Springs, AR 71901	501-262-4695 aac143@cablelynx.com	Creasy
CRONE, ** Glenn W & Jane A. (Kinnaird)	318 Morphew Rd. Hot Springs, AR. 719--	501-767-3373 janeandbillc@cablelynx.com	Crone, Crow, Gilbert, Kinnaird, Ridgeway.
DAVIS, ** B. Leon & Priscilla (Johnston)	242 Oakdale Terrace Hot Springs, AR 71913	501-767-4077 prisdavis731@cablelynx.com	Honeycutt, Johnston, Mallet, Millet, Pettit, Rinkle, Ward, Webb.
DUREN, Don & Cecilia	2508 Banner Elk Cir Plano, TX 75025	972-618-2501 dcduren@verizon.net	Duren
ERDMANN, Barbara Golden	196 Donda Lane Hot Springs, AR. 71913	Erdmann6@cox.net	Erdmann, Golden, Teirney, Kuhn, Patin, Dupre, Dupuis, Girod, Roeschlaib, Sisson
ERICHSEN, Vivian Lucile Gray	172 Trapview Tr. Hot Springs, AR 71913	501-525-4326 jameserichsen@live.com	Ashley, Bradford, Bradley, Goodman, Gray, Killian, Prince.
FELTS, Wanda (Wylie)	102 Fernwood St. Hot Springs, AR 71901	501-262-2049 felthat@webtv.net	Felts, Gill, Womack, Wylie
FLEISCHNER, Mark & Patti	402 Central Ave. Hot Springs, AR 71901		Fleischner
FRAHM, Jeanette Ellen (Warren)	24 Doblez Circle Hot Springs Village, AR 71909	501-922-9220 J44F65@yahoo.com	Albrecht, Duval, Fell, Flin/Flinn, Huxtable, Hardesty, Klein, Kramme, Lazenby, Osborn, Page, Petri, Priest, Shemate, Thornborough, Vaughn, Warren, Wetzler.
GADE, Jean (Henry)	156 Wildcat Estates Rd. Hot Springs, AR 71913	501-623-6523 W5go@wildblue.net	Gade, Henry, Kimble, Kimbel, Wolkoff.
GALLAHER, ** Douglas P. (wife-Skevington)	177 Rainbow Drive #7779 Livingston, TX 77399	dpgallaher@coam.net	Cook, Gallaher, Messer, Spriggs, Tackett.
GARNER, *** Doug & Debra (Slater) *(Corresponding Sec.)*	238 Oak Grove Trail Royal, AR 71968	501-767-3325 debig@wletc.com	Bain, Boone, Castleberry, Childers, Davis, Fox, Garner, Gross, House, Howell, McCollum, Poor/Poore, Reid, Robbins, Sharp, Slater, Stracener, Strasner, Thornton.
GIBSON, Nancy (Smith)	121 Bugler Ct. Pearcy, AR 71964	501-525-3236 jimnan@direclynx.net	Bradley, Brannam, Gibson, GOOCH, Grantham, Hill, Jack, Knight, Little, Mulder, Noddings, Orrell, Wood.
GILLIAM, Robert & Martha (Hampton)	123 Westgate Terr. Hot Springs, AR 71913	501-767-2637 hamgill@earthlink.net	Badgett, Barber, Barnes, Brisco, Gilliam, Grady, Hampton, Hawkins, Morgan, Price, Southard, Turner, Veach, Viars, Zachry.
GREBE, Jane (Robinson)	101 Westbrook St. Hot Springs, AR 71901	501-625-3886 gas4jobs@aol.com	Givens, Jenkins, Robinson.
GREGG, Mignon E. & Micah	276 Veranda Tr. Pearcy, AR 71964	501-282-4203 mgregg@mnbbank.com	Gregg, Graves
GRILLS, Paulette (Home)	485 Rollins Rd. Forest City, NC 28043	828-245-5596 paula7890@hotmail.com	Horne, York, Florida, Clark, Crawley, Crowley, Pettis, Furr, McClard
HALL, Patsy Ruth (Schran)	101 Oak Bend Loop Hot Springs, AR 71913	501-520-0467 pjhall@cablelynx.com	Bradley, Hall, Hamilton, Patterson, Schran, Schrand.
HALSELL, Joyce (Davis)	1870 E. Grand Ave. Hot Springs, AR 71901	501-624-4452	Austin, Bradley, Davis, George, Halsell, Mann, May, Masengill.
HARRELL, R. P.	#9 Crow Road Perryville, AR 72126	501-889-5601 rpharrell@windstream.net	Abney, Arnold, Ebbs, Ervin, Gregg, Harrell, Honeycutt, Keasler, Kemp, Kinsall, Parker, Raby, Rasberry, Ross, Stephens, Tackett, Walden, Wallace, Warnock, Wornock, Wray.

MEMBERSHIP LIST

Full Name	Address	Phone and E-mail	SURNAMES RESEARCHING
HAYNES, ** Terry and Nancy (Cotton)	113 Island View Cove Hot Springs, AR 71901	501-262-1995 terrynancy@cablelynx.com	Barnett, Brumbelow, Cooper, Cotton, Dover, Duff, Dunn, Fowler, Gillentine, Gooch, Hamm, Haynes, Hearle, Holloway, King, Lawler, Leavitt, Lewis, Mahaffey, Matlock, Mitchell, Murphree, Powell, Sherburn, Smith, Srygley, Steadman, Tate, Tennyson, Tribble, Vaughn, Vaughter, Ward, Weatherly, Whitaker, Wilson, Wright.
HAYS, William.Dave & Patti (Vance) *(Webmaster)*	210 Michael St. Hot Springs, AR. 71913	pvhwdh@cablelynx.com	Austin, Boyd, Caldwell, Fletcher, Hays, Henderson, Houser/Howser, Matthews, Peeler, Roberts, Vance, Wilson.
HILL, *** Teddy & Margie (Weatherford) *(President)*	5458 Sunshine Rd. Pearcy, AR 71964-9744	501-767-5474 mwh14@sbcglobal.net	Chadick, Couch, Hill, Johnston, Kelley /Kelly, Moore, Tankersley, Weatherford.
HOLZER, ** Nicholas C. & Janice C. (Stover)	321 Ranchester Terrace Hot Springs, AR 71913-8883	501-767-1138 jholzer321@cablelynx.com	Clawson, Davidson, Davis, Dunbar, Dunejtsik/Dunjtsek, Herrington, Higginbotham, Holzer, Keyser, Moody, Murphy, Nave, Perdue, Perry, Quinney, Smith, Snyder/Snider, Stover, Thorpe, Williams, Wilson, Woodhull.
HUBBARD, Marge	1411 Shady Grove Rd. Hot Springs, AR 71901	501-262-4513 mhubbardar5@aol.com	Hubbard
IRWIN, Kathy (Hammond)	128 Delight Lane Royal, AR 71968	501-760-3964 irwinkathy1@yahoo.com	Hammond, Heath, Henry, Helsey, Irwin, Jefferson, Shell, Tabors, Teague, Morgan, Young.
JOHNSON, Donald L.	111 Patrick Lee Ct. Hot Springs, AR	501-760-1880	Johnson, Barnett, Hines, Robinson, Meeks (Bradley & Calhoon Counties)
JONES, Merle & Jimmie Lois (Caton)	258 Catherine Heights Rd. Hot Springs, Ar 71901	501-262-4975 jimmie@hsnp.com	Caton, Harvey, King, Jones, Maughan, Reid, Simmons.
KING, Ron & Marsha (Oliver)	1608 Summer St. Hot Springs, AR 71913	501-624-0815 we3kings@hotsprings.net	King, Oliver.
LEDFORD, Francelle	127 Orchard St.	501-623-3045 francelle@cablelynx.com	
LOONEY, Mary Ann	5879 Sunshine Canyon Dr. Boulder, CO 80302	303-449-5325 Maryann.Looney@ionsky.com	Bingham, Caldwell, Caruth, Danuser, Rasberry, Scarborough, Winter.
MANNING, Foster T.	8917 W. Hawk Ridge Rd Coeur D'Alene, Id 83814	208-769-7991 manning@signet.com.sg	
MARTIN, ** Betty (Parker) LTM**	600 Pakis No 34 Hot Springs, AR 71913	501-525-0807 bpmartin@cablelynx.com	Cox, Davis, Syer, Green, Hobbs, Lewis, Martin, Money, Parker, Rice, Rowe/Roe,Tankersley, Whitworth, Williams.
MAUS, Frances Blyth	1925 Malvern Ave. #401 Hot Springs, AR 71901	501-321-1443	Maus, Williams, Zinn, Blyth
MAUS, Robert D.	224 Henderson St. Hot Springs, AR 71913	501-624-7551	Bottom, Bradley, Craig, Hawk, Leatherman, Maus, Ransbottom, Ramsbottom.
McGOWAN, Mary Ann (Carpenter)	601 Rector St. Hot Springs, AR 71913	501-624-3272	Carpenter, Harris, Lowe, McGowan, Ratliff, Shelley.
MERCHANT, Nan	210 Halteria Pt. Hot Springs, AR 71913	501-767-6625 NanTMerc@aol.com	Garner, Hart, Herron, Turner.
MERRITT, Stephen	156 Donald Lane Pearcy, AR 71964	501-767-5640 CODream@aol.com	Merritt, Merriott, Marriott.
MEYERS, Janice (Huston)	2133 Malvern Rd. Hot Springs, AR 71901		Huston, Meyers.

MEMBERSHIP LIST

Full Name	Address	Phone and E-mail	SURNAMES RESEARCHING
MILLER, Linda	302 Mississippi Hot Springs, AR 71901	501-318-6062 Lsmgen1957@yahoo.com	Brewer, Brothers, Chamlee, Craft, Garner, Gollham, Hammond, Heath, Henry, Holtclaw, House, Hudson, Hulsey, Mathis, Miller, Reynolds, Stonecipher, Sherrill, Nabers, Lindsey, Vasseau, Watson, Young.
MOORE, David A.	948 E. Parker Hamburg, AR 71646	damoore@hotmail.com	Moore
MYERS, Andrew & Jan	807 County Rd 19 Norwich, NY 13815		Greene, Parks, Hodges
NELSON, K. Ray & Jo Ann	P. O. Box 4055 Hot Springs, AR 71914	501-767-0202 krynels@aol.com	
NOBLES, *** Charleen (Cook) *(Vice President)*	523 Rockdale Rd. Hot Springs, AR 71901	501-321-4159 charleen@praize.com	Dodd, Garrett, Graves, Lynch, Nobles, Sammons, Terry, Vaughn, Ward.
O'NEAL, Thomas & Gay	100 McCurry Terr. Hot Springs, AR 71913	501-760-7002 onealtg@yahoo.com	O'Neal
PERKINS, Emma	Box 1814 Hot Springs, AR 71909	501-262-1115 Cell 501-545-5581	
POULTER, Glen H. & Myrna	169 Sky Canyon Tr Hot Springs, AR 71913	501-767-4343 gpoulter@hotmail.com	
REYNOLDS, Mary Jane (Maus)	109 Ellis Ct. Hot Springs, AR 71913		
RICHARDSON, Ted	2700 Leisure World Mesa, AZ 85206		
RIGGINS William (Bill) Sledge & Gloria Anette (Amisano)	108 Lu Juan Terr. Hot Springs, AR 71913	501-767-0464 billriggins555@gmail.com	Amisano, Edwards, Jones, Phillips, Means, Fracchia, Riggins.
ROBBINS, Elizabeth Lynn (Liz)	501 Sunrise Hot Springs, AR 71913	501-624-4729	Robbins
ROBBINS, *** Marguerite (Holzer) *(Corresponding Sec.)*	P. O. Box 752 Hot Springs, AR 71901	501-623-5755	Cloninger, Holzer, Reader, Robbins, Rowe.
ROSE, Joy (McKinney)	1004 Richard St. Hot Springs, AR 71913	501-623-3256	Cockburn, Crabb, Erwin, Fryar/Friar, Perrin, Smith
SKOOG, Kay G.	105 Earls Pt. Hot Springs, AR 71913	501-767-5451 skoog@direclynx.net	Skoog.
SLATER, Frances	238 Oak Grove Tr. Royal, AR 71968		Slater
SMITH, Billy Jack & Jo Ann (Selig)	128 St. Charles Circle Hot Springs, AR 71901	Bjs9@sbcglobal.net	Cobb, Selig, Smith, Miller
SMITH, Charles W. & Geraldine	829 Bellaire Dr. Hot Springs, AR 71901	501-624-0107	Smith
SNIDER, Norma		501-318-7578 diannhoward@live.com	Blair, Howard, Osteen, Parker, Petis, Powell, Snider.
SORRELLS, ** Klugh, E	6321 Albert Pike Royal, AR 71968	kesorrells@aol.com	Cockrell, Fisher, McDowell, Merriott, Rachills, Reich, Sorrells.
SPAINHOUR, Mike	358 Sadie Dr. Matthews, N. C. 28105		Spainhour
THEXTON, Pete & Barbara	137 Lake Forest Shores Dr. Hot Springs, AR 719--	501-760-3837 bthexton@cablelynx.com	Thexton, Perkins, Palmer, Ahlers, McKahey, Klotz, Prediger, Weber
THOMASON, Jan Sargo	3822 Park Ave. Hot Springs, AR 71901	501-623-2302 janthomason@cablelynx.com	Sargo, Thomason
THOMPSON, Sherrod & Judy (Livingston)	705 Rector St. Hot Springs, AR 71913	501-622-0337 Sjt940@yahoo.com	Cox, Livingston, Parker, Rippetoe, Snodgrass, Thompson, White.

MEMBERSHIP LIST

Full Name	Address	Phone and E-mail	SURNAMES RESEARCHING
THORNTON, Neil E. & Joyce (Stonecipher)	113 Forest View Cir. Hot Springs, AR 71913	501-624-0946 jnthornton@att.net	Emery, Shipley, Stonecipher, Thornton.
TILLMAN, Rodney V.	740 Weston Rd .#707 Hot Springs, AR 71913	501-760-6331	Tillman.
TREMÉ, Pamela A.	2914 Lake Saxon Dr. Land O'Lakes, FL		Tremé
VACCARO, Amy	220 Brantley Cir. Hot Springs, AR 71913	501-767-3742	Vaccaro
VANN, Robert H.	P. O. Box 1897 Huntsville, TX. 77342	936-291-2906	Vann
VEASEY, Kathy Stroope			Stroope, Veasey
WALKER, John & Joyce (Wtherell)	106 Silverwood Point Hot Springs, AR 71913	501-760-7559 johjoy@aol.com	Atnip, Bain, Gardner, Hulsey, Johnson, Launius/Lanius, Smith, Walker, Witherell.
WALLACE, Roberta (Ragsdale)	741 South Porter Tyler, TX 75701	903-593-0453 robertaharold@juno.net	Allen, Bashaw, Campbell, Green, Holley, Kinsey, Plemmons, Ragsdale, Stanford, Wallace.
WILSON, Martha (Wylie)	110 Watson St. Hot Springs, AR 71901	501-321-4337	Arnold, Avant, Ennis, Gill, Horn, Overby, Steed, Womack, Purdy.
WILSON, Paula Sue (Phillips)	663 Danville Rd. Hot Springs, AR 71901	501-624-5915 Suewilson4048@sbcglobal.net	Alexander, Cook, Phillips, Stricklin/Stricklen/Strickland, Wilson.
ZIEGLER, Norval F.	113 Caldwell Dr. Oak Ridge, Tn 37830	865-483-4108 nfziegler@bellsouth.net	Norman, Riley, Rippetoe, Ricker, Ziegler

** Denotes: Life Time Membership MPGS
*** MPGS Board Member

CORPORATE MEMBERSHIP

2008 **SIMMONS FIRST BANK OF HOT SPRINGS**
100 Werner Street
Hot Springs, AR 71913
501-318-1000

Steve Trusty,
President & CEO

2009 **SEIZ SIGN COMPANY**
1231 Central Avenue
Hot Springs, AR 71901
501-623-3181

David Hamilton
President

BENEFACTORS

2010   **HOT SPRINGS AREA COMMUNITY FOUNDATION**

2010   **HOT SPRINGS HIGH SCHOOL CLASS OF 1949**

LOWE (Social Hill) CEMETERY

Transcription by Linda Miller & Kathy Irwin

GPS Coordinates: Latitude: 34.50940, Longitude: -93.28530

Directions to Lowe Cemetery from Central Avenue at Grand Avenue: Take Highway 270 West past Royal, AR, past Sunshine Road, left on Ragweed Valley Road. Cemetery is on the left.

In transcribing Lowe Cemetery in 2010, the 1995 transcription by Debra Garner was used, especially for information on tombstones that can no longer be read or have been destroyed. Other records used were obituaries, funeral home records, Social Security Death Index, Census records, family records and personal information.

Photographs were taken of most of the tombstones by Linda Miller. Linda also has further family and genealogical information on many of those buried in Lowe Cemetery. Anyone with additional information to contribute or corrections to be made should contact Linda at Lsmgen1957@yahoo.com.

There is a section of Lowe Cemetery that is referred to as the Cain/Crumpton Section. It is included in this transcription. This section borders on the Cain/Crumpton property that abuts Lowe Cemetery.

JAMES ALEXANDER CARY, PARK RANGER

James Alexander Cary was born December 19, 1895 and died March 12, 1927. He was survived by a wife, son, and daughter. Ranger Cary had been with the United States Department of the Interior's National Park Service for four years. He was the first National Park Service Ranger to be killed in the line of duty. He was ambushed and killed by bootleggers while patrolling on West Mountain on March 12, 1927, and his body was found the next day. His killers were never found.

NAME	BIRTH	DEATH
Abbott, Grave Maybell Ray	12/21/1920	8/7/1996
Abbott, Irven Burley	12/27/1918	5/21/2001
Abernathy, Columbus Eugene	4/1/1925	4/26/1996
Abernathy, Randy	8/17/1955	6/27/1996
Abramson, Robert	5/23/1928	6/22/2001
Acord, Billy Wayne	6/10/1936	7/25/2000
Adams, David Eugene	3/6/1944	6/1/2000
Adams, James Michael	10/3/1969	2/2/1992
Ahl, Elizabeth	11/12/1913	7/8/1995
Allen, Charlotte Ione Muncrief	08/22/1890	11/21/1941
Allen, Sam W. (Rev.)	02/11/1880	7/12/1950
Anderson, Otis R., Sr.	3/9/1926	2/21/2005
Armon, Susie Reese	04/01/1898	5/7/1964
Armstrong, Julia Houser	02/22/1887	7/18/1961
Armstrong, Thomas Edward	02/01/1883	3/22/1953
Arnold, Carrie E. Coleman	7/8/1900	2/2/1998
Arnold, Eva O. Coleman	04/27/1896	6/19/1962
Arnold, Jane	7/22/1950	10/19/1997
Ashley, Ralph Doyle	9/27/1926	11/20/2003
Atkins, Cleta	1906	1978
Baker, Opal Lahoma Pate	6/12/1927	8/13/1944
Baker, Pearl E. Gillham	12/27/1903	2/18/1965
Bales, J. L. "Baby"	4/19/1929	4/19/1929
Bales, James L. "Roy"	1/29/1904	11/4/1989
Bales, Lessie V. Chitwood	2/20/1908	7/10/1991
Bales, William C.	6/1/1940	3/28/2000
Barrows, Ruth Ryan	6/6/1922	7/17/1987
Bashaw, Doshie L. McInvale	3/5/1907	5/25/1974
Bass, Earl Ray	2/14/1902	9/29/1928

NAME	BIRTH	DEATH
Bass, Gordon D., Sr.	1942	1990
Bass, James Stanley	07/07/1874	11/10/1922
Bass, Sally Mobley	11/24/1876	12/28/1927
Beals, Gregory, Deshawn	2/27/1978	2/25/1997
Beals, Monroe Henry	2/14/1906	11/18/1988
Beals, Ona Roach Garrett	7/11/1903	2/16/1985
Bearfield, Imogene	4/17/1931	5/20/2007
Bearfield, Robert L.	8/19/1922	8/18/1995
Beck, Eric	8/4/1983	3/8/1999
Berry, Annie McCaslin	04/10/1899	8/28/1978
Berry, Billie June	1/18/1932	6/5/1933
Berry, Chester D, Sr.	10/8/1915	2/24/1992
Berry, Ernest	1/26/1915	11/29/1993
Berry, Ernestine	9/20/1942	10/7/1942
Berry, Eva L. Fikes	2/6/1906	10/31/1975
Berry, Fannie V. Reeves	11/25/1887	3/1/1968
Berry, Floyd	5/14/1920	3/29/2003
Berry, Frances Runyon	3/1/1935	10/2/1999
Berry, Francis Wade	12/02/1856	4/6/1924
Berry, Hamp	1/29/1902	9/5/1981
Berry, Herman	1928	2004
Berry, Ishamel	1913	1914
Berry, James D.	12/23/1881	10/23/1959
Berry, James O.	12/20/1916	10/8/2009
Berry, John B.	06/24/1875	2/10/1956
Berry, Lee	09/26/1848	3/13/1928
Berry, Marion Juanita	1932	1932
Berry, Mary	04/18/1877	4/22/1925
Berry, Mildred Maxine	5/9/1925	6/27/1942

NAME	BIRTH	DEATH
Berry, Minnie L. Garrett	09/11/1880	10/25/1963
Berry, Nissie M. Armstrong	6/16/1930	4/9/2004
Berry, Paul Douglas	3/23/1924	12/21/1924
Berry, Pauline Wallace	12/6/1918	3/7/2004
Berry, Rosemary Frances	3/1/1935	10/2/1999
Berry, Ruby Warwick	1/13/1928	2/11/1997
Berry, Sherl	10/7/1941	10/8/1941
Berry, W. Jo Ray	8/20/1922	6/17/2003
Berry, William A.	1908	1909
Berry, William B.	04/19/1891	10/27/1968
Bertrand, Cora L.	04/11/1855	3/30/1902
Bettis, Algie	09/19/1894	6/16/1980
Bettis, Gladys Hughes	9/26/1908	3/28/2000
Bettis, John	11/9/1939	9/27/1991
Black, Annie Lewis	8/21/1921	9/27/1997
Black, Gary Wayne	1957	1959
Black, Peggy Ann	1949	1949
Blackburn, Lawrence David	7/4/1931	1/20/1990
Blackmon, JoAnn Little	12/29/1938	2/16/1994
Blackshear, Virgil	9/24/1929	8/28/2000
Blocker, Edmond James	01/15/1896	6/2/1979
Boatwright, Buelah Maebel Neighbors	4/28/1935	6/21/2007
Bouton, Rena Lou Orrell	9/30/1932	1/5/1964
Bowers, Betty Lee	5/11/1933	12/13/2002
Box, Helen Marie	5/8/1904	1/31/1994
Boyd, Joseph A.	1895	1918
Bradley, Charley Nathan	4/17/1915	2/20/1991
Bradley, Glenna Faye White	2/21/1939	6/15/2007
Bradley, Harley J.	6/13/1915	3/7/1974

NAME	BIRTH	DEATH
Bradley, Harvey O.	6/13/1915	9/14/1973
Bradley, J. Edith Shannon	6/27/1920	11/15/1998
Bradley, Madge Burrough	12/31/1914	4/29/1990
Bradley, Ruth F. Ennis	10/30/1914	10/25/2000
Braughton, Freddie Lee	2/14/1922	4/10/1986
Braughton, Lewis T.	09/19/1896	4/2/1973
Braziel, Holland O.	3/26/1916	1/17/2000
Braziel, Ida	08/03/1898	6/14/1973
Braziel, Joe Virgil	7/2/1910	7/22/1997
Braziel, Laura J. Metcalf	8/15/1913	4/15/1995
Braziel, Lillie J. Houser	01/21/1875	4/15/1949
Braziel, Nancy C. Reynolds	11/25/1945	8/8/2006
Braziel, Newt B.	01/27/1870	1/29/1934
Braziel, Ollie	4/12/1900	11/1/1900
Braziel, Sadie E.	12/2/1904	12/31/1995
Braziel, Thirra Bernice Tisdale	3/8/1920	8/11/2008
Braziel, Wilbur Ray "Buddy"	5/24/1949	12/1/1984
Breshears, Larry C.	10/21/1950	2/18/2000
Brewster, Ava L. McKelroy	6/17/1910	6/11/1986
Brewster, Lon L.	10/07/1871	8/1/1944
Brewster, Lydia Helton	05/21/1870	2/14/1951
Brewster, Ralph	11/27/1910	3/18/1987
Brown, Darren Edward	9/29/1972	6/21/1978
Brown, Della Mabra S.	2/6/1904	11/23/1992
Brown, Ella Christine Armstrong	6/25/1920	11/15/2000
Brown, Ellaine E. Ennis	2/25/1945	11/30/1992
Brown, James T.	07/15/1894	7/25/1926
Brown, Mark Anthony	1964	1964
Brown, Mearl Elisha	11/8/1916	7/21/1979

NAME	BIRTH	DEATH
Burnett, Mary Jane	09/16/1880	9/18/1952
Burnett, Roberta Gail	12/29/1983	12/29/1983
Burrow, Agnes	9/29/1925	5/23/1991
Burrow, Coleman	3/9/1916	5/4/1919
Burrow, I. M (May be L. M.)	02/24/1855	4/10/1923
Burrow, Julia Coleman	03/15/1888	6/13/1967
Buttrum Macuis	11/12/1905	1/18/1911
Buttrum, Carolyn Darlene Oliver	1/20/1956	8/18/1991
Buttrum, Curtis C.	11/1/1918	9/24/1984
Buttrum, Daisy Leora Brown	9/8/1922	12/12/2002
Buttrum, Ellen C. Fikes	03/01/1887	12/21/1975
Buttrum, Mary E.	06/04/1865	10/3/1939
Buttrum, Mary Hall	1887	1914
Buttrum, Mitchell	10/16/1879	03/35/2955
Buttrum, Seeman	06/15/1887	12/25/1968
Cain, Bessie Jewell Gillham	02/20/1894	7/27/1978
Cain, Billy Ray		No Dates
Cain, Carmon E.	7/17/1911	7/17/1968
Cain, David Victor	5/20/1900	1/1/1941
Cain, Henry A.	08/23/1860	8/5/1929
Cain, Isabelle Ina Lynch	8/6/1913	2/9/1954
Cain, John Dixon	10/13/1880	5/10/1952
Cain, Loyd C.	8/26/1933	5/5/1978
Cain, Nancy M. Cearley	02/25/1836	5/14/1919
Cain, Nora E. Coleman	02/11/1886	11/13/1960
Cain, Richard Joe	1/17/1959	3/19/2004
Cain, Runnah Mayberry	08/13/1872	3/11/1947
Cain, Vivian Graves	1/30/1924	12/8/1998
Cain, W. H.	08/22/1889	2/11/1967

NAME	BIRTH	DEATH
Brown, Muriel Glenn	11/3/1928	3/1/1951
Brown, Myrtle Goodman	11/13/1910	3/1/1962
Brown, Ralph Edward "Butch"	7/28/1944	8/2/2005
Brown, Roy E.	10/08/1893	10/30/1984
Brown, Tharon M.	5/12/1924	2/24/1992
Brown, William H.	7/30/1900	11/17/1966
Brown, Willie Ray	9/23/1931	4/21/2005
Brumley, Louisa Chitwood	04/01/1844	01/29/1898
Brumley, Melissa	12/22/1881	09/02/1896
Bryant, Dorothy E.	9/5/1936	3/15/1937
Bryant, John F.	03/16/1859	4/7/1928
Bryant, Mabel P.	5/20/1932	2/15/1933
Bryant, Martha J. Morgan	11/27/1864	03/16/1887
Bryant, William N.	11/7/1907	11/25/1968
Bulice, Rebecca E. Lavendar	12/18/1879	5/24/1920
Bullard, Irene Land	9/10/1904	4/4/1999
Bullard, Loris O.	10/26/1891	3/16/1979
Bump, Amelia Orrell	3/11/1921	8/15/2007
Bump, Charles Freddie	7/24/1941	9/23/2008
Bump, Charlie	11/02/1883	10/01/1891
Bump, Coy Dean	11/24/1916	11/24/1916
Bump, Della B. Owen	11/7/1900	1/15/1998
Bump, Fred O.	07/29/1894	5/12/1977
Bump, Julia Elizabeth Rouse	07/29/1866	11/28/1954
Bump, Lenora Ola	9/20/1919	3/31/2009
Bump, Nathan	08/31/1886	06/18/1888
Bump, Phylander H.	02/16/1865	11/7/1928
Burch, Sarah Ellen Connell	03/04/1878	7/1/1942
Burnett, James M.	7/22/1910	3/29/1975

NAME	BIRTH	DEATH
Caldwell, Annie J.	10/1/1909	7/24/1998
Caldwell, Hilda Etta Housley	7/16/1918	10/26/1997
Carpenter, Ira Walter	10/03/1884	11/29/1903
Carter, Everett Earl	3/31/1918	6/4/1994
Cary, James Alexander	12/19/1895	3/12/1927
Casada, Barbara A.	10/25/1949	10/27/1949
Case, Elma	10/22/1913	9/4/1920
Case, Guy	03/30/1892	8/28/1929
Cavnor, David D.	1/25/1940	12/25/1981
Cearley, Clarence E.	12/6/1933	9/13/1980
Cearley, Clement Walter (Jr.)	04/19/1893	2/5/1969
Cearley, Clement Walter "C. W."	1846	1935
Cearley, Elvira A. Parks Lowe	10/17/1850	1/18/1916
Cearley, James Walter	10/26/1931	1/1/2002
Cearley, Vela E. Pittman	10/25/1900	2/11/1988
Chambers, Lukas Raymond	2/26/1992	2/27/1992
Chatman, Cecil Virginia	4/2/1918	9/5/1968
Chitwood, Isabelle Ratliff	10/05/1876	12/19/1951
Chitwood, Adney G.	12/26/1868	08/18/1876
Chitwood, Andrew R.	02/26/1842	5/30/1922
Chitwood, Charles W.	07/21/1866	8/21/1963
Chitwood, Edmund Dee	11/18/1877	7/2/1902
Chitwood, Elisabeth Pinson	09/19/1814	11/21/1886
Chitwood, Ellen	Abt 1827	
Chitwood, James Obed	04/27/1888	1/27/1968
Chitwood, Janie Drucilla	08/13/1892	5/14/1902
Chitwood, Jessie Lee Smith	10/14/1915	6/16/2006
Chitwood, Joel M. D.	Abt 1832	
Chitwood, Kitty Stroud	01/27/1875	11/15/1958

NAME	BIRTH	DEATH
Chitwood, Marion	07/02/1871	Died young
Chitwood, Martha Jane	09/22/1842	12/10/1921
Chitwood, Moses A.	08/21/1869	Died young
Chitwood, P. Alice	02/06/1870	2/8/1932
Chitwood, Riley J.	11/16/1868	3/21/1951
Chitwood, Roy Stephen	1/8/1937	9/26/2004
Chitwood, Stephen D.	3/30/1914	4/26/1999
Chote, Nona Pierce	9/1/1927	9/25/1957
Church, Ethel F. Sutton	2/24/1914	5/23/1996
Clark, Jerry Joe	12/12/1955	12/19/2003
Clay, Ann Hollihan Lamkin	9/23/1905	12/15/1974
Cline, James H.	7/17/1909	6/26/1971
Cobb, Daniel Albert	7/23/1954	9/21/1994
Cobb, Patricia Jo Kennedy	8/5/1941	11/6/2002
Cockrell, Johana Rouse	05/01/1857	5/27/1935
Cockrell, Nancy A. Dorris	10/08/1868	6/7/1902
Cockrell, Rev. Wm. L.	06/27/1855	5/22/1940
Cockrell, Vander	01/14/1894	15/26/1917
Cogburn, Ethel Vernell	1/13/1922	7/11/1995
Cogburn, Orba Noral	10/11/1916	3/7/1992
Coker, Delcie Berry	11/19/1904	7/15/1990
Coker, F. L. "Fate"	3/20/1904	6/22/1978
Coker, John Hood	02/08/1894	4/1/1983
Coker, Richard Kurt	11/12/1962	8/15/1983
Coleman, Annie Cain	10/1/1909	7/24/1998
Coleman, Cleo Reese	8/11/1904	5/18/1987
Coleman, Elizabeth D. Rouse	April 1823	6/26/1916
Coleman, Glynn Reece	1933	1934
Coleman, James A.	04/20/1855	7/25/1937

NAME	BIRTH	DEATH
Coleman, James Arthur	06/27/1893	7/6/1947
Coleman, Joel	08/06/1899	9/14/1976
Coeman, Lavern		3/21/1936
Coleman, Lavone		3/21/1936
Coleman, Mary Jane	08/28/1856	7/20/1928
Coleman, Rilla Lee	1/26/1946	5/30/1998
Collins, Dyllan Lee	11/14/2000	11/14/2000
Conger, Chester Clyde	06/04/1891	03/14/1893
Conger, Floy Willard	11/24/1898	9/27/1905
Conover, Charles H.	3/15/1908	9/29/1992
Conover, Joseph Lee	09/29/1893	12/20/1978
Conover, Wilbur L.	05/15/1892	5/22/1973
Cooley, Lackey B.	1852	1/9/1941
Coomer, Mark	12/19/1958	12/19/1958
Coston, Otis Ray	11/3/1950	4/12/2006
Cox, Etta Houser	08/09/1888	9/14/1968
Cox, Leslie T.	12/06/1887	10/6/1959
Cox, Lizzie Nelson	08/08/1891	1/30/1969
Cox, Sammy Wayne	7/15/1948	11/16/1993
Cox, Sidney S. "Babe"	03/24/1886	1/22/1969
Crowder, Dortha Irene Orrell	2/11/1924	12/11/2006
Crumpton, Sue Abernathy	8/10/1947	9/13/1996
Crumpton, Willie Ray	4/15/1943	3/6/1996
Culliford, Cecila Maria	4/18/1960	6/11/1992
Culliford, William C.	11/26/1953	3/29/2004
Cunnigham, Amanda E. Wheeler	08/26/1868	6/9/1907
Cunningham, Della W. Muncrief	11/02/1868	6/8/1958
Cunningham, James A.	01/09/1871	04/17/1894
Cunningham, John B.	1859	1915

NAME	BIRTH	DEATH
Cunningham, John D.	01/17/1868	12/18/1951
Cunningham, Mary E. R.	1869	1945
Cunningham, Mary Jane	08/16/1844	8/9/1922
Cunningham, Rev. Thomas J.	10/17/1843	5/5/1900
Cunningham, W. T. "Bill"	7/14/1905	3/2/1976
Cunningham, William J.	05/17/1873	1/29/1921
Daniel(s), Jarrell F.	7/3/1936	8/25/1990
Daniel, Henry Oscar	10/20/1894	3/3/1960
Daniel, Jo Anna	1/31/1946	4/9/1979
Daniel, Joseph C.	8/19/1905	10/16/1974
Daniel, Julia Jane Hughes	8/20/1906	12/4/1998
Daniels, Belva O. Houpt	4/10/1937	6/25/2007
Daniels, Jennifer Amber	4/19/1977	4/19/1977
Darnell, Phillip Duane	9/8/1952	6/30/2008
Davidson, John		Age 71
Davis, Janet Virginia	6/24/1928	4/18/2005
Davis, William "Bill"	1870	1905
Dean, Thomas Sherman	01/12/1895	8/13/1973
DeBoard, Dianna Lynn Gillham	5/20/1971	9/11/1997
DeLee, Ben Day	09/24/1873	8/10/1927
DeLee, Kenneth Ben	9/25/1910	11/3/1966
DeLee, Mary Ault	10/30/1883	7/24/1968
DeLee, Raymond Day	1/29/1915	1/11/1970
DeLee, Virginia Alma Graves	8/20/1912	10/10/1984
Digby, Delphia	04/10/1899	4/15/1995
Digby, John Henry	10/02/1875	9/28/1961
Diggs, Elender Lonetta Kinsey	6/30/1915	4/25/2008
Diggs, Martin Curtis	3/8/1911	9/12/1993
Diggs, Patricia Ann	11/16/1938	12/14/2005

NAME	BIRTH	DEATH
Dillard, Jessie Lee Muncrief	4/4/1930	1/6/2008
Dobson, Joseph		No Dates
Dobson, Robert O.	05/21/1882	7/4/1948
Dodd, Lee	1913	1979
Dolphus, Frank	09/08/1859	11/9/1927
Dorris, Dora Garrett	1871	1906
Dorris, James M.	04/18/1874	2/14/1945
Dorris, Sackie Muncrief	12/13/1879	1/14/1946
Dorris, Zelma	1899	1916
Double, R. H.	12/22/1863	10/8/1905
Duckett, Amery-Ary	04/12/1894	_/11/1969?
Duckett, George R.	08/03/1875	6/19/1950
Duckett, George W.	5/18/1917	9/14/1947
Duckett, Jermiah O.	09/02/1873	3/19/1904
Duckett, Lizzie	06/07/1877	3/16/1956
Dunn, W. Dwayne	7/25/1984	9/9/2007
Dush, Irene Buttrum	9/22/1916	8/25/2006
Dush, Noah B.	3/19/1907	5/11/1992
Eberwein, Damien Vance	9/17/2007	3/25/2009
Eddleman, James Grundy	1825	02/01/1897
Eddleman, Lucy Ann Chitwood	01/10/1835	12/10/1924
Edgin, Robert Raymond	5/25/1913	2/16/1985
Edgin, Robert Raymond, Jr.	7/14/1934	4/6/1991
Edgin, Wilma Dora Harper	8/28/1917	8/16/1983
Elmore, Howard R.	2/14/1926	12/1/1960
Embry, Orice R.	12/8/1921	12/22/1992
Emerson, Albert Paul "Bub"	8/12/1926	4/6/2007
Emerson, Floyd Waldo	06/22/1898	8/20/1963
Emerson, John Annie Lynch	4/16/1903	2/21/1993

NAME	BIRTH	DEATH
Ennis, Allen Burr	1/2/1901	10/30/1972
Ennis, Audrey Keener	5/1/1929	9/17/1999
Ennis, Ben	1851	1914
Ennis, Betty L. Wallace	09/16/1896	7/29/1981
Ennis, Carlos H.	03/21/1894	9/22/1916
Ennis, China Saline Pate	03/31/1875	9/4/1916
Ennis, Elizabeth	1853	Unreadable
Ennis, Elizabeth Echols	12/25/1861	12/19/1931
Ennis, Ella B. Savage	07/07/1894	4/10/1963
Ennis, Gary		No Dates
Ennis, Hilda Mackey	7/29/1908	4/11/1927
Ennis, Infant		No Dates
Ennis, Jack A.	12/19/1881	5/18/1952
Ennis, James W.	09/02/1875	8/9/1959
Ennis, Joe	03/03/1882	11/7/1930
Ennis, Leon	02/29/1925	7/17/1997
Ennis, Margie E. Henry	3/2/1921	3/31/2004
Ennis, Martha A. Rawls	1858	1876
Ennis, Martha E. Cunningham	03/15/1876	4/3/1906
Ennis, Odie Ray	12/11/1903	7/22/1967
Ennis, Ordis	4/4/1923	9/13/2001
Ennis, Plez	7/27/1909	1/8/1943
Ennis, Settie Pate	09/02/1882	1/24/1974
Ennis, Squire	06/27/1890	10/7/1957
Ennis, Tilford	5/11/1920	7/7/1989
Ennis, Victoria Lewis	4/10/1915	1/24/1998
Ennis, Wilton	12/24/1920	6/13/1981
Erwin, Emma Riley "M. O."	5/24/1915	7/17/1960
Erwin, Infant		No Dates

NAME	BIRTH	DEATH
Erwin, May	1894	1930
Everright, Robert Jon	5/8/1981	4/17/2005
Farr, Mae Ennis	6/27/1910	12/19/1994
Farr, Tom Winford	7/27/1909	2/16/1974
Felton, Tiny Ellen Whitehead	3/18/1959	12/15/2006
Fendley, Alvin E.	12/2/1921	3/7/1986
Fendley, Claudia Lucille Pope	11/5/1924	11/30/2007
Fikes, Arlis	9/20/1912	9/20/1912
Fikes, Curtis	1/17/1904	07/07/19__
Fikes, Elizabeth S. Tucker	08/13/1867	10/6/1957
Fikes, George E. "Jack"	12/1/1910	1/2/1942
Fikes, John Andrew	03/07/1856	10/19/1934
Fikes, Johnny D.	8/26/1923	5/10/1999
Fikes, Luther G.	11/27/1884	1/28/1952
Fikes, Mary C. "Mollie" Tucker	10/20/1860	9/7/1946
Fikes, Morris R.	7/1/1920	6/22/2009
Fikes, Pearl Inez	8/21/1902	5/30/1921
Fikes, Ramsey A.	04/20/1861	8/22/1954
Fikes, Sadie M. Muncrief	10/28/1886	7/23/1960
Fisher, Era Elizabeth Cunningham	10/11/1900	2/11/1954
Fisher, George	1888	1920
Fisher, James B.	02/27/1897	1/27/1977
Fisher, Mary E.	12/12/1892	08/02/1893
Fisher, Myrta B. McCaslin	09/24/1872	1/15/1938
Fisher, Wade F.	1860	3/24/1928
Fisher, William Owen	02/05/1857	3/30/1934
Ford, Polly Ann	2/24/1922	1/31/1998
Frazier, Casada W. "C. W."	11/6/1917	2/12/2008
Frazier, Lois Marie Braughton	4/9/1925	3/10/1992

NAME	BIRTH	DEATH
Freeman, A. Pearl Weston	1916	1990
Freeman, Al	4/15/1924	4/20/1994
Freeman, Al Cecil Lee Freeman	1/16/1945	2/22/1976
Freeman, Cloie Clinton	10/14/1903	4/5/1978
Freeman, Emma Mackey	1/29/1903	8/28/1966
Freeman, Everett	03/06/1896	4/16/1969
Freeman, John E.	07/17/1874	11/17/1949
Freeman, Ray J.	6/26/1920	3/12/1984
Fryar, Deltha D. Kirk	11/22/1918	9/1/2007
Fryar, Vernon F.	5/25/1914	5/3/1981
Gardner, Austin P.	6/19/2000	6/19/2000
Garrett, Ada F.	11/15/1893	2/10/1977
Garrett, Ardis Zelma Hatmaker	8/16/1919	7/13/2008
Garrett, Clifton E.	11/22/1925	3/23/2007
Garrett, Columbus Elmer	7/1/1919	10/29/1955
Garrett, Della Thomason Koppersmith	1903	1952
Garrett, Ella M. Boswell	1895	1978
Garrett, Frank	01/05/1883	8/19/1928
Garrett, Gary Lee	11/2/1948	10/14/1975
Garrett, Gary Lee, Jr.	8/23/1973	8/25/1975
Garrett, Henry Frank	8/19/1923	6/14/1944
Garrett, Homer		No Dates
Garrett, Iva Rhodes Muncrief	09/17/1896	10/1/1993
Garrett, James Henry	1855	1912
Garrett, John Columbus	01/10/1887	7/30/1951
Garrett, Julia A. Chitwood	02/15/1885	1/13/1905
Garrett, Lottie		No Dates
Garrett, Luella Lansdell	8/1/1924	2/1/2007
Garrett, Lum	2/28/1917	1/4/1986

NAME	BIRTH	DEATH
Garrett, Merdie Lee	1897	1897
Garrett, Nancy Stapp	1858	1932
Garrett, Nannie	1891	1891
Garrett, Ruie Cockrell	1879	1918
Garrett, Vander	01/18/1899	8/20/1953
Garrett, William H.	07/17/1876	11/11/1971
Geary, Ruby DeLee	9/17/1906	7/24/1978
Genero, Grace Clara Spiva	9/22/1904	2/5/1963
George, Bethie Lee Hall	9/11/1915	9/11/2003
Gibson, Ruby Lou		4/18/1991
Gillham, Bulah Manning	9/1/1903	3/28/1986
Gillham, Doyle F.	10/25/1920	9/23/1959
Gillham, Elizabeth Jane Sexton		12/28/1916
Gillham, Enoch E.	10/23/1872	10/16/1921
Gillham, Enoch N.	12/16/1902	2/22/1996
Gillham, Frances E. Moore	01/30/1891	5/28/1945
Gillham, Genevieve Eugenia Ihly	4/18/1920	9/22/1999
Gillham, George	4/4/1923	4/4/1923
Gillham, James Lowell	4/7/1919	4/28/1987
Gillham, John	1774	1864
Gillham, John A.	1877	4/5/1932
Gillham, Johnny		02/10/1881
Gillham, Lydia Jane Savage	5/8/1926	12/10/2000
Gillham, Mary Hubble	6/20/1911	8/9/1983
Gillham, Phillip P.	02/07/1854	Bet 1870-1880
Gillham, Phillip Phagen	10/24/1828	9/30/1908
Gillham, Rachel	04/22/1871	10/20/1871
Gillham, Ronald Eugene	9/11/1948	1/10/1999
Gillham, Rosa McQuerter	1776	1863

NAME	BIRTH	DEATH
Gillham, Ruby Marie	1952	6/1/2005
Gillham, Sarah A. Rogers	06/21/1824	02/19/1885
Gillham, Sarah E. Howerton	10/22/1875	2/17/1974
Gillham, Thomas Newton	02/07/1849	4/16/1915
Gillham, Walter	12/25/1895	8/9/1902
Gillham, William C.	11/12/1927	10/14/1992
Gillham, William C. "W. C."	10/13/1899	12/29/1978
Glass, Ernest Cole	10/5/1910	1/31/2002
Goines, Peggy J. Ragsdale	6/7/1944	3/4/1989
Goodwin, James Louis	03/30/1885	8/24/1972
Goodwin, Nettie Maude	02/04/1885	10/27/1962
Gray, Mary Ann	9/10/1958	9/10/1958
Green, Ronald Gene	12/20/1947	9/9/2003
Green, Rosie Sutton	1868	1909
Griffin, Florence Elizabeth Burnett	10/24/1905	11/2/1992
Griffin, Leo Doyle	4/2/1928	8/16/1972
Griffin, Loraine	5/26/1923	7/14/1940
Griffin, Louis Raymond	10/3/1911	6/15/1930
Griffin, Luella Howton	02/23/1884	12/24/1955
Griffin, Mildred Beatrice Thomason	3/9/1921	6/19/1993
Griffin, Ozziro B.	03/30/1889	11/3/1922
Griffin, Ray	5/20/1918	2/14/1994
Griffin, Raymond Z.		No Dates
Griffith, Nettie Maude	03/22/1889	08/30/1891
Griffith, W. M.		No Dates
Grisham, Mary A.	6/20/1918	10/20/1972
Grisham, Virgil Ray	12/2/1919	3/24/1989
Gwinn, Mary Ann Sutton Martin	1850	1876
Hall, Barbara S.	12/15/1948	2/10/2005

NAME	BIRTH	DEATH
Hall, Barney John	08/13/1889	2/29/1976
Hall, Beulah F. Madison	4/1/1917	1/5/1984
Hall, Della Ussery Maynard	07/15/1890	11/20/1967
Hall, Helen Ruth	12/31/1940	4/18/2009
Hall, Leffie Andy	11/6/1960	12/12/1960
Hall, Leffie Isaac, Sr.	1/21/1914	2/13/1998
Hall, Mary Etter	12/06/1887	07/18/1890
Hall, Nathan R.	12/18/1919	4/25/1998
Hall, Nettie	1895	1914
Hall, Roy Allen	5/4/1952	10/21/1954
Harbin, Hazel Lorene"Blue Dot"	5/11/1927	10/14/1993
Harper, Susie K. Powell	12/11/1911	1/10/1997
Harrington, Katherine A. DeLee	10/21/1946	9/17/2006
Harris Margaret Addah E. Houser	01/28/1871	8/21/1964
Harris, Henry Edmond		06/27/1888
Harris, James P.	1865	1923
Harris, Lewis	12/22/1889	June 1899
Hart, Beatrice A.	11/10/1897	2/4/1980
Hart, Ceola L.	08/06/1891	7/10/1981
Harvey, Jesse Curtis	3/8/1992	6/10/1993
Hayes, Imogene L.	5/16/1954	12/22/1984
Hedrick, Hattie Reece	1900	1975
Helms, Willis C.	8/16/1919	4/5/2001
Helton, Amanda	11/05/1851	8/2/1933
Helton, John	07/23/1872	5/4/1954
Henderson, Dutch Webb	4/15/1910	1961
Henderson, Ola		12/26/1987
Hester, Mildred B.	6/27/1919	9/26/1998
Hester, Rev. Marvin	11/3/1917	6/12/1995

NAME	BIRTH	DEATH
Hickman, Richard Wilson	11/16/1923	10/7/2005
Hicks, Alice V. Hurst	02/18/1886	4/5/1974
Hicks, Edward T.	10/15/1885	9/5/1967
Hicks, Harlen R.	7/18/1924	6/11/1982
Hicks, Mary Rhodes	4/22/1927	1/23/1993
Hill, Anna Mae Cass	6/13/1910	6/10/2002
Hill, Clyde Eugene	8/25/1928	3/22/1995
Hill, Epp Leonard	3/1/1905	1/23/1974
Hill, Etta J. Braziel	3/28/1914	12/17/2003
Hill, Jeff M.	7/28/1908	3/14/1986
Hill, Lois Ellen Humphreys	7/30/1931	5/25/2000
Hobgood, Archie Columbus	6/18/1915	5/21/1998
Hodgeman, John I.	9/13/1920	9/11/1944
Hodges, Claude H.	05/23/1894	10/20/1957
Hodges, Janetta Runyan	12/23/1921	12/2/1998
Hollihan, John M., Sr.	11/14/1898	3/28/1981
Hollingsworth, Calvin T. "C. T."	6/19/1927	11/17/1995
Hollingsworth, Elzie B. "Crickett"	3/30/1932	8/11/1996
Holloway, Ezra Ola	12/20/1901	7/23/1954
Homan, Glen Thomas	8/15/1943	6/30/2004
Hopkins, Sabra Jane Rouse	1842	1874
Hopkins, Simon Newton		No Dates
Hopper, Glen Lee	2/18/1903	5/1/1984
House, Infant		No Dates
House, Terry Dean	06/10/1869	8/8/1935
Houser, Andrew J. "A. J."		No Dates
Houser, Charley R.	02/13/1885	3/29/1920
Houser, Doyle Charles "Charley"	4/25/1922	8/25/2003
Houser, Edgar J.	09/18/1881	09/25/1882

NAME	BIRTH	DEATH
Houser, Gertie Cockrell	06/16/1885	11/29/1964
Houser, Joel Anderson	01/20/1883	1/2/1969
Houser, Joseph Nimrod	10/28/1845	8/3/1919
Houser, Little Annie May	11/01/1893	12/20/1896
Houser, Little Arthur	10/17/1896	01/01/1897
Houser, Mary M.	09/02/1851	03/17/1879
Houser, Sarah Elizabeth Chitwood	03/18/1852	3/29/1932
Howard, Ocie N.	7/31/1913	2/17/1989
Howard, Opal Maxine	11/16/1923	3/28/1996
Howell, Birdie A. Bauchman	05/10/1898	7/15/1996
Howell, Donald L.	12/13/1909	10/18/1972
Howell, James N.	10/29/1930	9/25/2003
Howell, John E.	10/18/1893	2/21/1984
Howell, Ottis H.	4/19/1906	5/3/1962
Howell, Ruby Muncrief	10/4/1909	6/28/1958
Howell, Vera N. Cooper	6/2/1915	2/7/1981
Huber, Peter	11/01/1898	10/28/1931
Hughes, Arthur E.	8/27/1912	12/25/1988
Hughes, Bobbie J. Smith	6/28/1929	12/16/1966
Hughes, Carolyn Joyce	7/21/1943	7/22/1943
Hughes, Stella Alice Garrett	1886	1935
Hughes, Thomas William	09/03/1872	4/18/1952
Hughes, W. H. "bill"	10/116/1904	7/17/1989
Hughes, Wilford Earl	2/17/1917	5/25/1989
Humphreys, Daniel		No Dates
Humphreys, David		No Dates
Humphreys, Dera V. Godwin	11/10/1906	9/13/1981
Humphreys, Ethel M. Jones	12/21/1904	9/8/1999
Humphreys, Etta Weston	12/26/1902	4/10/1997

NAME	BIRTH	DEATH
Humphreys, Eunice	03/29/1889	01/10/1899
Humphreys, Gabriel	1860	1948
Humphreys, Glenn	1906	1908
Humphreys, James	4/5/1946	4/5/1946
Humphreys, Jerry	4/5/1946	4/5/1946
Humphreys, Jesse L.	9/1/1902	12/2/1979
Humphreys, John R.	6/21/1906	12/18/1982
Humphreys, Kittie Clyde Muncrief	12/14/1869	11/28/1950
Humphreys, Matilda J.	1832	1910
Humphreys, Nancy Betsy Howell	03/25/1867	11/6/1936
Humphreys, Richard A.	11/04/1855	8/15/1935
Humphreys, Richard Benjamin	7/20/1904	5/22/1932
Humphreys, Richard Ross	9/3/1945	8/19/2005
Humphreys, Roxy	1895	1913
Humphreys, Roy	1904	1909
Humphreys, Samuel J.	10/18/1897	4/6/1974
Humphreys, Samuel Robert	2/18/1935	10/9/2009
Humphreys, Steven Robert	6/22/1970	7/4/2006
Humpreys, William Leonard	1/3/1900	11/10/1902
Hunter, Carl M.	10/9/1924	7/12/1925
Hunter, Dillard A.	02/27/1877	11/5/1955
Hunter, Floyd E.	6/20/1903	12/28/1965
Hunter, James M.	09/15/1860	4/13/1938
Hunter, Minnie Cantrell	09/05/1879	12/7/1938
Hunter, Pearl Odessa Noles	7/22/1905	9/5/1977
Hunter, Shirley Ann	6/2/1935	2/13/1940
Hurst, Andy C.	10/09/1873	4/27/1946
Hurst, Beulah Maebel Neighbors	4/28/1935	6/21/2007
Hurst, Brian Allen	1/16/1985	1/3/1999

NAME	BIRTH	DEATH
Hurst, Donna May	10/7/1959	10/7/1959
Hurst, Elizabeth Noles	07/14/1856	12/19/1933
Hurst, Leroy	11/28/1928	4/1/1998
Hurst, Nancy Bird Hurst	1870	1959
Ivey, Raymon F.	9/6/1922	3/16/2002
James, Irene	8/2/1918	9/17/1935
Jennings, Damie L. Lucking	08/28/1879	12/2/1958
Jennings, Dr. Orville	07/10/1872	10/28/1933
Jewell, Clarence	3/13/1902	6/10/1996
Jewell, Effie C. Hagler	10/03/1873	4/5/1948
Jewell, Elsie Mae Heath	5/12/1905	9/8/1997
Jewell, James Bruce	05/21/1858	3/28/1913
Jewell, James Russell	06/29/1894	2/7/1975
Jewell, Roy Hagler (Hager)	05/14/1896	9/15/1918
Johnson, Margaret M. Gillham	5/1/1914	2/14/2002
Johnson, Betty Lou	4/2/1947	2/13/1948
Johnson, Charles E.	1/24/1906	12/11/1960
Johnson, Edward L.	10/15/1926	10/31/2002
Johnson, Ezra O. Cranford	1902	1954
Johnson, J. Y.		No Dates
Johnson, James Dennis	11/20/1950	10/31/1981
Johnson, Thomas R.	8/23/1929	6/27/1998
Jones, Christopher M.	12/16/1960	8/22/1978
Jones, Christy Gayle	3/28/1982	10/24/2002
Jones, Donald Wayne, Jr. "Donnie"	7/10/1966	8/3/2004
Jones, Fred	1861	1893
Jones, Larry A.	12/10/1956	11/25/2005
Kassaw, Geneva S.	11/27/1917	8/8/1988
Keenom, Ira R.	11/20/1903	11/21/1985

NAME	BIRTH	DEATH
Keenom, Lois Outler	8/24/1905	11/8/1988
Kellar, Clifford Daniel	8/4/1959	2/16/1981
Kellum, Dolen J.	11/24/1913	7/26/1986
Kellum, Sylvia B. Neighbors	9/4/1925	8/5/1983
Kelton, Baby		No Dates
Kelton, Bertha E. Orrell	03/26/1884	11/17/1951
Kelton, Eugene	07/09/1867	2/9/1950
Ketzer, Edward, Jr.	6/2/1951	8/21/2000
Kilby, Cindy Lou	12/9/1948	12/9/1948
Kilby, Dovie Pearl	2/18/1905	2/5/1953
Kilby, John Paul	10/31/1963	12/21/1997
Kilgore, Georgie	8/19/1908	4/23/1912
Kilgore, John T.	10/10/1910	11/3/1982
Kilgore, Ted T.	1910	1982
Kimery, Earl Henry	5/3/1931	1/23/1984
Kimery, Willie Mae Rowland	4/25/1914	12/14/2001
King, Alfred M.	1833	1864
King, Alph		07/10/1862
King, Joshua		08/13/1864
King, Mary Jane	1860	1890
Kinsey, Daniel C.	10/19/1930	11/14/1933
Kinsey, James Leon	5/31/1926	2/21/1984
Kinsey, Jim W.	06/08/1882	3/20/1948
Kinsey, Ruth E. Humphreys	11/30/1900	5/11/1954
Kipp, Tina Elizabeth Hargrove	9/2/1971	6/18/1994
Kirby, Appie	8/26/1907	12/25/1922
Kirby, Mary Catherine Chitwood	02/03/1871	1916
Kirby, Rado	5/8/1913	10/28/1913
Kirby, Sarah Jane Pate	06/21/1867	3/24/1952

NAME	BIRTH	DEATH
Lay, Paul W.	3/8/1938	3/29/2005
Lee, Effie Crystal Jewell	2/14/1900	1/10/1990
Lee, James Ray	1/23/1934	1/23/1934
Lee, Mary L. Black	03/17/1869	2/8/1947
Lee, Robert	4/12/1900	9/10/1965
Lee, Robert "Bob"	1860	1902
Lee, Will E.	1872	1898
Lee, Willis Earl	07/28/1893	3/7/1947
Lee, Willis Earl, Jr.	9/25/1932	9/25/1932
LeJeune, Sidney Paul, Sr.	7/17/1936	5/22/2006
Lewis, David W.	08/02/1896	6/28/1992
Lewis, Thelma McCaslin	8/22/1903	8/26/1976
Lindley, Minnie Keener	5/17/1900	12/23/1979
Lindsey, Ethel Baker	2/29/1924	1/25/2005
Lizotte, Vesta Mackey	2/21/1901	11/10/1932
Long, Esther Sutton	2/16/1904	2/7/1988
Lott, Arnold G.	12/11/1923	5/24/2003
Lott, Clara Beatrice "Bea" Donahoe	12/19/1925	4/26/1994
Lowe, Archie L.	6/30/1933	10/18/1987
Lowe, Dillard	12/29/1856	4/1/1905
Lowe, Eliza Catherine Anderson	1836	2/27/1922
Lowe, James Henry	1828	12/5/1908
Lowery, Bonnie Harper	4/26/1932	9/18/1997
Lowery, Clem F.	3/19/1928	12/19/2004
Lowery, Martin	12/15/1924	4/25/1998
Lowrey, Nonnia E.	12/18/1944	2/12/2009
Loy, Alvin Leon	6/15/1939	11/20/2006
Lucking, Henry C.	1857	1932
Luttrell, William Allen	11/01/1893	7/10/1951

NAME	BIRTH	DEATH
Kirby, Wesley D.	04/18/1874	7/29/1938
Kirkpatrick, Fannie Mae Tuberville	5/5/1910	3/13/1982
Krest, Patsy Inez	12/19/1940	6/6/1973
Kunkel, Eleanor Josephine Neighbors	8/31/1922	7/8/2001
Kunkel, John Martin	3/15/1912	12/18/1996
Lair, Sheila Victoria Sorter	5/2/1957	6/11/2007
Lamkin, Gene	1922	1978
Lancaster, Infant	1924	1924
Land, Alvis A.	04/24/1874	3/25/1961
Land, Dacus Thomas	3/15/1915	2/23/1995
Land, Henry Quintin	9/24/1907	2/1/1978
Land, Hubert B.	1/24/1903	8/22/1988
Land, Iva Louella Berry	10/5/1921	9/20/2007
Land, Mary Ellen Cain	11/27/1885	11/7/1951
Land, Pearl I. Dacus	04/18/1881	2/15/1960
Land, Ruby	1/19/1909	2/13/1950
Land, Ruth M. Butler	11/10/1910	5/23/1981
Land, Thomas Levi	03/29/1879	12/5/1958
Land, Tommy L., Jr.	9/25/1923	7/2/1975
Landsdell, Bobby Ray	2/11/1929	7/28/1940
Landsdell, Loyd Eugene	3/23/1920	9/17/1985
Lankey, Alfred J.	4/21/1921	4/4/1996
Lankey, Bernice Muncrief	9/12/1913	1/27/1999
Lavender, Ernest E.	1898	3/15/1938
Lavender, John T.	1843	8/8/1919
Lavender, L. E.	1877	1973
Lavender, Matilda Griffin	03/07/1844	3/15/1923
Lavender, Nettie	1880	1959
Law, Sherry Ann	7/1/1956	12/18/2008

NAME	BIRTH	DEATH
Luttrell, Zelma Lee	07/17/1897	2/16/1978
Lynch, Ernest Edward	12/22/1918	4/16/1995
Lynch, Mary T. Nelson	07/12/1895	3/31/1970
Lynch, Oleeta Pearl Trammell	6/8/1918	8/9/2008
Lynch, Tom E.	01/07/1894	8/26/1967
Lyons, Clara Weaver	1905	1990
Mackey, Andrew J.		No Dates
Mackey, Lucinda Lavender	1871	1959
Macon, Rosco A.	1/2/1922	10/24/1994
Martin, Nathaniel Lee	3/29/2005	11/7/2005
Mason, Daisy Goodwin	8/12/1912	3/3/2005
Mason, Leonard Ray	10/3/1914	5/8/1994
Mathews, Charles A.	1953	1954
Mathews, O. P. (Rev)		01/02/1892
Mathis, Olive Owen	1/29/1906	4/18/1995
Mathis, Wilton C.	10/30/1902	12/23/1986
Maxwell, Betty Rose	12/10/1929	11/10/1998
Maxwell, Howell Earl	7/14/1928	12/13/1987
Mayberry, Walter W.	9/11/1927	10/5/1997
Mayo, Agnes	9/29/1925	5/23/1991
Mayo, Clarence Dale	7/30/1925	3/23/1948
Mayo, Claudia	No Dates	Infant
Mayo, Vernon D.	1/13/1943	1/27/1943
Mayo, Virgie Dona Pate	1917	1943
McCall, Juanita L.	1/11/1942	2/11/1996
McCall, W. Eron	7/20/1940	3/10/1998
McCalsin, Robert E.	07/31/1881	10/4/1940
McCaslin, B. G. (baby)		Nov-33
McCaslin, Charles Baxter	03/26/1864	8/13/1940

NAME	BIRTH	DEATH
McCaslin, Iva Lee	8/25/1915	7/6/1998
McCaslin, James	1826	1907
McCaslin, james W.	01/21/1875	4/2/1934
McCaslin, John David	04/24/1868	10/4/1949
McCaslin, John G.	4/20/1932	4/25/2002
McCaslin, John Leland	11/13/1906	10/22/1963
McCaslin, Maria Orrell	1829	1924
McCaslin, Melissa Abigale "Abbie"	03/25/1872	2/19/1947
McCaslin, Princess Luvenia Muncrief	10/09/1871	9/9/1953
McCaslin, Sarita Renee	11/7/1966	11/24/1966
McConnell, Nathan, Dr.	12/01/1840	08/08/1894
McDaniel, Sarah Gillham	05/20/1852	03/06/1898
McElroy, Mayme E.	12/09/1886	11/20/1976
McElroy, Opal P.	6/27/1910	9/30/1998
McElroy, P. Ivan	3/15/1906	4/22/1983
McInvale, john E.	02/24/1851	12/16/1928
McInvale, Lucinda McClendon	06/13/1875	8/29/1965
McInvale, Lydia	02/14/1894	12/14/1990
McKinney, Karen Michelle	8/26/1963	8/26/1963
McKinney, Lum Doyle	3/16/1937	9/12/2007
McKnight, Charles Allen	1892	1/27/1919
McKnight, Mary Alice Ennis	01/29/1888	2/27/1976
McKnight, William Andrew	08/29/1889	11/6/1957
Mellott, Della Weaver	1901	1989
Melton, Luther D.	9/23/1903	12/4/1990
Melton, Ruth S.	10/4/1912	6/10/1983
Melton, Ruth Vera Conover	01/16/1898	7/5/1983
Meredith, Burlen David	7/20/1909	3/24/1991
Meredith, Daisy Cathleen Land	10/3/1915	11/7/2000

NAME	BIRTH	DEATH
Millard, James	12/29/1944	10/12/1997
Miller, Virda Jane Ayers	4/28/1909	8/25/2001
Mindt, Mary K.	10/4/1938	1/17/1940
Mitchell, Robert L. "Bob"	10/22/1916	4/9/1995
Mitchell, Walter L. H.	10/12/1962	8/6/1987
Moore, Gladys Griffin Jones	12/23/1925	12/31/1986
Moore, Henry E.	11/18/1900	12/2/1975
Moran, Tom E.	2/27/1912	9/14/1989
Moser, Kaye S.	10/5/1921	2/12/1999
Moser, William J. "Jack"	9/12/1911	2/4/2008
Mothershed, Dolores C.	6/17/1969	11/29/2002
Mulens, Calvin		No Dates
Muncrief, Annie	1920	1920
Muncrief, Bessie Lee	4/4/1930	1931
Muncrief, Billye Jean Stewart	7/15/1933	10/16/1986
Muncrief, Carrie A.	1876	1878
Muncrief, Charles Stroud	12/26/1861	2/13/1936
Muncrief, Clifford D.	6/11/1941	6/12/1941
Muncrief, David L., Sr.	07/05/1895	7/19/1986
Muncrief, Earl	05/11/1898	3/20/1969
Muncrief, Edsel M.	11/15/1939	11/15/1939
Muncrief, Floyd	09/21/1896	1/21/1900
Muncrief, Harold H. "Bunny"	9/30/1911	10/28/1995
Muncrief, Hugh G.	02/24/1872	7/1/1933
Muncrief, Ida Lee	1882	1887
Muncrief, Iona Barthena McCaslin	05/15/1865	12/12/1925
Muncrief, Iva	7/4/1902	10/22/1918
Muncrief, James L. (Dr.)	04/01/1832	9/21/1921
Muncrief, James L., Jr.	03/19/1885	12/14/1963

NAME	BIRTH	DEATH
Muncrief, Jennie M. Jewell	09/30/1897	1/11/1981
Muncrief, Leona Fikes	09/17/1878	6/11/1961
Muncrief, Leslie Dennis	4/15/1933	7/8/1977
Muncrief, Mary E.	1878	1886
Muncrief, Oma Sutton	3/10/1902	12/14/1918
Muncrief, Ona Ethel Chitwood	09/15/1895	7/28/1979
Muncrief, Robert Eldon	3/9/1918	9/21/1992
Muncrief, Robert Jefferson	02/06/1897	10/21/1962
Muncrief, Roger		3/2/1945
Muncrief, Sarah N. Stroud	10/07/1838	12/28/1920
Muncrief, Tom G.	03/27/1874	11/20/1953
Muncrief, Wendell D.	6/20/1934	10/21/2005
Muncrief, Willie Rowe	7/18/1907	7/12/1988
Murders, Sammy L.	10/19/1950	10/19/1950
Murphy, Virginia Smith	10/17/1928	12/13/1992
Murry, Oliver K.	9/25/1917	12/30/1994
Neal, Helen K. Howell	8/10/1914	7/13/1998
Neal, W. G.	9/13/1928	9/25/1930
Neal, William E.	1/22/1912	8/6/1981
Neely, Darius Melvin	8/10/1923	10/21/2002
Neighbors, Baby		No Dates
Neighbors, Dorothy Jane Hiebert	2/23/1934	8/13/2002
Neighbors, George	2/10/1924	10/11/1936
Neighbors, Gwendolyn	1/29/1976	12/31/1989
Neighbors, James A.	11/4/1906	8/2/1942
Neighbors, Jerry	8/9/1947	8/9/1947
Neighbors, John W.	1/21/1957	7/25/2008
Neighbors, Stanley Wayne	2/27/1931	1/1/2000
Neighbors, Velma Cunningham	4/8/1903	4/24/1967

NAME	BIRTH	DEATH
Neighbors, Walter	05/23/1896	5/26/1978
Nelson, Annie	3/16/1901	4/4/1924
Nelson, Fay Elizabeth	8/26/1925	9/7/1925
Nelson, Henry J.	12/07/1858	11/22/1928
Nelson, Johnny	08/23/1886	3/16/1962
Nelson, Mary T. Benze	1866	2/9/1939
Nelson, Myrtle Bump		No Dates
Nelson, Safronia "Fronie" Benze	11/22/1867	2/21/1947
Nelson, Sylvester S.	06/10/1852	12/27/1927
Noles, Charlie B.	6/14/1900	7/7/1979
Noles, Dewey	08/21/1898	5/19/1942
Noles, Emily Rowena Chitwood	12/08/1873	2/11/1935
Noles, Laura Estelle Howell	1/6/1903	6/28/1961
Noles, Lillie Kinsey	1903	1976
Noles, Otis E.		May-45
Noles, William Samuel	10/23/1872	12/27/1937
Norris, William W.	05/29/1837	01/14/1895
Olenski, Daisy O.	5/23/1918	6/23/1960
Oliver, Judy L. Dush	8/3/1942	4/28/1992
Oliver, Robert Kyle	11/27/1963	10/23/1984
Orrell, Annie Lee Robbins	05/07/1893	10/16/1972
Orrell, Charles Clifford	10/14/1917	11/1/1974
Orrell, Charles Henry	12/26/1887	3/16/1964
Orrell, Christine	1/6/1926	1/10/1926
Orrell, Edward Warren	11/2/1920	2/24/1935
Orrell, George R.	6/8/1919	5/20/1924
Orrell, Glovan (Glovon) Rayburn	8/18/1926	8/16/1993
Orrell, Infant		No Dates
Orrell, James T.	12/29/1922	12/15/2001

NAME	BIRTH	DEATH
Orrell, James Thomas	09/30/1844	1/26/1928
Orrell, James Thomas, Jr.	03/28/1894	9/7/1973
Orrell, Mary Clarinda Lewis	10/16/1859	3/5/1949
Orrell, Mella Smith	4/17/1902	11/30/1978
Orrell, Opal Minetta Sutton	1/3/1902	8/1/1991
Orrell, Paul Edward	4/1/1927	6/17/1996
Orrell, Robert F.	08/04/1899	3/10/1968
Orrell, Rosa Aline Hill	9/14/1932	8/3/2008
Orrell, Teddy L.	10/22/1929	8/31/2005
Orrell, Tilitha O.	8/3/1913	7/4/1914
Orrell, Timothy	6/7/1981	4/1/2007
Outler, Arnold	12/20/1917	6/7/1972
Owen(s), Jane Eddleman		No Dates
Owen(s), John		No Dates
Owen, Emma L. Houser	12/24/1877	3/7/1974
Owen, John H.	08/04/1885	8/16/1964
Owens, Baby		No Dates
Owens, Baby		No Dates
Owens, Cora Chitwood	1873	1910
Owens, Hurman	8/2/1902	9/14/1902
Owens, Thomas	1874	1943
Palmer, Elmer M.	10/8/1902	7/12/1988
Palmer, Katherine Muncrief	4/22/1906	9/3/1989
Parker, Sylvia Elmore	5/7/1927	7/13/2007
Pate Adaline Stewart	Aft 1845	Aft 1900 Census
Pate, Allen P.	Abt 1844	Aft 1900 Census
Pate, Alonzo Clay	02/05/1892	6/6/1965
Pate, Angeline Ennis	02/09/1852	12/1/1931
Pate, Clifford M.	10/8/1909	9/28/1974

NAME	BIRTH	DEATH
Pate, Daisy A. Hensley	1905	1980
Pate, Edward Argus	1915	6/10/1930
Pate, Edward M.	11/28/1840	6/6/1914
Pate, George W.	09/10/1888	11/7/1981
Pate, Ida M. Gillham	09/27/1878	1/2/1915
Pate, Ida Rowena Young	08/15/1893	1/28/1977
Pate, James T. "J. T."	06/16/1874	9/16/1964
Pate, Saphronia "Fronie" Nelson	09/20/1890	5/29/1952
Peavyhouse, Mary F.	6/19/1969	8/8/1935
Pennington, Ella Noles	05/13/1896	5/17/1932
Pennington, Jessie Pearl	4/27/1929	5/4/1961
Pennington, Richard G.	8/15/1919	8/26/1992
Pennington, Virginia Jones	7/8/1924	11/8/2002
Phelps, Vernon H.	4/23/1927	3/5/1996
Phillips, Dona	7/22/1905	1981
Phillips, Florence Adell	5/21/1930	2/22/1997
Phillips, John D.	01/07/1888	10/18/1980
Pierce, Edna "Susie"	12/06/1890	11/27/1958
Pierce, Jess W.	05/06/1883	3/17/1953
Pierce, Mary L.	11/12/1869	7/18/1949
Pierce, Larry R.	9/25/1944	9/25/1944
Pittman, Clara Thrantham	03/01/1889	2/4/1982
Pittman, James Marshall	07/07/1889	10/4/1961
Pittman, Laura Williamson	10/04/1869	3/3/1937
Pomplum, Clarence B.	09/06/1885	8/13/1980
Pomplum, Lorene E. VanWay	06/20/1899	4/16/1989
Pomplum, Wallace W., Sr.	06/16/1893	10/29/1977
Pope, Cecil G.	12/4/1917	5/26/2000
Pope, Johnnie Wayne	9/20/1947	11/4/2003

NAME	BIRTH	DEATH
Pope, Louis D.	9/23/1926	11/28/2006
Pope, Virginia E. Hodgemn	1/29/1923	9/16/2006
Porter, Rex T.	10/16/1910	10/10/1982
Porter, Tessie Pearl Orrell	11/9/1914	8/12/1983
Posey, Allen	1812	09/14/1892
Posey, Charles T.	06/11/1861	2/28/1931
Posey, Mollie Sutton	1856	1883
Posey, Mrs. Allen	1830	1880
Posey, Tennie E. Melson	03/28/1871	9/15/1960
Powell, Barbara Ann McIntos	9/2/1930	3/30/2000
Powell, Nora E. Wallace	04/22/1891	8/23/1975
Prince, John J.	07/23/1872	2/26/1958
Puckett, John A.	03/27/1897	11/21/1968
Puckett, John Wesley		11/04/1854
Puckett, Lowduskie I.	02/11/1899	9/5/1972
Puckett, Mayuma Huffstettler	09/22/1872	3/25/1962
Rachilla, Allie Cunningham	01/28/1898	12/1/1929
Rachilla, Anthony A.		10/17/1918
Rainwater, Delta Lynn Harmen	10/18/1960	6/5/1997
Randle, John W.	6/22/1945	5/19/2004
Randolph, Robert E.	1/3/1901	5/24/1999
Randolph, Lafayette Henry	11/7/1919	1/5/2001
Randolph, Rena Eva Farr	1/28/1921	2/3/1995
Rash, Albert D.	7/9/1901	5/24/1979
Rash, Elsie I. Fikes	7/23/1911	8/28/2008
Ratliff, Amanda Evelyn Houser	01/07/1880	7/27/1947
Ratliff, James E.	8/10/1905	6/3/1958
Ratliff, Johnnie E. Lowe	09/01/1880	2/15/1960
Ratliff, Lou Mims	10/10/1834	5/28/1909

NAME	BIRTH	DEATH
Rawls, Clarence	1908	1908
Rawls, Hulda Ann Drucilla Redwine	09/19/854	6/30/1945
Rawls, John Felix	09/15/1844	2/18/1908
Rawls, Rado Spiva	03/28/1871	7/30/1946
Rawls, Sarah Throgmartin		1852
Rawls, Thomas Felix	03/04/1874	8/21/1943
Ray, Nancy V.	06/22/1834	10/22/1917
Ray, Phillip M.	4/29/1932	9/29/2000
Ray, Verna Mae	4/10/1928	4/17/1928
Reed, Melba O. Hunter	7/19/1927	7/10/2002
Reed, W. Franklin	8/14/1926	7/25/1994
Reed, Wayne F., Jr.	4/17/1947	8/7/1998
Reeves, Henry Clay	03/02/1880	11/15/1915
Reeves, Katherine Lee	02.04/1924	10/19/2008
Reeves, Lenard Earl	9/18/1942	1/16/1993
Reeves, Lenard L.	10/8/1918	9/15/1995
Reich, Delia Staggs	09/29/1875	8/16/1959
Reich, Kiley	02/25/1872	6/4/1945
Renegar, Charles B. "Shorty"	Aug-11	Apr-69
Ressie, Pauline Johnson	8/5/1938	11/2/1986
Reynolds, Elbert James	2/9/1909	2/3/1997
Reynolds, Grace J. Wehunt	9/28/1935	11/29/1911
Reynolds, Patsy Jean		8/5/1940
Reynolds, Pearl Berry	6/15/1912	6/7/1964
Rhodes, Docia T. Minton	02/24/1893	4/10/1974
Rhodes, Dorothy Mae Sutton	12/13/1924	3/3/2008
Rhodes, Joseph Emery	12/26/1919	9/4/1975
Rhodes, Minnie O.	6/10/1903	4/15/1971
Rhodes, Thomas H.	09/10/1893	6/20/1976

NAME	BIRTH	DEATH
Richardson, Blanch M.	02/16/1885	3/26/1983
Richardson, George T.	03/14/1891	5/1/1974
Risques, Franco Antonio	3/23/1950	9/14/2003
Ritchy, Elizabeth Terry		1896
Roach, Bertha Garrett	03/22/1897	11/15/1990
Roach, Delmar	3/12/1938	12/1/1971
Roach, Frank	10/7/1902	3/31/1956
Roach, Joseph Newton	04/22/1896	4/27/1987
Roach, Will		No Dates
Robbins, Baby Boy	7/1/1968	7/1/1968
Robbins, Dorothy Emerson	2/4/1924	5/17/2007
Robbins, Kenneth Gary	7/7/1970	7/8/1970
Robbins, Kenneth Morris	4/27/1922	8/26/1968
Robson, James L.	04/05/1894	8/14/1975
Robson, Myrtle D. Floyd	3/22/1907	1/14/1987
Ross, Emma Rosetta Orrell	08/18/1891	7/20/1971
Ross, Irene Marie	6/19/1910	1/19/1919
Ross, Thomas	10/14/1872	1/2/1967
Rouse, Wiley	04/10/1823	07/18/1887
Rowe, Blanch E. Tillery	10/10/1898	10/1/1994
Rowe, Clarence O.	7/14/1904	4/4/1984
Rowe, Elsa	10/09/1885	10/09/1885
Rowe, Horace A.	02/02/1896	11/30/1975
Rowe, Ida V. (Coleman)	1893	1917
Rowe, Infant Son	8/28/1930	8/31/1930
Rowe, Jessey D.	1899	1899
Rowe, Luther	10/24/1889	10/24/1889
Rowe, Marshall C.	02/24/1863	1913
Rowe, Mary Blanche McCaslin	11/11/1903	3/2/1992

NAME	BIRTH	DEATH
Rowe, Roy E.	1902	1902
Rowe, Sarah L. Gillham	1866	1918
Rowland, Alex Aaron	3/12/1912	1/19/2003
Rowland, Billy G.	5/6/1942	9/19/1998
Rowland, E. Mayola Sheets	8/18/1914	2/4/2005
Rowland, Johnny A.	3/4/1935	9/1/1988
Rowland, Mary E. Gillham	12/31/1873	2/13/1932
Rowland, Nellie M. Harper	9/12/1915	7/15/2007
Rowland, Orba Henry	12/26/1908	12/21/1989
Rowland, Paul	8/20/1933	5/3/1983
Rowland, Paulette	1957	1958
Ryan, Claudie B. Rawls	02/22/1889	7/5/1925
Ryan, Lester H.	07/24/1884	8/2/1970
Ryan, Ruby	11/6/1919	8/19/1931
Ryan, Tina M.	1/12/1918	8/18/1932
Sargent, Bonnie F.	5/27/1942	7/27/2000
Savage, Rena E. Boswell Hughes	12/6/1915	2/17/1987
Schnell, Dorothy I. Kilgore	1/18/1916	12/13/2003
Scott, Christine Iva Rhodes	12/18/1927	1/16/2008
Scully, James P.	7/16/1917	4/5/1980
Scully, Roxie Catherine	12/16/1920	8/24/1985
Sexton, Clara Pittman	12/25/1892	9/8/1979
Sexton, Dillard	05/07/1876	8/21/1937
Seymore, Margaret R.		No Dates
Seymore, W. E.	07/01/1869	06/16/1888
Seymore, William T.	09/13/1848	6/28/1928
Sherman, James Luther	11/16/1962	9/14/1994
Shook, Randy Neal		1/18/1994
Sigmon, David Wayne	12/12/1957	10/29/2004

NAME	BIRTH	DEATH
Simpson, Estelle	4/13/1908	11/28/1968
Simpson, Eunice L.	9/8/1915	8/8/1999
Simpson, Harry Kenneth	8/10/1912	3/15/1995
Simpson, Warren C.	5/12/1938	7/26/1982
Simpson, Wilma Land	6/5/1909	5/4/1951
Siverson, Marvin Albert	5/23/1932	2/20/2001
Siverson, Mary Lillian Dorant	2/28/1932	7/17/2004
Skillern, Stanley Athan	4/27/1927	11/22/1998
Sloan, Norman Virgle	4/1/1930	6/11/2001
Smith, Artie B.	1/25/1904	12/29/1993
Smith, Catherine Schverch	10/28/1951	7/1/2003
Smith, Charles A.	06/24/1885	11/19/1961
Smith, Faye Burch	6/17/1909	5/11/2001
Smith, Floyd V.	08/01/1895	5/18/1979
Smith, James Gilford	3/12/1949	3/12/1949
Smith, Jepson	1853	1912
Smith, John Henry	12/18/1904	7/7/1980
Smith, Lee E.	10/6/1909	5/28/1979
Smith, Linton L.	6/13/1930	0518/1997
Smith, Martha E.	03/12/1887	6/26/1952
Smith, Melia Jarusha	11/26/2000	2/25/2001
Smith, Muriel D.	8/14/1928	11/26/2007
Smith, Olene Montgomery	9/23/1908	9/22/2002
Smith, Rhoda Rowe	1859	1908
Smith, Roberta (infant)		1938
Smith, Shannon Denise	3/1/1973	8/20/1996
Smoot, Geraldine	1924	1989
Smooth, Jack	1928	1996
Sorrells, Wanda June Tennessee Fisher	4/9/1938	9/3/2000

NAME	BIRTH	DEATH
Sorter, Betty Lou	1/22/1960	1/22/1960
Sorter, Joyce J. Neighbors	1/30/1933	8/25/2000
Sorter, Louie G.	9/23/1926	6/24/1984
Spiva, Beulah Ward	1894	12/5/1945
Spiva, Donald Elisha	5/25/1907	12/29/1976
Spiva, Dora Alice Orrell	07/04/1878	11/25/1927
Spiva, Elisha	11/04/1838	08/11/1899
Spiva, Elizabeth Kilgore	10/31/1882	2/7/1954
Spiva, James Arnold	9/15/1945	6/12/2003
Spiva, James Henry	07/18/1873	4/26/1911
Spiva, Jonas		No Dates
Spiva, Jonas B.	1812	1868
Spiva, Katie Reese	7/19/1902	2/14/1984
Spiva, Mary Ann		No Dates
Spiva, Tessie Lee	12/1/1944	11/29/1992
Spiva, Ward E.	1915	1959
Spiva, Zelma Julia	5/23/1908	9/4/1997
Spoon, Annie E. Ward	01/06/1873	12/17/1956
Spoon, Betty Warwick	10/30/1913	12/27/1998
Spoon, David Allen	7/1/1912	3/4/1989
Spoon, Eddie E.	10/7/1909	3/14/2001
Spoon, Genie Wilson	12/15/1913	8/24/1993
Spoon, James David	7/1/1928	12/8/2006
Spoon, Roy L.	12/24/1914	2/3/1985
Spoon, William Fredrick	4/7/1907	4/16/1941
Sprinkle, Esther Humphreys	1894	1992
Stallings, John W.	4/20/1924	11/4/1972
Standefer, Albion	8/31/1917	9/1/1917
Standefer, Arthur	3/18/1907	11/14/1991

NAME	BIRTH	DEATH
Standefer, Ethel P.	12/27/1889	7/21/1969
Standefer, Hershell Lee	10/14/1914	12/7/1914
Standefer, John C.	12/28/1878	1/25/1973
Standefer, Sibyl M.	2/24/1919	9/16/2003
Standerfer, Delcie C.	7/1/1914	7/14/2007
Standridge, Jodie	8/3/1901	2/5/1976
Standridge, Zora Burch	12/31/1907	7/8/1998
Stapp, Elmia	1837	1908
Stark, Sherry Law	7/1/1956	12/18/2008
Steiskal, James E.	6/16/1939	1/30/1997
Stillwell, Bobby Gene	10/13/1943	5/10/2009
Stipe, Betty Jo Ennis	6/16/1945	5/27/2001
Stoyak, Velma Rhodes	12/6/1924	5/2/1993
Street, Nettie M. Daniels	1892	1958
Street, William	02/18/1892	3/5/1957
Sutton, Allen R.	11/15/1877	11/2/1969
Sutton, Andrew J.	11/22/1872	5/17/1960
Sutton, Archie	7/9/1922	7/22/1986
Sutton, Arvil William	11/3/1919	7/26/1921
Sutton, Floyd Erwin	1/2/1927	12/2/1932
Sutton, Fronie	1874	1882
Sutton, Grace Tuberville	4/8/1913	6/8/1989
Sutton, Hubert C.	12/11/1928	10/1/1992
Sutton, Jonas	1871	1883
Sutton, Mary E. McConnell	04/10/1892	4/2/1972
Sutton, Minnie Moore	10/03/1878	9/25/1972
Sutton, Monroe S.	04/15/1883	7/8/1960
Sutton, Peter		No Dates
Sutton, Peter	1853	1911

NAME	BIRTH	DEATH
Sutton, Polly Spiva	1825	1880
Sutton, Rosella "Rosie" Green		No Dates
Sutton, Roy S.	10/12/1916	1/24/1996
Sutton, Tom Alford	10/6/1926	4/4/1929
Sutton, Violet M.	01/31/1886	1/6/1981
Sutton, Virgil G.	3/6/1907	4/11/1976
Sutton, William	3/4/1908	3/25/1975
Sutton, William Owen	07/22/1875	4/4/1928
Tackett, Gwen Bradley	8/23/1948	1/22/1993
Tankersley, Bobby Gene, Jr.	2/14/1959	2/19/1959
Terry, James W.	1855	1/13/1933
Thornton, Cecil C.	1907	1986
Thornton, Kenneth J. P.	12/20/1932	4/22/2009
Tichacek, A. Cleo Orrell	2/19/1912	8/20/1947
Tillery, Anna Eugenia "Jennie"	1867	1945
Tillery, James Cawfield	06/22/1896	11/22/1980
Tontsch, Helena M.	1921	1980
Trantham, Eunice F. Rowe	07/25/1891	12/25/1945
Trantham, George Robert	07/09/1891	5/7/1959
Trantham, Luther Morris	8/23/1920	6/2/1998
Trantham, Luther O.	10/16/1880	8/29/1957
Trantham, Richard	01/04/1856	2/15/1910
Trantham, Susie Ethel Johnson	11/09/1898	6/28/1964
Treadway, Barbara Ann Johnson	12/26/1937	2/24/2008
Treadway, Lana Archer	11/15/1939	2/21/1994
Treece, Vicki Lynn	1/19/1972	1/19/1972
Tuberville, Doris H.	3/22/1923	12/26/2007
Tuberville, Effie Howton	02/22/1889	8/30/1956
Tuberville, Freddy G.	6/5/1947	7/24/2008

NAME	BIRTH	DEATH
Tuberville, Grover	6/4/1918	4/14/2004
Tuberville, Lester O.	1/6/1916	8/18/1991
Tuberville, Nicky Wade	3/5/1968	7/24/2008
Tuberville, Ollis W.	07/09/1884	8/30/1956
Tucker, Billy Ray	9/1/1934	1/1/1958
Tucker, Dorthy	5/22/1927	7/6/1928
Tucker, Eula Mae West	7/17/1906	12/18/1980
Tucker, Imogene	9/28/1930	2/13/1931
Tucker, Jess G.	6/1/1903	6/21/1971
Tucker, Oscar W.	03/24/1868	6/28/1943
Tucker, Roger Lee	12/11/1947	7/26/2001
Turner, Boone C.	05/08/1886	9/2/1963
Ulmer, Holly Nicole	12/17/1993	12/19/1993
Upchurch, Rex D.	12/11/1935	9/11/1986
Upchurch, Wanda I. Lambert	11/12/1937	6/15/1982
Ussery, Albert Charles	02/08/1887	1/4/1906
Ussery, Albert Chase		No Dates
Vanderslice, Thomas D.	11/09/1886	5/11/1957
Vasseau, Charles Paul	4/20/1955	9/14/1998
Vasseau, John	8/5/1914	11/13/1991
Vasseau, Lois Ann Wehunt	9/9/1952	4/17/1981
Vasseau, Nellie Mae Mathis	8/8/1920	11/15/2000
Volentine, Altha A.	07/06/1894	06/06/1896
Wagner, Elsie B. Sargent	04/06/1899	5/23/1980
Wagner, John	08/31/1896	10/6/1978
Walker, Christine	12/25/1925	6/4/1998
Walker, John Harvey	12/26/1913	1/26/1980
Wallace, Bobby Lee	7/24/1934	4/15/1937
Wallace, David Frank	7/11/1902	5/16/1978

NAME	BIRTH	DEATH
Wiley, James Edward	2/10/1927	6/20/1988
Wiley, Paul David	12/14/1957	10/7/1976
Williams, Catherine	12/10/1941	12/10/1941
Williams, Infant	12/10/1918	12/10/1918
Williams, Infant	2/3/1934	2/3/1934
Williams, Kristen Eric Rowland	3/11/1980	9/6/1981
Williams, Mary Elizabeth Fisher	2/3/1932	09/30/200
Williams, Tray Gene	10/20/1942	10/20/1942
Williams, William J.	08/29/1851	6/19/1942
Williamson, Faye	1/2/1913	8/11/1940
Williamson, Leland	07/23/1869	5/7/1914
Williamson, Leslie Lucille	1/9/1906	3/4/1906
Williamson, Oliver	1/12/1910	1/24/1984
Williamson, Panzie Jewell Cornish	8/17/1914	9/19/2000
Wilson, Clarence Lonnie	11/6/1911	10/7/1949
Wilson, Kittie Ruth Sprinkle	1/28/1935	2/12/1974
Wilson, Matthew Max	5/25/1928	4/7/1991
Wilson, Minnie	1894	1916
Wing, Joshua Issac	6/24/2008	11/16/2008
Winstead, Joe M.	1870	1949
Winston, Edra Madge	9/6/1910	4/1/1939
Winters, Shirley F.	2/13/1927	4/9/1928
Wood, Jardone	1891	1896
Wood, Margerette V.	10/9/1929	10/9/1929
Wood, Mary Elizabeth Carpenter	12/21/1942	2/9/2002
Wood, Ruben Thomas	11/01/1898	6/25/1938
Wood, Vera Virginia Cunningham	12/18/1901	2/13/1985
Woodall, Keri Lynn	3/28/2006	5/26/2006
Woodruff, Arville Leon	9/15/1917	3/12/1987

NAME	BIRTH	DEATH
Wallace, Donnie Frank	11/30/1938	12/7/1988
Wallace, Hilda M. Land	6/3/1900	9/26/1981
Wallace, Idella Mae	9/28/1920	11/18/1934
Wallace, James E.	8/11/1925	3/12/1971
Wallace, Jeff E.	3/7/1923	6/21/1984
Wallace, Jim	1866	1904
Wallace, John H.	07/31/1899	6/29/1964
Wallace, Loyd D.	6/2/1932	8/28/1998
Wallace, Margorie Dell Tribble	9/26/1927	3/7/1999
Wallace, Richard E.	11/14/1894	04/08/1899
Wallace, Robert Earl	11/22/1954	4/17/1994
Wallace, Winnie Pearl Mathews	2/8/1905	7/4/1983
Walter, Cleo E. Garrett	7/31/1921	5/1/2000
Walter, David O.	8/26/1915	8/19/1987
Ward, William W.	6/3/1905	8/8/1967
Watson, Larry	11/18/1917	1/17/1981
Watson, Pauline Renegar	3/6/1923	6/1/1994
Weaver, Lauren		2/22/1989
Webb, Elvira Redwine	02/20/1862	9/17/1949
Webb, Henderson Dutch	4/15/1910	1961
Webb, Ollie Anderson	1922	1983
Weber, Bernice P.	6/4/1913	7/11/1996
Weber, Harry J.	4/26/1915	5/24/1991
Weiss, Patsy Elizabeth Burnett	1/7/1950	11/16/2000
Weldon, Arthur J.	08/24/1865	11/9/1933
Westerman, Martha L. Chitwood	0/24/1886	2/19/1926
White, Infant		No Dates
Wiley, Audrey Ruby	6/5/1924	1/10/2002
Wiley, Gilbert	1/13/1923	12/30/1991

NAME	BIRTH	DEATH
Woodruff, Judy Crane	7/27/1947	2/24/1986
Worley, Travis S.	12/4/1940	1/1/2001
Wright, Aubrey Lynn	9/1/1926	5/30/1983
Yarbrough, Avodrie Marie	2/18/2009	9/11/2009
Yarbrough, Bertha Burton	5/26/1916	6/11/1977
Yarbrough, Birtha Ann	7/13/1978	7/13/1978
Yarbrough, Kenneth H.	11/12/1937	12/6/2003
Yarbrough, William S.	6/10/1932	1/19/1994

JOHNNIE WAYNE POPE, a True Arkansas Hero

Johnnie Wayne Pope was born Septembe 20, 1947, in Hot Springs, AR to Cecil G. and Virginia E. Hodgeman Pope. Johnnie died on November 4, 2003, in Royal, AR. He was a member of the Crystal Springs Church of Christ located in Crystal Springs, AR. Johnnie's ashes are buried in Lowe Cemetery.

Johnnie lived as he died, a "Good Samaritan." He would help anybody he knew that was in need. Johnnie literally gave his life for his brother as well as for many others. His tombstone reads: "He gave his life so that others might live. Greater Love hath no man than this, that a man lay down his life for his friends. John 15:13." According to Larry Sanders, Garland County Sheriff's Captain, "He was obviously thinking about the safety of others."

Shortly after 2:00 p.m. on November 4, 2003, Johnnie had just finished filling his pickup with gas at C & H Gas and Grocery, 6052 Albert Pike, Royal, AR, when the truck burst into flames. Instead of thinking of himself, Johnnie drove the vehicle more than fifty feet away from the gas pumps before the pickup exploded. The explosion and fire killed him. If it had not been for him, many would have perished and/or would have been seriously injured. Johnnie's brother, Gary, had accompanied him to the store and was inside paying for the gas when the incident occurred.

On December 16, 2003, the State of Arkansas, 84th General Assembly, Second Extraordinary Session, 2003, honored Johnnie Wayne Pope as a True Arkansas Hero. The document states, *"WHEREAS, the giving of one's own life to save others is one of the most noble acts a man can commit toward his fellow man, requiring a rare combination of selflessness, courage, kindness, and respect for human life."*

Sources: 1.) *The Sentinel Record*, Wednesday, November 5, 2003, Pages 1A and 10A and 2.) Thursday, November 6, 2003, Page 8A
      3.) *House Memorial Resolution*, Call item ## HMR 1003, December 16, 2003